Could It Be Adult ADHD?

Could It Be Adult ADHD?

A Clinician's Guide to Recognition, Assessment, and Treatment

JAN WILLER

OXFORD
UNIVERSITY PRESS

OXFORD
UNIVERSITY PRESS

Oxford University Press is a department of the University of Oxford. It furthers the University's objective of excellence in research, scholarship, and education by publishing worldwide. Oxford is a registered trade mark of Oxford University Press in the UK and certain other countries.

Published in the United States of America by Oxford University Press
198 Madison Avenue, New York, NY 10016, United States of America.

Library of Congress Cataloging-in-Publication Data
Names: Willer, Jan, author.
Title: Could it be adult ADHD? : a clinician's guide to recognition, assessment, and treatment / Jan Willer.
Description: New York, NY : Oxford University Press, [2017] |
Includes bibliographical references and index.
Identifiers: LCCN 2016048019 (print) | LCCN 2016049934 (ebook) | ISBN 9780190256319 |
ISBN 9780190256326 (ebook) | ISBN 9780190670139 (ebook)
Subjects: | MESH: Attention Deficit Disorder with Hyperactivity—diagnosis |
Attention Deficit Disorder with Hyperactivity—therapy | Adult
Classification: LCC RC394.A85 (print) | LCC RC394.A85 (ebook) | NLM WM 165 |
DDC 616.85/89—dc23
LC record available at https://lccn.loc.gov/2016048019

CONTENTS

FOREWORD

I am one of those people who did not go looking for a particularly specialty, but one found me. Namely, I am a psychologist who specializes in the assessment and psychosocial treatment of attention deficit hyperactivity disorder (ADHD) in adults.

My colleague, my friend, and top-notch psychiatrist, Dr. Anthony Rostain, approached me on March 8, 1999, about his vision for a specialty program focused on evidence-supported assessments and treatments for adults with ADHD. (Tony is truly a "visionary," because he had previously had a vision that ended up becoming the Children's Hospital of Philadelphia's ADHD Program, which continues to be at the forefront of the treatment of children and adolescents who have ADHD.) He was already an expert in the pharmacotherapy options, but he recognized that most ADHD adults need more than medications to improve functioning and overall well-being. Having completed a two-year postdoctoral fellowship in cognitive behavioral therapy (CBT) at the Center for Cognitive Therapy at the University of Pennsylvania, and just paddling out into the waters of the faculty track at Penn as an instructor, I signed on for what has turned out to be an ongoing professional collaboration and friendship, with my distinct contribution to the program being to adapt CBT to the needs of adults with ADHD.

I was not sure how long my role in this project would be necessary. The going wisdom at the time was that medications were the only treatment option for adults with ADHD. Frankly, I was quite surprised as we and other groups published data on the benefits of CBT for adult ADHD (most often in combination with medications), and I continue to observe its benefits in my day-to-day clinical practice through our program.

The Penn Adult ADHD Treatment and Research Program continues as a fully functioning clinic offering diagnostic assessments, medication management, individual CBT, and, most recently, coping skills training groups for adults with ADHD. The range of services offered by our program and other adult ADHD clinics is a testament to the fact that ADHD has wide-ranging effects on those with the diagnosis as well as others in their lives.

Apart from the clinical aspects of assessing for and treating ADHD, the very letters A-D-H-D trigger an array of reactions, ranging from individuals and families affected by ADHD who describe how an accurate diagnosis and treatment have been life-changing to the opposite end of the continuum with those who renounce the validity of the diagnosis. In terms of a clinical specialty, ADHD offers all the clinical challenges of practice and research, and the benefits of seeing the positive difference that competent assessment and treatment can make in the lives of real people, as well as confronting the topics of how a disorder is defined, whether ADHD is a "gift," gene–environment interactions, the nature of will and self-control, and a gamut of other provocative questions. Any one of these topics could be the focus of one's life work.

This back story is meant to set the stage for Jan Willer's ambitious book herein. Even the title, starting off with the seemingly innocent but common question, "Could it be adult ADHD?" requires the much broader "A Clinician's Guide to Recognition, Assessment, and Treatment" to provide an answer. With this book, Dr. Willer takes on the challenge of painstakingly enumerating and addressing all the practical clinical facets of identifying and treating ADHD in adults, as well as tackling the main questions and controversies that surround these endeavors. She provides a lovely and comprehensive overview of the contemporary scientific understanding of and clinical standards for treating ADHD in adults.

Make no mistake about it, though, this book is a useful, hands-on clinical guide that practicing diagnosticians and clinicians will no doubt find themselves retrieving from the shelf as they evaluate and treat adult clients with ADHD. In addition to clinician-friendly therapeutic strategies and illustrative case examples, Dr. Willer examines in great detail the official symptoms of ADHD that comprise the diagnostic criteria with various other features of ADHD that help to differentiate it from other conditions. She tethers these symptoms to the real-world difficulties and impairments that lead adults with ADHD to seek help. Last, she provides a thorough framework for carrying out psychosocial treatment, including a review of evidence-supported treatments and clinically informed wisdom for managing the realities of treatment with this clinical population. First-line medication treatments and complementary-alternative treatments are also reviewed to provide clinicians with an overview, both to inform treatment plans and to provide accurate information to clients who may ask about these topics.

In sum, Dr. Willer's book will be very useful for practicing clinicians who treat adult clients with ADHD, particularly those providing psychosocial treatment. Dr. Willer provides direction for navigating through all the unique clinical issues that arise in therapy for adult ADHD, allowing treatment to be adapted to the client's needs. There is useful information about medications and adjunctive treatments that provides a foundation for psychoeducation for clients, with some information provided in the form of useful handouts. Last, graduate or medical students in psychology or psychiatry or any clinicians-in-training will find this book to be a useful overview of adult ADHD. So, however adult ADHD may have found you in your clinical practice, you are fortunate to have found Dr. Willer's excellent book.

—J. Russell Ramsay, Ph.D.,
Codirector, Adult ADHD Treatment and Research Program and
Associate Professor of Clinical Psychology in Psychiatry,
Perelman School of Medicine, University of Pennsylvania;
coauthor, *Cognitive Behavioral Therapy for Adult ADHD: An Integrative Psychosocial and Medical Approach* (2nd ed.)
and *The Adult ADHD Tool Kit: Using CBT to Facilitate Coping Inside and Out*, and author, *Nonmedication Treatments for Adult ADHD: Evaluating Impact of Daily Functioning and Well-Being*

ACKNOWLEDGMENTS

Thanks to my editor, Sarah Harrington, for her valuable input and support regarding the content and structure of this book. I would like to thank J. Russell Ramsay for his helpful suggestions and advice. I would also like to thank the following for reading various portions of this book and providing their professional feedback and suggestions: Renanah Lehner, Ph.D., Sara Dittoe Barrett, Ph.D. and Shona Vas, Ph.D.

For their insights into the struggles and successes of college students with adult ADHD, I thank Michael Pietrus, Psy.D., and Jacqueline Pardo, M.D., both at the University of Chicago Student Counseling and Resource School, and Judy Kolar, Director, Center for Students with Disabilities, DePaul University. Also, I thank Donald Bliwise for providing input and direction regarding assessing sleep quality and sleep disorders through questionnaires.

Special thanks go to my father, David Willer, for instilling an appreciation of lifelong learning in all his children. And extra special thanks go to my husband, Mark Osing, for his unwavering support of my writing endeavors.

SECTION I

Recognition

1

Meet Clara and Troy, Two Adults with ADHD

Clara: I've always felt that there was something wrong with me. I felt like an imposter. But I didn't want other people to know that I couldn't do the things that they could do. I just had to work harder, and I could usually pull it together, even though it was usually at the very last minute. Only my husband knows what a slob I am. Whenever anyone comes over, I just hide the mess in closets, drawers, or behind closed doors. All this makes me very anxious.

Troy: I was diagnosed with ADHD when I was a kid, but I always thought I'd outgrown it until my daughter was diagnosed with ADHD as well. The school psychologist asked whether anyone else in the family had ADHD, and I said that I did when I was a kid. Then my wife and I started to look up adult ADHD online and the descriptions of it are just like me.

One out of every 5 to 10 adult psychotherapy clients probably has attention deficit/hyperactivity disorder (ADHD; Asherson, 2013). Have you been recognizing them? Like many others, for years I did not recognize ADHD in my adult clients. I graduated with my Ph.D. in 1991, when adult ADHD was not known to exist. Key studies and writings emerged in 1995 supporting the idea of adult ADHD (Biederman et al., 1995; Wender, 1995). It took many years of reading and research for me to confidently recognize and appropriately treat adult ADHD. I hope this book will help all of us recognize, assess, and treat our clients with ADHD.

Adult ADHD continues to be underrecognized by mental health clinicians, even when clients with ADHD are already in treatment for other mental illnesses (Kessler et al., 2006). Dissemination of clinically relevant findings to practicing psychotherapists remains a problem. Many—even most—graduate students in the mental health fields are still not being trained to assess or treat adult ADHD. My informal poll of psychology interns found that no graduate training about adult ADHD remains the norm. In another informal poll, most psychologists who received their doctorates between 1990 and 2010 reported having received no graduate education about adult ADHD. Occasionally, information is filtering through to graduate students, but the information can be erroneous and outdated. Mental health practitioners in Europe have a similar lack of education about adult ADHD (Kooij et al., 2010). This book aims to fill that gap.

Throughout the book, I use the cases of Clara and Troy to demonstrate key points about the experiences and difficulties of adult ADHD. Additional clients are sometimes mentioned in brief vignettes to provide a fuller understanding of the range of symptoms and experiences. Note that Clara, Troy, and all the other clients discussed in this book are composites and do not represent any one specific adult with ADHD.

ADULT ADHD MYTHS

Considerable misinformation circulates about adult ADHD. Consider these myths and the facts that disprove them:

Myth: Adult ADHD is a controversial and trendy diagnosis. It does not really exist.

Facts: False. The existence of adult ADHD is strongly supported through multiple converging lines of evidence, including genetics, symptomatology, impairment, neuropsychological testing results, and differences in brain structure and functioning (Barkley et al., 2002; Castellanos & Proal, 2012; Faraone et al., 2000; Nigg, 2006). ADHD is highly heritable (Coghill & Banaschewski, 2009) and about as heritable as bipolar disorder and schizophrenia, which were previously considered to be the two most heritable mental illnesses.

Myth: Everyone is distractible sometimes. Those people are just making excuses for being lazy and unmotivated.

Facts: Like most other mental disorders, symptoms of ADHD are on a continuum, and the people whom we diagnose with ADHD are in the extreme tail of that distribution (Brown, 2006). The continuum of ADHD may partially explain the difficulty that doubters have with understanding that ADHD is a true disorder. Of course, everyone is occasionally distractible and disorganized. So it's easy for some to say, "she's not sick; she just needs to try harder" or that ADHD is "an excuse." This attitude is both uninformed and emotionally damaging to individuals with ADHD (Ramsay & Rostain, 2008b).

Myth: ADHD is a result of our modern technological lifestyle.

Facts: False. Technology may certainly contribute to distractibility in all adults, including those with ADHD. However, individuals of all ages, including those who grew up with technology and those who did not, have problems with ADHD (Michielsen et al., 2012). Instead, in the past, ADHD was conceptualized differently as a character flaw: "lazy" or "unmotivated."

Myth: ADHD is caused by bad parenting, too much TV, and so on.
Facts: False. ADHD is primarily a genetically inherited neurological difference (Coghill & Banaschewski, 2009). However, childhood stress can increase the likelihood that ADHD develops in a person who is genetically at risk (Biederman, Faraone, & Monuteaux, 2002; Spencer, Biederman, & Mick, 2007).

Myth: A good diet can cure ADHD.
Facts: In general, no. However, there are a few caveats to this: (a) in a recent meta-analysis, about 30% of children with ADHD were found to improve on a diet free of food additives (Nigg, Lewis, Edinger, & Falk, 2012); (b) there is preliminary evidence that environmental toxins, such as lead and pesticides, may increase ADHD symptoms in children (Bouchard, Bellinger, Wright, & Weisskopf, 2010; Nigg, 2010; Nigg, Nikolas, Knottnerus, Cavanagh, & Friderici, 2010); and (c) the addition of omega-3 fatty acids does help cognition in children with ADHD (Hawkey & Nigg, 2014; McGough, 2014), although not nearly as much as stimulant medication, so it is not recommended as a primary treatment (Ramsay, 2010b). Not much is known about diet and adults with ADHD.

Myth: ADHD is a socially constructed disorder.
Facts: Every disorder is a socially constructed way of cutting reality into categories. ADHD is no different from anxiety, depression, or any other mental illness in this regard.

Myth: ADHD is a culture-bound syndrome in the United States.
Facts: False. Multiple international studies of ADHD have documented the presence of this disorder in countries across the globe, including but not limited to Canada, France, Germany, Italy, the Netherlands, the United Kingdom, Japan, and Korea (Brod, Pohlman, Lasser, & Hodgkins, 2012; Davis, Takahashi, Shinoda, & Gregg, 2012; Park et al., 2011).

Myth: Most children outgrow ADHD by adulthood, so there is a low prevalence of adults with ADHD relative to children with ADHD.
Facts: False. Over two-thirds of adults who had ADHD as children still have significant functional impairment as adults (Biederman, Petty, Evans, Small, & Faraone, 2010; Faraone, Biederman, & Mick, 2000, 2006).

Myth: Most adults with ADHD are diagnosed as children.
Facts: False. Many individuals with ADHD—especially those who are women, did not have childhood behavior problems, had inattentive type ADHD, are in disadvantaged groups, or are now age 40 and above—were never recognized to have ADHD as children (Barkley, 2006a; Barkley, Murphy, & Fischer, 2008; Michielsen et al., 2012; Ramsay, 2010b; Rucklidge & Kaplan, 1997; Wasserstein, 2005).

Myth: Adults with ADHD are rare.
Facts: False. At least 4% to 5% of the US adult population has ADHD, and this is probably an underestimate (Barkley, 2006a; Biederman, 2011; Buitelaar, 2011; Fedele, Hartung, Canu, & Wilkowski, 2010; Kessler et al., 2006; Kessler et al., 2010; Ramsay, 2010b).

Myth: Only a trained neuropsychologist can diagnose ADHD in adults.
Facts: Not necessarily. A well-trained mental health practitioner can, in most cases, diagnose ADHD from a careful clinical interview. In other cases, a well-educated psychologist can clarify the clinical picture by administering appropriate ADHD rating scales, conducting a careful developmental interview, and obtaining observer ratings, if necessary. Nonetheless, neuropsychologists are the one group of mental health practitioners who are well trained to recognize ADHD in adults. Be aware that about 60% of adults with ADHD have normal neuropsychological test results of executive functioning (Biederman, Mick, et al., 2011), probably because life is more complicated than neuropsychological tests (Barkley et al., 2008). So neuropsychologists often diagnose ADHD from history, symptoms and behavior during testing rather than test results. Also, neuropsychological testing can be helpful in very complex cases with multiple comorbidities, especially those with learning disabilities.

CORE CHARACTERISTICS OF ADHD

ADHD is a real and serious disorder affecting millions of people worldwide. Differences in the brain cause ADHD symptoms. People with ADHD are not making excuses, lazy, or unmotivated. ADHD is not a fad. Currently there is no laboratory, genetic, or brain functioning test that can diagnose ADHD (Toone, 2004) because individuals with ADHD vary considerably from each other. So ADHD remains a disorder that is diagnosed based on symptoms, which is also the case for depression, anxiety, bipolar disorder, and most other psychiatric conditions. The following are the core characteristics of ADHD:

- ADHD has *developmental* aspects: The brains of children with ADHD tend to mature 3 to 5 years later than those of peers (Brown, 2013). By adulthood, 70% of childhood hyperactive/impulsive symptoms are in remission versus only 40% of inattentive symptoms (Dias et al., 2013).
- ADHD is very highly *heritable*—as much as schizophrenia or bipolar disorder—which are the most heritable of mental illnesses (Banerjee, Middleton, & Faraone, 2007), and it is also genetically heterogeneous (Dias et al., 2013).
- ADHD is a *neurological* disorder, affecting the structure and activation of the brain, as well as *cognitive* functioning and *self-regulation* (Brown, 2013; Ramsay, 2008).

- ADHD is a *disorder* because it impairs behavior and functioning in major life activities, such as education, social interactions, occupational functioning, and emotional functioning (Brown, 2013).

EVERY FIFTH TO TENTH CLIENT PROBABLY HAS ADHD

The most commonly cited estimate of prevalence of ADHD in US adults is 4.4% (Kessler et al., 2006). International prevalence rates are 2.5% to 5.3% (Polanczyk, de Lima, Horta, Biederman, & Rohde, 2007; Simon, Czobor, Bálint, Mészáros, & Bitter, 2009). *So a good estimate is that 1 out of every 25 American adults has ADHD as defined by the Diagnostic and Statistical Manual of Mental Disorders* (fifth ed., American Psychiatric Association, 2013).

Since adults with ADHD usually have other mental illnesses and problems with adaptive functioning, *more* than 4% of any clinical population is likely to have ADHD. In fact, ADHD was found in 10% to 20% of people with other common mental health problems in the UK (Asherson, 2013). These findings suggest that *1 out of every 5 to 10 psychotherapy clients is likely to have adult ADHD.*

Interestingly, in a random national telephone survey, Faraone and Biederman (2005) found that about 17% of their sample had some impairing symptoms of adult ADHD, whether they had the full diagnosis or not—that is *one out of every six adults.* This illustrates the continuum of ADHD symptoms in the general population. No one is arguing that 17% of the population should be medicated for ADHD. However, recognizing even mild symptoms of ADHD and providing individuals with appropriate skills training may enhance the effectiveness of their psychotherapy.

EMOTIONAL DISTRESS IN ADHD

Clara: I've always had problems off and on with depression and anxiety. Lately, my mood has been better, but I still feel down on myself really easily. Anxiety is still a major issue, though.

Emotional distress is nearly universal in untreated adults who have ADHD because of the following:

- *Comorbid mood and anxiety disorders*: Most adults with ADHD have a comorbid mental health diagnosis. Depression and anxiety are common, but other diagnoses such as bipolar disorder are also more commonly found in adults with ADHD than in the general population.
- *Emotional dysregulation*: About half of adults with ADHD struggle with difficulties controlling their own emotions. They are easily overwhelmed with everyday stressors and can easily become angry, impatient, irritable, and excitable.

- *Distress over life problems relating to ADHD*: Individuals are upset about life difficulties stemming from ADHD, such as running up to deadlines, having communication problems, and being error-prone.

Emotional problems can include the following:

- *Shame and low self-esteem*: Many social blunders can stem from ADHD: blurting out responses, being overly blunt and tactless, and being overly talkative (Weiss, Gibbins, & Hunter, 2011). Most adults with ADHD compare themselves to other people they know who do not have ADHD and find themselves lacking. They wonder why some things are so difficult for them but so easy for others and then blame themselves.
- *Feeling stigmatized:* Many individuals who had ADHD as children will stop their medications when they become adults. They reject the stigma of mental illness by rejecting the diagnosis of ADHD instead of rejecting the stigma itself. Unfortunately, in most of them, the ADHD symptoms continue and contribute to many life problems. Later, when the diagnosis is accepted, they struggle with whom to inform about it and with their understanding that others may be dismissive and critical.
- *Feelings of underachievement:* Because they run up against deadlines and do things at the last minute, they know that they could have done these tasks better if they had started earlier. Most likely, they missed many opportunities because of procrastination and disorganization. All of this leads to chronic feelings of underachievement. It can also lead to a self-image as an individual who is lazy and unmotivated.
- *Rumination and perfectionism:* Because of many difficulties that have arisen through errors and impulsiveness, some adults with ADHD develop a ruminative and perfectionistic style to compensate.
- *Learned helplessness, hopelessness, pessimism, and emotional pain*: The symptoms of ADHD affect many different domains of functioning, which adults with untreated ADHD have struggled unsuccessfully to address (Ramsay, 2010a).
- *Grief*: An adult who learns that ADHD caused so many life problems can go through a period of grief about lost opportunities (Murphy & Gordon, 2006; Ramsay, 2010a).

COMMON FUNCTIONAL IMPAIRMENTS IN ADHD

Troy: I've quit jobs too many times to count. But I've mostly worked for relatives, so they've always taken me back. I didn't go to college out of high school, but in my early twenties, I did finish up an auto mechanic program at the community college. My wife and family were very proud of me for following through on that. We had our first kid when I was 19 years old. That was tough.

Clara: My husband gets mad at me because he has to tell me things over and over. He says that I must not care because I don't listen to him. I feel terrible about this, but I don't know what to do.

The following is a summary of the functional impairments that individuals with ADHD are more likely to have (Barkley, 2002; Wilens, Faraone, & Biederman, 2004). Be sure to examine both obvious and subtle dysfunction. Some examples of each are also given.

- *Academic problems*: These range in severity from being high school dropouts to taking extra time to complete a college degree. They are likely to obtain lower grades in classes that they do not consider interesting, and chronically run up against deadlines.
- *Work problems*: These range in severity from being fired, being unemployed, and frequent job changes to underperformance at work, including struggling with getting everything done in a timely and organized manner. Adults with ADHD often have a lower socioeconomic status than we might predict, given the verbal intelligence they display during psychotherapy sessions.
- *Social problems*: These may range from having few or no friends to having good friends, who either are irritated with or joke about their impulsiveness, forgetfulness, and lateness.
- *Family problems:* When these are more severe, the individual might have been a teen parent and is more likely to be separated or divorced. When these are mild, the individual may have communication problems with the spouse, conflicts around organization in the home, and problems with parenting in a consistent manner.

This is only a small snapshot of some of the life problems that individuals with ADHD experience. Further information about adaptive functioning is presented in chapter 8.

EXCERPTS FROM CLARA'S INITIAL SESSION: PRESENTING PROBLEMS

Our first client, Clara, requested evaluation and psychotherapy for ADHD. She is a 28-year-old married Latina high school chemistry teacher. Her parents emigrated to the United States from Guatemala before she was born, and she is fluent in Spanish and English. She has had problems with ADHD throughout her life but only recognized this recently when one of her students was diagnosed with ADHD. On the phone, she said that she's worried because she's having difficulty keeping up with the demands of her job. The psychotherapist noted that she was still filling out her intake paperwork in the waiting room prior to her first session, and gave her a little more time to finish it. The following are excerpts from the first psychotherapy session.

Psychotherapist: It's good to meet you in person. Have a seat . . . Thanks for filling out this paperwork. Can you tell me some more about what brought you to therapy?

Clara: Well, as I told you on the phone, I was at an educational planning meeting for one of my students, and the school psychologist started to talk about this kid's symptoms of ADHD, and I realized that I was just like that when I was a kid.

P: Sounds like this insight came as a surprise to you.

C: Yes, and then the parents started to talk about the kid.

P: What did they say?

C: It was spooky. The parents are second-generation Polish, and my parents are first-generation Guatemalan, but the things they said about her were almost identical to what my parents said about me: "She's smart but lazy, she doesn't apply herself enough, she just doesn't pay attention" and so on. My teachers would say the exact same things on my report cards.

P: What was it like for you to hear this?

C: It was like I was hit by lightning! All of a sudden, I learned what had been wrong with me as a kid. I talked to the school psychologist afterwards—Whitney, she's a friend of mine—and she told me that ADHD doesn't necessarily include hyperactivity. When I was in college and learned about ADHD, I always thought that since I hadn't been a hyperactive kid, I couldn't have had ADHD. I don't know why I missed that. So then Whitney told me that sometimes ADHD persists to adulthood and suggested that maybe I talk to someone who is knowledgeable about adult ADHD. So that's how I came to you.

P: I find that it's common for people to come see me for ADHD because they realize a similarity between themselves and someone else. Often it's one of their own kids, but I see that in your case it was one of your students. So what are your thoughts about what Whitney said? Do you think that you have ADHD?

C: Well, I have to wonder. Everyone at school says I do such a good job. But they don't really know how I do things. Sometimes I wing it in the classroom since I haven't prepared enough the night before. And I feel really guilty because it takes me too long to grade the kids' lab write-ups, homework, and tests. I keep putting the grading off, and then all of a sudden I feel so bad about it that I stay up until 2 AM just to finish it and hand it back the next day. At the end of every quarter, I have lots of grading backed up and have to spend every spare minute on it. I've been lucky that the parents haven't complained to the principal.

P: How are you feeling about all that?

C: I feel ashamed. No one but my husband knows that I'm like this. I try to keep it a secret from my coworkers because I don't want them thinking negatively about me.

P: How are you feeling about yourself when you think about this?

C: It makes me feel like I'm a terrible teacher and I'm just hiding it from everyone. Like no one would like me if they knew how I really am.

P: I find that most adults with ADHD have a lot of negative thoughts about themselves. It seems like you've had quite a surprise to realize that you might have been a kid with ADHD instead of a difficult, lazy kid like your parents and teachers said. As you know, that kind of feedback has a negative impact on a kid's self-image and feelings about themselves. I can see that you're still having some of these feelings today, since you talk about being ashamed and feeling like a terrible teacher. I want to ask you some more questions to get a better handle on how you've been doing, but I suspect that you're right—that you were a kid with ADHD and that some of these symptoms may well have persisted to adulthood. What are your feelings about your student, the one that has ADHD?

C: She's a good kid, a really talented artist, and I can see that she's struggling.

P: Given what you know now about ADHD, do you think she's a bad kid or that she's not applying herself enough?

C: No, she's a great kid. Whitney explained to me that the functioning of the brain in a kid with ADHD is different and that's why she struggles with paying attention and getting things done.

P: And the same thing may be true of you, that you're a person who tries hard but struggles with some cognitive differences that, at this point, are beyond your control.

C: I understand your point, but it may take a while for that to sink in.

P: That's understandable. It's a big deal to rethink your ideas about yourself and your past in this way. I noticed that you had difficulty getting your intake paperwork done on time. Do you often wrestle with paperwork?

C: Yes, all the time. I try to hide it, but sometimes people can tell. I have a question. Some of the parents and teachers at my school say that ADHD isn't a real disorder and that those kids just need more support, better parenting, or better teaching. So sometimes I wonder whether ADHD really even exists and what that means for me.

P: I've heard people say these things too. Actually, there's good scientific evidence that a diagnosis of ADHD is related to real changes in the structure, biochemistry, and functioning of the brain.

C: Also, I've been talking about this with my friends, and some of them say that they don't think that ADHD is a real diagnosis either.

P: There is a lot of misinformation out there about ADHD. Considerable research about genetics, brain functioning, and ADHD symptoms has shown that ADHD is a valid condition. We can talk more about this research later if you are interested. For now, can I get some more information about how you've been doing and see if we can pin this down?

EXCERPTS FROM TROY'S INITIAL SESSION: PRESENTING PROBLEMS

The second client, Troy, was diagnosed ADHD in childhood and is still having problems. Troy is a 34-year-old white married father of three and a car mechanic. On the phone, he said that he had been diagnosed with ADHD as a child, and now his youngest daughter has been diagnosed with ADHD as well. His wife has been encouraging him to come to therapy for a while. He and his wife have conflicts about communication, organization, and parenting. The following is an excerpt from the first session.

Psychotherapist: I'm glad you could make it in. So tell me more about why you decided to come to psychotherapy.

Troy: My wife encouraged me to. We really love each other and we've been together forever, since we were teenagers. We have three kids. My youngest daughter's teacher recently told us that she thought our daughter had ADHD. I guess I wasn't too surprised, since I had ADHD myself when I was a kid.

P: So what's going on at school with your daughter?

T: The school psychologist tested her and confirmed that she has ADHD. We've had a meeting with the teachers and the school psychologist. They've given us some good advice for working with her at home. We hope that she will be able to make better progress at school now that we know what is going on.

P: I'm glad to hear that you're feeling that she's getting the help she needs. Do you have your intake paperwork for me? That will help us sort out your issues.

T: Here it is. [Troy hands over the intake paperwork. The pages are filled out with different colors of pens and the pages are mixed up and not in the original order. He didn't finish filling out the ADHD questionnaire.]

P: Here, I'll give this questionnaire back to you. Can you fill it out and bring it in next week?

T: Sure. Sorry I didn't get to it before the session.

P: No worries. I have to tell you that I often find clues about whether someone has ADHD in how they fill out their paperwork. So I'm seeing that you didn't get to part of it, and the rest of it is a bit disorganized. Do you often have problems organizing tasks in your life?

T: Sometimes. At work, I usually don't have many problems because I just go step-by-step to make a repair on a car. My cousin owns the shop that I work at. He always says that I'm the best at figuring out what's wrong with a car when everyone else is stumped. But then, if a car needs several things done to it, he has to go over the list with me afterwards because sometimes I forget to do one or two of the repairs.

P: What about at home? Do you have any problems being organized there?

T: That can be a big problem. There's always a lot going on at our house with three kids. Aimee—that's my wife—sometimes blows up and says that she feels like she's got four kids instead of three. I feel bad because I do try.

P: What kinds of things make Aimee angry?

T: All kinds of things. I leave my clothes all over the floor, and she has to pick them up. I start doing the laundry, but then I get distracted and don't finish it. I'll tell her that I'm going to clean up the breakfast dishes, but then they'll still be there when she's ready to start making dinner. I really mean to do them, but she says I don't get credit for it unless I actually get them done. Aimee says that she's been reading about adults with ADHD since our daughter was diagnosed, and she thinks I never did outgrow it.

P: Have you been reading about adult ADHD too? What else have you noticed that makes you think you still have ADHD?

T: I had hyperactivity as a kid, and I'm not bouncing off the walls anymore, but sometimes Aimee asks me to sit down and chill out, and I just can't unless I've been smoking pot. I interrupt people a lot when they are talking, which I see is a common problem for adults with ADHD.

P: Sounds like you're thinking you still have some issues with hyperactivity and impulsiveness.

T: Yes, sometimes the only thing that can chill me out is smoking some weed. Maybe I do it too much.

P: I've heard a number of clients who still have hyperactivity as adults say that marijuana helps them chill out. However, I'm a bit concerned, because sometimes marijuana use can be related to motivation problems and people with ADHD can have problems with motivation even before they smoke any marijuana. Maybe we can help you figure out some other ways to manage hyperactivity. Would you be open to that?

T: Okay, I'm willing to consider that.

P: So getting back to impulsiveness—is that still a problem?

T: Yes, I can be hot-tempered sometimes. I yell at my cousin at work when I'm angry at him, but he's family, so he gets over it. Still, I don't feel very good about behaving that way. I get upset with myself because I think I'm still acting like a kid.

P: I can see that you have a lot of great things in life—you have a steady job that you like, a loving wife, and three kids. But I can also see that you're still struggling on a regular basis and it's creating some distress for you and your wife. People used to think that kids outgrew ADHD. But it turns out that most kids with ADHD just grow up to be adults with ADHD. You were diagnosed with ADHD as a kid, so that makes our assessment easier. All we need to do is figure out if you are still having ADHD symptoms. I'm hearing already that you're having some problems with hyperactivity, impulsiveness, hot temper, and organization. Let's get more details about these difficulties so we have a good understanding of what you are wrestling with.

KEY POINTS

- One out of every 5 to 10 psychotherapy clients is likely to have adult ADHD.
- ADHD is a real problem that affects the functioning, emotions, and self-esteem of millions of Americans, at least 4% of the population. At least 1 out of every 25 adult Americans has ADHD.
- ADHD has the following core characteristics: it is a neurological disorder that has developmental aspects, it is highly heritable, and it affects cognitive and adaptive functioning.

2

Adult ADHD Symptoms

Understanding the symptoms of adult ADHD is an essential starting place. Misinformation about ADHD floats around constantly in the popular press. Researchers have learned a lot about the symptoms of adult ADHD in the past 10 years or so. Unfortunately, most of this information is buried in journal articles and in interesting—but somewhat technical—professional books, which most busy clinicians do not have time to access and review.

I start with *Diagnostic and Statistical Manual of Mental Disorders* (DSM; American Psychiatric Association, 2013) symptoms and then move on to other adult ADHD symptoms that have been well documented in multiple research studies. Following a description of each symptom are suggested interview questions for assessment. The clinical interview questions about ADHD in this chapter—some verbatim and some modified—are from many sources (Adler & Cohen, 2004; Asherson, 2005; Barkley & Brown, 2008; Barkley, Murphy, & Fischer, 2008; McGough, 2014; Murphy & Gordon, 2006; Ramsay, 2010b; Surman, 2013a; Weiss & Murray, 2003). The questions that are in *italics* are especially predictive of a diagnosis of ADHD (Barkley et al., 2008; Buitelaar, 2011; Riccio et al., 2005; World Health Organization, 2003). Not all questions need to be asked of all clients. Instead, only enough questions need to be asked to determine whether there are significant symptoms and difficulties with functioning.

DSM SYMPTOM: INATTENTION/DISTRACTIBILITY

Troy: My family has always said that I'm flakey and forgetful. I can't tell you how many gloves and hats I lost as a kid. My wife gets mad at me because I sometimes go off to work without my keys or phone and she can't reach me or someone has to let me back into our house. I do okay at work, but sometimes people get frustrated with me because they say that they already told me something and I don't remember them telling me at all.

Clara: I don't lose things very often because I have a system for where everything goes and I carefully stick to it. Otherwise, I would. I used to lose a lot of things when I was a kid. When I'm talking to my husband, sometimes I will zone out and have to drag my attention back to what he's saying. I really do care, but I can have a hard time concentrating on the details of what he's saying to me, especially if I don't know the people involved.

Over 90% of adults with ADHD have inattentiveness symptoms (Wilens et al., 2009). So, in the vast majority of cases, inattention and distractibility will be present in adults with ADHD. (The other 10% have hyperactivity alone.)

Inattention and distractibility are common among many mental illnesses (Riccio et al., 2005), so inattention and distractibility should not be used to diagnose adult ADHD without examining the full clinical and developmental picture. Questions to assess inattention and distractibility during the clinical interview include the following (italics indicate questions that most reliably predict an ADHD diagnosis):

- *Do you find yourself being distracted by your own thoughts? Are you prone to daydreaming?*
- *Do you lose track of what is being discussed even when you're trying to pay attention?*
- *Are you easily distracted by extraneous noises and events?*
- *Do you have difficulty sustaining attention at work or school?*
- *Are you often losing things such as your keys, cell phone, or important documents? How often do you spend more than 10 minutes a day looking for things?*
- Do you often lose track of plans or appointments?
- Do you have a hard time keeping track of things when you get interrupted?
- Do you have difficulty sustaining attention during classes or meetings?
- Do you have a hard time comprehending written materials and need to reread them?
- Do you forget the point you're trying to make when you're talking to other people?
- Do you feel that the quality of your work is inconsistent or that you could get a lot more work done if you could concentrate?
- Do you struggle with attention to details?

DSM SYMPTOM: IMPULSIVENESS

Troy: I've been impulsive ever since I was a kid. My wife says sometimes I don't know when to shut up, and she says I don't have any tact. I know she's right about that. I just blurt things out and then I feel bad afterwards because I know I was rude. Sometimes she gets mad at me because I've gotten something new for my bike and didn't check with her first about the budget, like we agreed. Our budget is tight with three kids, and she tells me that I spend too much, which I know I do.

Impulsiveness alone cannot be used to diagnose adult ADHD because individuals with other mental illnesses are often also impulsive (bipolar disorder and antisocial personality disorder, for example). Again, impulsiveness has to be evaluated in the context of the individual's full developmental and clinical picture. Although I describe impulsiveness and hyperactivity separately here, and we may conceptualize them differently, research shows that hyperactivity and impulsiveness tend to co-occur and are generally part of the same symptom cluster (Matte et al., 2015). Questions to assess impulsivity during the clinical interview include the following (italics indicate some of the questions most predictive of ADHD diagnosis):

- *Do you tend to make decisions impulsively?*
- *Do you like to drive your car faster than others drive? Are you especially impatient when you drive?*
- *Do you tend to blurt out responses and interrupt others when they are talking? How often do other people ask you to let them finish?*
- *Do you have difficulty being quiet when you are engaging in leisure activities or doing fun things?*
- Do you find yourself being impulsive? In what areas of your life? (This could include social situations, spending, work, and other situations.)
- Do you have a reputation for making tactless remarks?
- Do you have any problems with spending impulsively?
- Is it difficult for you to behave appropriately at times?

DSM SYMPTOM: HYPERACTIVITY

Troy: I like to always be on the go. I have an active job, but when I get home, I like to run around and play ball in the yard with the kids for a while. Then I'll come in and fix dinner. And in the evening, I play softball with two different teams, and I also coach. Aimee says she can't keep up with me.

Some adults with ADHD have residual symptoms of hyperactivity, but others never had any hyperactivity at all. Hyperactivity in adulthood is generally a much subtler condition than hyperactivity in childhood and is often reported as an internal sense of restlessness (Kessler et al., 2010), rather than considerable inappropriate movement like children have. However, one study found differences in the amount of small movements between ADHD and control subjects, with the ADHD subjects shifting around in their chairs three times as much as controls during a task (Lis et al., 2010).

Clinically, I tend to observe two types of adults with hyperactivity. The first type has obvious adult hyperactivity, such as Troy (see previous quote). He talks quickly, has tangential thoughts, gets easily excited, tends to be expressive with his hands and body movements during the session, and always gives the feeling of being quickly in motion. It is clear that he has a high energy level and has difficulty staying still for long. Keeping up with his rapid speech and tangential topic changes during the session can be tiring. However, he can often concentrate well during the session because it is an interesting and novel experience. Sometimes it is difficult to tell the difference between an individual like this and someone who has hypomania. However, a few questions will clearly reveal that the individual with ADHD is always hyper and does not have the severe mood swings of bipolar disorder.

The second type of adult with hyperactivity is subtler. She does not speak as rapidly, nor is she as obviously hyperactive during the session. However, she tends to be tangential in her speech. Also, when you talk to her about her daily life and activities, you find that she is always on the go, has difficulty sitting still, often feels restless, has difficulty relaxing, and has an energy level that is high for her age.

Interestingly, medication can help manage hyperactivity and improve tangential speech. However, the individual will maintain a very high energy level. Symptoms similar to hyperactivity can sometimes be found in other mental illnesses (agitated depression or mania, for example), so a careful clinical interview is often needed. Watch for these behavioral symptoms of hyperactivity:

- Pacing, leg shaking, playing with desk items, or rustling papers while talking (Wasserstein, 2005)
- Speaking rapidly in a tangential and somewhat disorganized fashion (Engelhardt, Ferreira, & Nigg, 2011; Knouse & Safren, 2013)

Even if the client is not obviously showing signs of hyperactivity, still ask:

- *Do you have difficulty relaxing and engaging in leisure activities quietly?*
- *Do you tend to be squirmy and fidgety?*
- *Do you tend to feel restless or want to be on the go all the time?*
- (For individuals middle-aged and above): Do you have a high energy level compared to others your age?

PROBLEMS WITH USING DSM CRITERIA FOR ADULT ADHD

The DSM criteria have always been significantly flawed and inadequate to diagnose adult ADHD for the following reasons:

- *The criteria were developed for children, not adults.* They have never been validated on adults, nor sufficiently adapted for use with adults (Buitelaar, 2011).
- *There is too much emphasis on hyperactivity.* In the fourth edition, text revision (DSM-IV-TR), criteria were insensitive to developmental changes across the lifespan (Deault, 2010). Hyperactivity is a major functional issue in children (Deault, 2010) but is much less important

in adults (Biederman, 2011). This has not been resolved with the fifth edition (DSM-5).

- *Too many symptoms are required for adults.* The number of ADHD symptoms usually decreases from childhood to adulthood, but the remaining symptoms are very impairing. The DSM-IV-TR criteria did not take this into account and therefore underdiagnosed ADHD in adults (Barkley, 2006a). DSM-5 changes this somewhat, but insufficiently (see later discussion).
- *The criteria ignore many well-documented adult ADHD symptoms, especially executive dysfunction.* DSM-IV-TR criteria did not include additional symptoms that adults with ADHD may have, such as difficulty regulating emotions, executive functioning problems, time management problems, and difficulties relating to the brain reward system. Experts considered it crucially important to add executive function deficits to the DSM-5 definition of ADHD (Kessler et al., 2010), but this did not happen.
- *The criteria emphasize categorization, not continuum.* ADHD is on a continuum, with some people having severe symptoms and others mild symptoms (Asherson, 2013). No version of the DSM reflects this.
- *There is too much emphasis on subtypes.* Considerable research shows that DSM-IV-TR subtypes (which are the same as what the DSM-5 calls "presentations") are unstable over time (Willcutt et al., 2012).
- *The criteria are not helpful for differential diagnoses.* DSM-IV-TR criteria for ADHD did not adequately distinguish between adults with ADHD and adults with other psychiatric disorders (Buitelaar, 2011). The DSM-5 did not fix this.
- *The criteria ignore many adult settings that can be impaired.* DSM-IV-TR criteria only specified school, work, and home as settings where impairment may be present. What about financial management, child rearing, marital functioning, and health maintenance activities (McGough & Barkley, 2004)?

The DSM-5 criteria for ADHD have improved somewhat over the DSM-IV-TR criteria (American Psychiatric Publishing, 2013a, 2013b). Specifically,

- *Symptom number change*: Children must have at least six symptoms from either the inattention or the hyperactivity/impulsivity group of symptoms, but now adults and teens ages 17 and up are required to have only five symptoms from either symptom group.
- *Age of onset change*: Instead of ADHD requiring an age of onset before 7 years old, the age of onset is now before 12 years old. This is more consistent with research and expert recommendations (Faraone, Biederman, Spencer, et al., 2006; McGough & Barkley, 2004), but current evidence suggests that this is still too young a cut-off age (Faraone, 2016)—15 or 16 years old is a more useful and valid cut-off age (Buitelaar, 2011; Ramsay, 2010b).

These changes move the DSM-5 in the right direction, but they do not catch up with current knowledge about adult ADHD. The cut-off of five symptoms for adults is still too high (Buitelaar, 2011; Matte et al., 2015; Solanto, Wasserstein, Marks, & Mitchell, 2012). For example, an adult with four symptoms of ADHD may not be able to pay good attention to what he is told, he may be highly disorganized, he may not be able to keep his attention on work, and he may be very forgetful. This level of symptoms is more than sufficient to result in job loss, relationship problems, and so on. For these reasons, the number of symptoms present may be more clinically useful than whether or not an individual is categorized with ADHD (Lahey & Willcutt, 2010).

Presentation (formerly called subtype) classifications are also problematic. The DSM-5 categorizes ADHD as the predominantly inattentive presentation, the predominantly hyperactive presentation, and a combined presentation (in which both types of symptoms are present). Researchers have not found much evidence that these subtypes are meaningful on a genetic level (Thapar, Langley, O'Donovan, & Owen, 2006), nor are these subtypes related to cognitive differences (Nigg et al., 2005) or stable over time (Willcutt et al., 2012). Also, experts conclude that it is premature to establish new subtype categories because data do not yet exist that fully support any particular new subtype scheme (Willcutt et al., 2012). Recently, Lahey and Willcutt (2010) proposed that ADHD be considered a single disorder without subtypes while specifying the degree of inattentive and hyperactive-impulsive symptoms the client has. For the purposes of this book, I follow their recommendation to consider ADHD a single disorder, while keeping in mind the importance of assessing and understanding each individual's particular symptoms.

Even the term used—attention deficit/hyperactivity disorder—can be considered problematic, although it is now firmly entrenched. As discussed earlier, hyperactivity is *not* a major problem for most adults with ADHD, although some—like Troy—still struggle with it. Attention problems are a more important part of adult ADHD, but attention problems alone do not adequately differentiate ADHD adults from adults with other mental illnesses (Kessler et al., 2010; Riccio et al., 2005). Nonetheless, as of now, the term ADHD is well established, and no one has proposed a commonly accepted alternative.

OVERVIEW OF ADDITIONAL ADULT ADHD SYMPTOMS

Attention problems, impulsiveness, and hyperactivity are important, but other ADHD symptoms *are* significant—especially for adults. The most important ones are:

- Emotion regulation problems
- Time perception, time management, and motor control problems
- Symptoms associated with a different brain reward system
- Executive functioning deficits (*executive functioning* refers to a person's ability to self-manage, self-control, plan, and organize life tasks across time to achieve desired outcomes)

Note that adults with ADHD are a very heterogeneous group, so not every individual will have symptoms from every group.

EMOTIONAL DYSREGULATION

Troy: Everyone says I have a hell of a temper, and I know they are right. I can just go off and start yelling. I say things that I regret later. I think my temper is better now, but sometimes I still struggle. I yell at people before I even think. I know that's not using good communication skills, and I feel bad afterwards. And I feel terrible after I yell at my kids.

ADHD researchers and experts consider emotional dysregulation (also called deficient emotional self-regulation, emotional lability, emotional impulsiveness, or affective instability) to be an important symptom cluster (Barkley, 2010; Barkley & Fischer, 2010; Matte, 2012; Retz, Stieglitz, Corbisiero, Retz-Junginger, & Rösler, 2012; Skirrow, McLoughlin, Kuntsi, & Asherson, 2009; Shaw, Stringaris, Nigg, & Leibenluft, 2014; Surman et al., 2011). Emotional dysregulation in ADHD involves intense fluctuating emotions that are difficult to control and result in impulsive emotional behavior (Barkley, 2010b). The emotional dysregulation of ADHD is characterized by the following (Barkley, 2010b; Barkley & Fischer, 2010; Brown, 2013; Haavik, Halmøy, Lundervold, & Fasmer, 2010; Reimherr, 2016; Skirrow et al., 2009):

- Irritability
- Frustration
- Impatience
- Anger/temper outbursts
- Easily excitable
- Frequent mood shifts but not meeting criteria for mood disorders
- Overreactiveness to stressors

This type of emotional dysregulation is characteristic of ADHD, rather than depression and anxiety (Skirrow & Asherson, 2013). A reasonable estimate is that *about half of adults with ADHD have emotional dysregulation* and about half do not (Shaw et al., 2014; Surman, Biederman, et al., 2013).

Adults with emotional dysregulation are usually more impaired than those without it (Barkley & Fischer, 2010; Surman, Biederman, et al., 2013). However, emotional dysregulation is much less studied than traditional symptoms that characterize adult ADHD (Skirrow, McLoughlin et al., 2009). Problems that ensue from emotional dysregulation include:

- Others feel that the individual overreacts to minor problems
- Minor life stresses are seen as crises
- Temper outbursts
- Moodiness leads to relationship problems

- Many episodes of socially inappropriate emotional outbursts
- Low frustration tolerance and other negative emotions may be a cause of unsafe driving (Oliver, Nigg, Cassavaugh, & Backs, 2012)

Expert opinions vary as to whether emotional dyscontrol should become an official symptom category for ADHD. However, because of the previously mentioned findings, any adult with chronic emotional lability should be evaluated for ADHD (Skirrow & Asherson, 2013) and all clients with suspected ADHD should be evaluated for emotional dysregulation. Questions to assess this clinically include:

- Are you moody?
- Do you often feel overwhelmed?
- Do you feel that you have difficulty managing your emotions, especially irritability, frustration, or impatience?
- Do you have problems with your temper?

TIME PERCEPTION, TIME MANAGEMENT, AND MOTOR CONTROL PROBLEMS

Clara: I can make it in to school on time every morning because I know if I don't, my job is at risk. Most everything else, I'm late for. I'm not as bad as I used to be—back when I was 20, all my friends would joke that they needed to tell me a time that was an hour earlier than the real time in order to get me anywhere on time. Now, I'm usually just 5 to 15 minutes late.

Many adults with ADHD are less able to estimate time intervals accurately than adults without ADHD (Aguiar, Eubig, & Schantz, 2010; Barkley et al., 2008; Seidman, 2006). Also, time management is often a significant problem (Riccio et al., 2005). The following time perception and time management symptoms are found to be common in adults with ADHD (Riccio et al., 2005, p. 265):

- Difficulty meeting deadlines
- Lack of forethought
- Less well-developed sense of time

Other symptoms of difficulty managing time include:

- Frequently late to important meetings, events, or classes
- Chronically underestimating time necessary to complete tasks or to make a trip

Difficulties with coordination are commonly found in children with ADHD (Nigg, 2006). This symptom is not often studied in adults, but occasionally symptoms emerge that may be related to motor coordination problems, such as being accident-prone (Fedele, Hartun, Canu, & Wilkowski, 2010). Timing is a key element of good motor control, so these two issues are probably related (Nigg, 2006). Motor and time differences are discussed further in chapter 10.

The following are some questions that can be used clinically to assess difficulties estimating time, managing time, and being uncoordinated:

- Do you miss deadlines for projects?
- Do you have trouble figuring out how much time it will take to do a task or to get somewhere?
- Are you often late to important meetings, events, or classes?
- Do you have a hard time keeping track of time?
- Are you accident-prone?
- Do you have difficulties with coordination or clumsiness?

ATYPICAL REWARD SENSITIVITY

Clara: I have this oddball hobby of fixing up old watches and clocks. I have a workbench in the garage with all my tools and the clocks I'm working on. My husband complains that I can stay out there for hours, without eating or going to bed at a reasonable hour. I know he feels neglected when I do that, but I just get into the zone. He says that I like the clocks more than I like him, and that makes me feel terrible.

Troy: When I was younger, I would just walk out of the grocery store, just leaving my groceries sitting there, if the lines were too long. I hate to wait. I would go shopping in the middle of the night, if I was still up, just to avoid the lines.

Many people with ADHD are strongly driven by immediate rewards, while longer term rewards, even if more valuable, are not nearly as motivating (Ströhle et al., 2008). Related findings are that they have (a) a very strong preference for interesting and novel stimuli and tasks—which are immediately reinforcing, and (b) a strong aversion to stimuli and tasks that are considered boring, tedious, and mundane—which are *not* immediately reinforcing. In other words, *Interesting = Easy* and *Boring = Hard*. These differences result in significant variability in performance from one task to another (Brown, 2008), which in turn contributes to the incorrect conclusion that variability in performance is due to lack of willpower. Instead, different reward system activation in the brains of people with ADHD contributes to this variability (Ströhle et al., 2008).

My ADHD clients often describe getting an enjoyable and energetic cognitive "buzz" when they immerse themselves in something interesting. The length of the task, its difficulty, the amount of thought necessary, and so on are not very important factors for people with ADHD. If they are interested in something, they dive right in (unless they are overwhelmed by the size of the task or are having difficulties organizing it). They then experience "hyperfocus," get extremely engrossed, and lose all sense of time and other priorities. However, once the task becomes boring, or a few tedious details need to be wrapped up, it may be abandoned. This leads to multiple abandoned projects, starts and stops in academic coursework, job changes, and sometimes even abandoned relationships (Solanto, 2011).

Most adults with ADHD want everything to happen immediately. They react to delays with overactivity, inattention, frustration, and irritability (Sonuga-Barke, Sergeant, Nigg, & Willcutt, 2008). They get easily frustrated and annoyed with situations that involve waiting and may even prefer to leave rather than wait. They understand delayed gratification intellectually but can have difficulty implementing the concept, so they procrastinate on long-term goals. They tend to do fun or interesting activities, which are immediately reinforcing, instead of focusing on necessary (but boring) tasks that only have long-term benefits (such as paying the electric bill so the lights stay on next month, filing income taxes in time to avoid late filing fees later, or organizing paperwork so important documents can be readily located when needed).

People with ADHD *can* concentrate on boring tasks *if* they are sufficiently motivated. However, this requires increased mental effort (Loo et al., 2009; Prox, Dietrich, Zhang, Emrich, & Ohlmeier, 2007), which is subjectively difficult and draining. Generally, they have difficulty staying alert and persisting with boring tasks. Active encouragement, structure, and companionship from others can help a person with ADHD maintain effort on tedious tasks (Ek & Isaksson, 2013). This is how many kids with ADHD get through school—with ample encouragement, structure, and close supervision from parents. An immediate deadline also helps to focus the mind of a person with ADHD. They tend to complete tasks just before deadline, or even miss deadlines, because the task was put off until the deadline was pressing and immediate.

In summary, *four factors tend to focus the mind of a person with ADHD: interesting stimuli, novel stimuli, a looming deadline, or others providing support and structure.* Medication helps with focus considerably as well.

Here are some questions to clinically assess your client's brain reward system:

- Is it difficult to continue to work on boring tasks?
- Do you sometimes have to exert a lot of mental energy to keep your mind concentrated? Especially on dull tasks?
- Do you have a hard time tolerating boredom? Are you easily bored?
- Is it hard to stay alert or awake in boring situations?
- Do you have a hard time doing things that may pay off far in the future?
- Do you find yourself searching for things that are new and stimulating?
- Do you sometimes find yourself being so engrossed in interesting things that you completely lose track of time for hours?
- Is it difficult to stop interesting activities?
- Do you have a hard time finishing things unless there is an immediate deadline?
- Do you sometimes miss deadlines at work or school?

- Do you tend to procrastinate or put things off until the last minute?
- Does having a deadline help you concentrate and get things done?
- Do you have a hard time waiting or being patient?
- How often do you avoid waiting in lines or leave them?

EXECUTIVE FUNCTIONING DEFICITS

Clara: I stopped at the grocery store. I needed to remember to pick up some soy milk, salsa, two cans of black beans, bananas, and something else—I forget what. I picked up some blueberries and bananas. Then I ran into my neighbor and got into a brief discussion about our condo building. After that, I went to check out and realized when I got home that I didn't have soy milk, salsa, or beans. But I'd brought home several other things, including junk food, which I've been trying to avoid.

Troy: Getting the bills paid has always been a challenge for me. Luckily my wife does it all now. The last straw was when our cable was cut off one time because I forgot to pay it. She still gets frustrated because I'll bring the mail in and leave it in various places all over the house instead of where she wants it.

Executive functioning (EF) involves the multiple cognitive abilities necessary to effectively decide on, organize, prioritize, plan, and carry out tasks (Jurado & Rosselli, 2007). Experts agree that EF deficits are a key behavioral problem in most adults with ADHD (Barkley, 2014a; Brown, 2013; Matte, 2012; Ramsay, 2010b; Riccio et al., 2005; Surman, 2013). These questions assess EF problems commonly found in adult ADHD (Barkley et al., 2008; Kessler et al., 2010; Wasserstein, 2005; World Health Organization, 2003). As before, italics indicate questions that are particularly predictive of an adult ADHD diagnosis.

- *Is it difficult for you to organize tasks or activities?*
- *Is it difficult for you to stop your activities or behavior when you should do so?*
- *Is it a challenge for you to plan ahead?*
- *Do you start projects or tasks without reading or listening to the directions carefully?*
- *Is it difficult for you to get things done in their proper order?*
- *Do you miss deadlines? Do you have difficulty getting started with projects until you are right up against a deadline?*
- *Do you often struggle with follow-through on your promises or commitments to others?*
- Do you have a tendency to dive into projects without first thinking strategically about how to do them?
- Do you feel that you often waste time or have difficulty managing it?

- Do you tend to forget things that you were supposed to do? Do you tend to lose track of appointments? Do you tend to lose track of your bills and paperwork? Do you get your taxes in on time?
- Do you have difficulty finishing tasks at work?
- Do you feel that the quality of your work is inconsistent and that you have poor attention to detail?
- Do you feel that some tasks take more effort than they should? What are those tasks?
- Is it hard for you to change your behavior when people give you feedback about your mistakes?
- Is it difficult to keep track of several activities at once?
- Do you sometimes find yourself switching from one task to another in a haphazard fashion?
- Can you get things done more easily if someone else helps and organizes the job for you?
- If you are interrupted while doing something, is it hard to get back to what you were doing before the interruption?

DO ALL CLIENTS WITH ADHD HAVE SYMPTOMS FROM EACH SYMPTOM GROUP?

Every individual with ADHD has a unique constellation of symptoms and deficits. ADHD is genetically, symptomatically, cognitively, and behaviorally *heterogeneous* (Dias et al., 2013). Not all individuals with ADHD have inattentiveness, hyperactivity, affective instability, or time management problems (Surman et al., 2011; Wilens et al., 2009; Willcutt, Doyle, Nigg, Faraone, & Pennington, 2005). Opinions among experts differ as to whether executive functioning problems are a core symptom of adult ADHD (Barkley, 2014a; Brown, 2013; Ramsay, 2010b) or whether some clients with ADHD do not have executive functioning problems (Sonuga-Barke et al., 2008), but it is commonly agreed that executive functioning problems are found among most adults with ADHD.

SLUGGISH COGNITIVE TEMPO: ANOTHER SYMPTOM CLUSTER?

Elizabeth is an agent for a large insurance company, and she works out of a storefront. She inherited a large caseload of clients from her mother, who is now retired. These clients provide a good income to her. She has a couple of employees who manage most of the work. She spends her days mostly lying on the couch watching TV. She reports feeling tired and sleepy much of the time. When she has to have a client meeting, she pulls it together and comes into the office but then lapses back into lethargy. When her mother comes from Florida to visit, she enjoys being more active but then quickly resumes lying on the couch and isolating herself when her mother is gone. She sometimes feels a bit down when thinking about how she is living her life and feels that she's wasting it. Her psychotherapist has recommended many interventions to activate her, but she only intermittently follows through.

Sluggish cognitive tempo (SCT) describes a subset of individuals with very specific behavioral, concentration, and cognitive problems (Barkley, 2012, 2014c; Becker, Marshall, & McBurnett, 2014; McBurnett, 2016; Saxbe & Barkley, 2014), including most of the following:

- Daydreaming
- Cognitive slowing, mentally foggy, easily confused
- Trouble staying awake and alert
- Drowsy and sleepy appearance
- Physical underactivity
- Slow to complete tasks
- Lacks initiative and/or effort fades
- Stares a lot
- Apathetic/withdrawn
- Underactive, slow-moving, sluggish, lethargic
- Seems distracted, "spacey," lost in thoughts
- Does not process questions or explanations accurately
- Working memory issues: becomes confused, loses track of thoughts, forgets what he or she was going to say

There is a movement to rename this condition concentration deficit disorder, since the term "sluggish" can be seen as pejorative (Barkley, 2014c).

It is likely that, in practice, most of these individuals have been diagnosed with the inattentive type of ADHD—if they are identified as having problems at all. There is significant overlap between SCT and ADHD, inattentive type, with many people having both (Barkley, 2012), but statistical analyses show that the symptom patterns are distinct (Barkley, 2012; Becker, 2013; Willcutt et al., 2014) and that some individuals have SCT without ADHD (Becker, 2013). In conclusion, SCT is strangely similar to hyperactivity, because—like hyperactivity—SCT can occur separately from inattention and other ADHD symptoms but commonly is comorbid.

Until 2012, all the research on SCT was done with children and teens (Barkley, 2012). Little was known about adults with SCT. Recent research has found associations between SCT and the following:

- *Decreased income*: Incomes of community adults with SCT (and with both SCT and ADHD) were found to be lower than those of control and ADHD-only adults (Barkley, 2012).
- *Academic impairment, anxiety, and depression*, among college students (Becker, Langberg, Luebbe, Dvorsky, & Flannery, 2014).

- *Worse sleep quality*, among college students (Becker, Luebbe, & Langberg, 2014)
- *Decreased psychological and physical quality of life* (Combs, Canu, Fulks, & Nieman, 2014)
- *Emotional dysregulation*, among college students (Flannery, Becker, & Luebbe, 2016; Jarrett, Rapport, Rondon, & Becker, 2014)
- *Executive dysfunction, especially with self-organization and problem-solving*, among college students (Jarrett et al., 2014)
- *High impairment in combination with ADHD*: The combination of SCT and ADHD was more impairing than either disorder alone (Barkley, 2012).

All of these findings are tentative because many of these studies were done with college students and, in most cases, only one research study supports each of the points.

No formal diagnostic criteria are available for SCT. The Barkley Adult ADHD Rating Scale-IV has been used to assess SCT in adults (see Appendix 1 for further information about this scale). Very little evidence is yet available regarding effective medication for SCT; however, the best evidence available suggests low doses of stimulants and/or atomoxetine may be effective (Barkley, 2014c; Wietecha et al., 2013). It is not completely clear how SCT can be treated effectively with psychotherapy because these clients are so difficult to motivate and activate.

So here are two take-home messages for psychotherapists about SCT. First, be aware that people who present primarily with attention, distractibility, concentration, and executive functioning problems can have all different levels of physical and mental activity, ranging from very high (hyperactivity) to normal to very low (SCT). Second, there is a group of individuals who may behaviorally appear depressed (low energy level, low motivation, low functioning), but actually are not clinically depressed and are mostly okay with this lifestyle—these people probably have SCT.

WORKING TOWARD A NEW DEFINITION OF ADHD

Expert consensus is emerging about symptom clusters that are central to adult ADHD:

- *Inattention/distractibility*: Clearly, inattention and distractibility remain a major problem for almost all adults who have ADHD. This is a key symptom cluster. However, people with other mental illnesses sometimes display these symptoms too. So these symptoms are not always helpful for differential diagnosis.
- *Impulsiveness*: Impulsiveness is a key problem for many adults who have ADHD.

- *Hyperactivity:* Most adults, although not all, outgrow obvious symptoms of hyperactivity. But many adults still have subjective restlessness and a greater tendency toward fidgeting or making small, frequent movements that may not be particularly noticeable to others.
- *Emotional dysregulation:* There is a growing consensus that emotional dysregulation is a key symptom cluster for about half of adults who have ADHD.
- *Executive functioning deficits:* There is universal consensus among experts that EF deficits should be considered an important symptom cluster for adults with ADHD. Although experts disagree as to whether all or most adults with ADHD have EF problems, they do agree that EF deficits are important and potentially debilitating symptoms when present.
- *Sluggish cognitive tempo:* SCT is not a diagnosis in the DSM-5. Multiple research studies show that SCT symptoms are distinct from ADHD inattentive symptoms, although they commonly coexist. No consensus has emerged about whether SCT is a separate but often overlapping diagnosis or another presentation of ADHD (Combs, Canu, Broman Fulks, Rocheleau, & Nieman, 2015).
- *Time perception, time management, and motor control problems:* These problems are common to adults with ADHD. Time management has considerable overlap with EF problems. How or whether to include these in diagnosis is not yet fully clear.
- *Atypical reward sensitivity:* While differences in reward sensitivity are commonly found in adults with ADHD, I have not heard suggestions that it should be a part of the diagnostic criteria yet. Clinically, however, keep in mind that acute differences in response to boredom versus interest is highly predictive of ADHD.

A PRACTICAL ISSUE: DIAGNOSING ADHD WITH THE ICD-10

Clearly, the science of diagnosing ADHD is in flux. Given that the DSM-5 is fairly recent and considerable flaws remain with its criteria, this situation will not be resolved anytime soon. In addition to the DSM, there is another set of diagnostic criteria, the International Classification of Diseases, tenth edition (ICD-10; World Health Organization, 1993). ICD-10 criteria for ADHD are even more problematic than those in the DSM, because the international edition *requires* hyperactivity as a symptom of ADHD and does not acknowledge the existence of ADHD without hyperactivity (World Health Organization, 2015). In fact, the ICD-10 label for ADHD is *hyperkinetic disorder*. However, the American modification of the ICD-10 includes ADHD without hyperactivity. Like the DSM-5, ICD-10 criteria focus on childhood behaviors and do not adequately address adults.

As you probably know, the American healthcare system converted to using a modified version of ICD-10 for all diagnostic coding and insurance billing in late 2015. The following are the ADHD categories for the American version of ICD-10 (ICD10Data.com, 2015):

- F90.0, ADHD, predominantly inattentive type
- F90.1, ADHD, predominantly hyperactive type
- F90.2, ADHD, combined type
- F90.8, ADHD, other type, includes adult residual
- F90.9, ADHD, unspecified type

Use the appropriate code for one of the first three options if a client meets the DSM-5 criteria for ADHD. If the client clearly has ADHD symptoms and dysfunction but the number of inattention or hyperactive symptoms is not sufficient for the diagnosis, use F90.8 or F90.9.

KEY POINTS

- Inattention, hyperactivity, and impulsiveness remain key symptoms of ADHD, but the DSM-5 does not fully describe all adult ADHD symptoms.
- Most adults outgrow obvious hyperactivity if they had it as a child. But they may still shift around more when sitting, feel restless, and have difficulty relaxing quietly.
- Additional key symptoms of adult ADHD are (a) affect regulation problems; (b) time perception, time management, and motor control problems; (c) symptoms associated with a different brain reward system; and, most importantly, (d) EF deficits.
- Like children, not all adults with ADHD have symptoms from every symptom group. These symptom differences probably are reflective of genetic differences.
- Distinguishing subtypes (otherwise called presentations in the DSM-5) is less clinically useful than understanding which symptoms adults do and do not have.
- Emotional dysregulation is found in about half of adults with ADHD. Irritability, frustration and anger are easily triggered in these individuals.
- For many adults with ADHD, interesting tasks (no matter how long) are easy, while boring tasks (no matter how short) are hard.
- Four things focus the mind of a person with ADHD: interesting stimuli, novel stimuli, a looming deadline, and others providing support and structure. The right medicine helps too.

3

Hidden ADHD

Presenting Problems and Comorbidity

Hidden ADHD is common. Most adults with ADHD—between 70% and 90%—have psychiatric comorbidity (Adler, Barkley, Willens, & Ginsbert, 2006; Ramsay & Rostain, 2007). When ADHD is comorbid with another disorder, it is often unrecognized and untreated (Kessler et al., 2006). A client with untreated ADHD will have difficulty following through with treatment recommendations, which will negatively affect treatment (Barkley & Brown, 2008). Whenever a client does not respond adequately to treatment, comorbid ADHD should be considered (Barkley & Brown, 2008). Recognizing hidden ADHD is essential for effective treatment.

LOOK FOR ADHD-SPECIFIC SYMPTOMS AND DEVELOPMENTAL PATTERNS

ADHD symptoms like inattention or executive dysfunction are the kinds of symptoms that physicians call "nonspecific" (Ramsay, 2010). In other words, a medical symptom such as nausea or fever is definitely clinically important, but it could indicate many different diseases, so it is nonspecific. Similarly, most ADHD symptoms could be indicative of many different mental health problems, especially when only the current symptoms are evaluated.

However, Ramsay (2010b) clarifies that ADHD has "a distinctive developmental and symptom profile that can be identified through thorough assessment" (p. 10). So, when making a diagnosis, think longitudinally. For example, depression and anxiety tend to wax and wane over weeks, months, or years. However, ADHD symptoms are present every day, although at certain times they may be less noticeable. So determining whether ADHD symptoms have been consistently present—even when depression or anxiety were absent—usually clarifies the diagnostic picture.

PRESENTING PROBLEMS

People who have ADHD decide to engage in psychotherapy for many different reasons (Adler & Cohen, 2004), some which are directly related to ADHD:

- Sudden or gradual realization that ADHD may be related to life problems
- Client's child (or other relative) has been diagnosed with ADHD, so now client is wondering about self
- Client's spouse or partner insists that client be evaluated for ADHD
- "Hitting the wall" or "crashing and burning"—all of a sudden, the client's executive functioning skills are exceeded by life demands and a crisis ensues—such as flunking out of college, losing a job, being unable to finish a thesis, and so on (Manos, 2010)
- Dissatisfaction with chronic life problems caused by impulsiveness, poor attention to detail, poor time management, and poor organization, such as legal or criminal issues, financial crises, job crises, and so on (Adler & Cohen, 2004)
- Dissatisfaction with chronic interpersonal problems, such as impulsively blurting out tactless remarks, irritability, temper problems, difficulty sustaining friendships, difficulty listening to others (Barkley, 2006a), conflicts with authority (Adler & Cohen, 2004), and frequent arguments with family members
- Dissatisfaction with procrastination, lack of motivation, and underachievement; complaints about how much effort it takes to accomplish tasks (Asherson, 2013)
- Emotional distress, pain, regret, and frustration with underachievement in life, leading to low self-esteem (Tuckman, 2007)
- Inability to parent or attend to child's medical issues consistently (Canadian ADHD Resource Alliance [CADDRA], 2011)
- Challenges due to poor mood regulation, low frustration tolerance, or angry outbursts (Adler & Cohen, 2004; CADDRA, 2011)

Clients with any of these life problems should be assessed carefully for ADHD.

LOOK FOR BEHAVIORS SUGGESTIVE OF ADHD

Some clients do not present with concerns about ADHD, but they exhibit behaviors suggestive of ADHD:

- Client comes to first session without the requested paperwork.
- Client brings paperwork in to first session, but it is incomplete, messy, and/or the pages are all mixed up.

- Client usually runs late to sessions.
- Client is squirmy and fidgets during the session.
- Client talks rapidly in a pressured and tangential fashion.
- Client discusses life events that suggest impulsiveness and risk-taking, such as frequent accidents, involvement in extreme sports, or problems with driving (CADDRA, 2011).
- Client describes own possessions or speech as "all over the place."

Clients who exhibit these behaviors should be carefully screened for ADHD (among other disorders).

However, many clients who have ADHD will *not* exhibit these behaviors, so do not necessarily expect to notice significant symptoms of ADHD during the session (Asherson, 2005). The things you may *not* notice include distractibility, hyperactivity, lack of motivation, or poor attention to the task at hand. Why? Psychotherapy is a novel experience, and of course clients are interested in talking about their personal challenges. These aspects of the psychotherapy experience help focus the client's mind and minimize obvious ADHD symptoms.

SUBSTANCE ABUSE

All clients presenting with a substance abuse disorder should be assessed for ADHD. Clients with known substance abuse problems have ADHD 10% to 25% of the time (Barkley & Brown, 2008; Ohlmeier et al., 2008; Wilens, 2006). Looking at it from the other angle, about half of clients with known ADHD have a substance use disorder (Adler et al., 2006; McGough, 2014). These statistics confirm a high degree of overlap between substance abuse and ADHD. So all clients presenting with substance abuse should be evaluated for ADHD, and all clients presenting with ADHD should be evaluated for substance abuse.

Making an accurate diagnosis of ADHD in an adult who has recently or is currently abusing substances is notoriously difficult (Mariani & Levin, 2007). The cognitive and emotional symptoms of substance use often mimic ADHD and other psychiatric disorders (Mariani & Levin, 2007). Also, the life problems of individuals with substance abuse and ADHD are similar—for example, relationship, financial, work, and driving problems—so historical information may not fully clarify the diagnostic picture either. Sometimes it is helpful to ask about functioning during periods of abstinence in the past. If the ADHD-like symptoms started around the time that the substance abuse started, ADHD probably is not an appropriate diagnosis. However, the client might not have sufficient periods of abstinence to clarify the diagnostic picture (Mariani & Levin, 2007). Once the client has been abstinent for at least a month but probably longer, assessing whether adult ADHD is present will be easier (Sobanski, Paslakis, Schredl, Daffner, & Alm, 2013). If it is unclear whether a substance abuse client has ADHD, refer the client for substance abuse treatment and provide support as a first step in psychotherapy.

Chronic exposure to substances through addiction can lead to cognitive dysfunction that is similar to ADHD (Adler et al., 2006). If the client has a long and/or severe history of substance abuse, with no clear signs of childhood ADHD, it may be wise to refer for neurological and neuropsychological assessment to see if the diagnostic picture can be clarified.

On the other hand, it is also possible that the diagnostic picture may be relatively clear. Your client may have been diagnosed with ADHD as a child. As we know, most people with childhood ADHD do not outgrow it. The client may also have had significant periods of abstinence. Careful inquiry into the client's behavior and symptoms during those time periods can clarify whether ADHD is present.

Clients with ADHD tend to have more severe substance abuse, including earlier onset of substance abuse, longer time necessary to achieve remission, a greater risk of relapse, more relapses, and greater difficulty remaining abstinent (Upadhyaya, 2007; van de Glind et al., 2014; Wilens, 2006). ADHD and substance abuse have a shared genetic risk, and both involve the dopamine system of the brain (Wilens, 2006).

Childhood ADHD is a risk factor in developing substance abuse disorders as an adult (Ohlmeier et al., 2008; Wilens et al., 2011). Nonetheless, children treated with stimulants for ADHD were *less* likely to develop adult substance abuse problems than unmedicated children with ADHD (Wilens, Faraone, Biederman, & Ganawardene, 2003). Unfortunately, while early diagnosis and treatment of ADHD in children or young adults may help prevent substance abuse problems (Ohlmeier et al., 2008), our adult clients often reach us with substance abuse present.

Marijuana is the most commonly used substance (Wilens, 2006), perhaps because it calms the internal sensations of restlessness (Wilens, 2011), but clients also can self-medicate ADHD symptoms with nicotine, caffeine, alcohol, and cocaine (Adler & Cohen, 2004; Asherson, 2005; Wilens, 2011). Nicotine dependence (Ohlmeier et al., 2007) is common, probably because nicotine reduces symptoms of ADHD, which makes smoking cessation difficult (Wilens, 2006).

ANXIETY DISORDERS

Clara: I'm always worrying about whether my husband will get into a wreck on the way home. Will we survive financially? Why am I such a failure? My husband says that I'm my own worst enemy.

All clients presenting with an anxiety disorder should be screened for ADHD. Over one-quarter of adults presenting to an anxiety disorders clinic in Canada had ADHD (Van Ameringen, Mancini, Simpson, & Patterson, 2011). Also, about 40% to 50% of adults with ADHD have an anxiety disorder (Adler et al., 2006; McGough, 2014). Individuals who have panic disorder should also be screened for ADHD. One study found that about 10% of panic disorder patients fulfilled DSM-III-R criteria for ADHD and about 15% had subthreshold diagnoses (Fones, Pollack, Susswein, & Otto, 2000). Obsessive-compulsive disorder can also be comorbid with ADHD, but the degree of comorbidity remains unclear (Schatz & Rostain, 2006). Anxiety and ADHD can be assessed simultaneously. While concentration problems are common to both disorders, most other symptoms are unique to anxiety or ADHD.

At times, posttraumatic stress disorder may present with some symptoms resembling the attention deficits of ADHD (Ramsay & Rostain, 2015). Also, individuals growing up in a household where abuse or neglect is present may not have had the opportunity to learn executive functioning skills at the developmentally appropriate time.

The symptoms and dysfunction associated with ADHD often cause worry and anxiety (Asherson, 2005), increasing the risk of generalized anxiety disorder developing. Individuals with ADHD and anxiety have a reality-based fear of deficient social or cognitive functioning (Schatz & Rostain, 2006):

- Fear of making commitments because of past lack of follow-through
- Worry about not meeting deadlines, as has often been a problem in the past
- Anxiety about forgetting possessions and obligations
- Fear of "failing again"
- Fear of acting or speaking impulsively—blurting out inappropriate comments
- Worry about social situations because their minds tend to drift off topic
- Worry about difficulties managing and modulating emotions (Brown, 2013)
- Fear of what will go wrong next

Then, they may hyperfocus on their worries and ruminations for hours. They may even ruminate as a way to keep track of things, instead of using more effective skills. Anxiety can make working memory and other cognitive deficits worse (Schatz & Rostain, 2006), which contributes to a vicious cycle of errors and worry about performance. ADHD aggravates anxiety symptoms, and then anxiety symptoms aggravate ADHD symptoms.

Oddly, anxiety does seem to have an adaptive function in some individuals with ADHD. Anxiety may actually cause some improvement in functioning by inhibiting impulsivity, response inhibition deficits, and poor social behavior (Schatz & Rostain, 2006). They may become perfectionistic to cope with disorganization and past errors. While this strategy has been somewhat helpful, improved coping skills for ADHD and anxiety will lead to better mental health. Stimulant medication helps many clients with anxiety-provoking cognitive deficits and thus reduces anxiety. However, in others, stimulants may increase anxiety because of "jittery" feelings.

DEPRESSION

All clients presenting with depression should be assessed for ADHD (Alpert et al., 1996); depressive disorders are often comorbid:

- *Major depression*: About one-third of adults with ADHD have major depressive disorder (Adler et al., 2006).
- *Dysthymia*: ADHD is generally agreed to contribute to dysthymia in many individuals (Asherson, 2005).
- *Seasonal affective disorder:* About one-fourth of adults with ADHD were found to have seasonal affective disorder (Amons, Kooij, Haffmans, Hoffman, & Hoencamp, 2006).

Life difficulties of adults lead to low self-esteem, poor self-image, guilt, feelings of failure, hopelessness, underachievement, and emotional pain about their struggles (Murphy & Gordon, 2006). They can hyperfocus for hours on negative, ruminative thoughts, which worsens depression.

One symptom of depression is decreased concentration, which may resemble ADHD (Adler et al., 2006). Individuals with significant depression also have problems with motivation and procrastinate on major projects because they do not have the energy to address them. So when a client is severely depressed, it may be best to treat the depression and reevaluate ADHD symptoms later. Do not forget to evaluate the severely depressed client for past episodes of mania or hypomania, indicative of bipolar disorder. Also, the severely depressed client can still be assessed for a history suggestive of earlier childhood ADHD, even though current ADHD symptoms may be best evaluated when the client is less depressed.

If the client has mild major depression or dysthymia, depressive symptoms may not be so prominent, and ADHD can be accurately assessed. A history of childhood ADHD may clarify the diagnostic picture.

Psychotherapists often see clients who have untreated ADHD and depression as resistant and noncompliant. When ADHD is identified, effective treatment is possible. Medications for ADHD help the client follow through on behavioral activation, socialization, and other treatment recommendations for depression.

BIPOLAR DISORDER

All clients with bipolar disorder should be screened for ADHD. There is significant comorbidity between bipolar disorder and ADHD (Faraone, Biederman, & Wozniak, 2012). Over 20% of adults with bipolar disorder also meet criteria for ADHD (Barkley & Brown, 2008). However, a client with a current depressed, manic, hypomanic, or mixed episode should be treated for bipolar disorder first. When the client has attained normal mood or mildly depressed mood (which is common among bipolar clients between major mood episodes), then assess for ADHD.

Clients may present with symptoms that could be viewed as either ADHD or bipolar disorder, so bipolar disorder can be an important differential diagnosis (Davidson, 2008; Wender et al., 2001). Bipolar disorder and ADHD have some similarities:

- Rapidly changing moods and periods of being energized are common symptoms (Ramsay and Rostain, 2008b), although they are expressed differently in each disorder over time.
- Both can involve impulsive and reckless behavior.
- People who have ADHD can be very excited by activities that are of interest to them. This excitement can result in spending unusually long hours on the activity, and they may sometimes stay up all night in a hyperfocused state and an enthusiastic mood. This can initially resemble mania.

However, there are key differences between this hyperfocused enthusiastic state and a manic state. After staying up all night, a person with ADHD is tired and needs plenty of sleep. A person who is manic will still be full of energy and will not feel a need for much sleep—maybe just two or three hours and then they are up, full of energy again. A person who is manic usually hops from one enthusiasm to another all night, whereas a person with ADHD is hyperfocused on one interesting activity. Other differences between ADHD and bipolar disorder include (from Asherson, 2005; Murphy & Gordon, 2006):

- ADHD usually has a much earlier age of onset.
- ADHD is constant and chronic, whereas bipolar symptoms are intermittent.
- In ADHD, if there are mood swings, they are less extreme and occur multiple times per day, whereas in bipolar disorder, extreme moods generally last for days, if not weeks or months.
- Grandiosity and expansive mood are not found with ADHD, although excitement and enthusiasm can be present.
- Psychosis is not found in ADHD but is often present in bipolar disorder (Adler et al., 2006).
- In bipolar disorder, thoughts are sped up and often experienced as especially clear or insightful—this is not the case in ADHD, where thoughts feel unfocused and disorganized.
- Generally, individuals with bipolar disorder are more severely impaired than those with ADHD (Adler et al., 2006).

Of course, it is quite possible that the client may have both ADHD and bipolar disorder. When both are present, both should be treated.

ADDITIONAL COMORBIDITIES AND DIFFERENTIAL DIAGNOSES

Why are so many disorders comorbid with ADHD? Executive functioning problems are analogous to computer operating system problems—there is dysfunction at a very deep, basic, and unconscious level, leading to increased vulnerability to environmental stressors and increased risk of additional disorders (Brown, 2013). Also, there is often common genetic vulnerability. The following conditions also have increased comorbidity with ADHD:

- Borderline personality disorder (Fischer, Barkley, Smallish, & Fletcher, 2002). Sometimes it is necessary to make the differential diagnosis between borderline personality disorder and ADHD (see Wender, Wolf, & Wasserstein [2001] for more advice on this)
- Passive-aggressive personality disorder (Fischer et al., 2002)
- Antisocial personality disorder (Davidson, 2008; Fischer et al., 2002; Retz & Rösler, 2009)
- Histrionic personality disorder (Fischer et al., 2002)
- Conduct disorder and oppositional defiant disorder (McGough et al., 2005)
- Eating disorders, such as binge eating disorder (Pagoto et al., 2009), bulimia, and anorexia nervosa (Bleck, DeBate, & Olivardia, 2015)
- Learning disabilities (Davidson, 2008)
- Tic disorders (McGough, 2014)
- Hoarding disorder (Brown, 2013)
- Autism spectrum disorders (Musser et al., 2014): Individuals who have Asperger's syndrome, now classified simply as milder autism, have significant overlap in symptoms with ADHD, specifically issues with interpersonal functioning and hyperfocus on their interest areas (Adler et al., 2006; Barkley & Brown, 2008)

KEY POINTS

- If a psychotherapy client is not improving with standard treatment, it is quite likely that ADHD is complicating the clinical picture.
- ADHD should be assessed in every client presenting with substance abuse, anxiety, depression, or bipolar disorder.

4

Recognizing Strengths

Strengths may come from ADHD itself or from the experience of living with ADHD. This topic has been neglected by researchers (Murphy & Gordon, 2006; Wiklund, Patzelt, & Dimov, 2016). Not much research exists that examines how people with ADHD can thrive or can even exceed those who do not have ADHD. So I cite the literature, when it exists, but some of this chapter is speculative, based on clinical observation and anecdote.

Consider conceptualizing ADHD with a "difference model" instead of a deficit model (Manos, 2010). Using a difference model, we help clients with ADHD appreciate what their brain *is* capable of, and possibly *more* capable of—instead of solely focusing on deficits.

HIGHER ENERGY LEVEL THAN SAME-AGE PEERS

April is a 73-year-old widowed farmer. She's been a farmer all her life, working the farm with her husband while he was alive and raising their four children. She's still highly active. She's cut back and rents out much of the acreage of the farm now, but she plants and maintains a large organic garden and a small orchard. She sells her organic vegetables at the local farmer's market every Saturday, and in the fall she sells homemade jam from the fruit. She also enjoys canning throughout the growing season, and all her children and grandchildren are thrilled to get her peach jam, spicy green beans, and other goodies.

Darnell is a 57-year-old married postal worker. He walks all day delivering mail. Then he enjoys multiple activities during the evenings and weekends: coaching softball, tutoring math at the local Boys and Girls club, playing drums at church, and getting together with his two daughters and his three grandchildren. His wife says that she can't keep up with him and that he doesn't like to sit still for long.

April and Darnell have high energy levels and are high-functioning individuals who are middle-aged or elderly. This high energy level may be due to hyperactivity. (It is difficult to determine whether young adults have a higher energy levels than their peers.) Both April and Darnell have learned how to channel their high energy levels productively. A qualitative study of Swedish entrepreneurs with ADHD found that many of them reported much higher energy levels than peers (Wiklund et al., 2016).

PASSION AND DEDICATION

Asif is a 20-year-old single man who works loading baggage onto planes at the local airport. He's always been interested in becoming a pilot. He taught himself to identify every type of airplane by sight and to understand instrument panels by researching them online by himself when he was in high school. He was determined to get a job at the airport because it takes him closer to airplanes. He lives with his parents so that he can use all of his income to take flying lessons.

Hideko is a 28-year-old first-year graduate student in English literature at a prestigious university. She's been interested in Victorian novels ever since she discovered them at age 13. She's read everything she can get her hands on at least once and rereads her favorites yearly. Her professors are impressed by her depth of knowledge in the field.

Individuals with ADHD generally have a different reward system in the brain (further discussed in chapter 10). So, for people with ADHD, interesting = easy and boring = difficult. The practical implication of this is that a person with ADHD can put off filling out a form that takes 3 minutes indefinitely, while he happily reads highly technical material in his field of interest for hours. Other aspects that most people would consider in determining whether a task was difficult—the time that the task takes, how much trouble it is, how much thought goes into it—are completely immaterial in comparison to how interesting it is to the individual with ADHD. Also, there may be a connection between impulsivity and passionate engagement with the subject matter at hand (Tymms & Merrell, 2011). So, when they find an interest or purpose, adults with ADHD will pursue it with an energy and passion that few others can match (Bush, 2010; Wiklund et al., 2016) and also with delight, excitement, and enthusiasm that can be infectious. For this reason, some individuals with ADHD can be dynamic public speakers, although they may struggle with organizing their remarks and remaining within the time allotted.

ABILITY TO POWER THROUGH A LARGE TASK, WHEN MOTIVATED

[When a founder of a consulting firm was] asked to write a book in two weeks, he reserved a business-class flight to Tokyo. When he got there, he drank a few espressos in the lounge, turned around, and came back. He finished the book in 30 hours. The trip cost $4,000 and was "worth every penny," he says. (Machan, 2011)

Clara admitted to the psychotherapist that she had over 1,000 email messages in her work and home email in-boxes. After they discussed how to manage email effectively, she went home and completely cleaned out both in-boxes the next day.

When individuals with ADHD have the motivation to start a task, they can have an amazing ability to power through a huge task in a short period of time. Many people with ADHD have stayed up all night multiple times powering through tasks that have caught their interest. This ability comes from their brain's tendency to "hyperfocus"; in other words, once their brain is locked onto one thing, they can stay focused on that one thing for many more hours straight than the average person. I, for one, would be completely incapable of staying awake for 30 hours and spending all that time writing an entire book, like Shankman in the previous vignette. (Note that he intentionally did it on a plane so he would be captive in his seat and there would be few distractions.) However, most adults with ADHD are quite capable of hyperfocusing for many, many more hours than the average person can focus.

Because of this ability, combined with the tendency to otherwise procrastinate, adults with ADHD often prefer to do tasks—even large ones—in just one concentrated session. This is because they know that planning multiple sessions of work may increase the likelihood that the task will not be completed.

CREATIVITY AND INNOVATION

Many adults with ADHD have tangential speech and thoughts. Once they start, the first idea connects to another and then keeps on connecting in a long chain that leads away from the original idea. I have heard many clients say (and others have long speculated, e.g., Bush, 2010; Cramond, 1994) that thought processes unique to ADHD can spark creativity and innovation—both with artistic projects and with other tasks.

Interestingly, two very recent studies found that creativity is linked to default mode network activity in the brain (Beaty et al., 2014; Kühn et al., 2013)—an area that tends to be overly active in adults with ADHD. Also, creativity is linked to a decreased capacity to screen irrelevant stimuli from conscious awareness (Carson, Peterson, & Higgins, 2003); similar difficulties with cognitive inhibition are well-documented in individuals with ADHD. What these tentative connections might ultimately mean remains unclear.

Small studies of creativity in children have found mixed results (Healey & Rucklidge, 2008). A study of gifted children and teens with ADHD found they had poorer working memory (a well-documented finding about ADHD; see chapter 9) *and* greater creativity as compared to equally gifted controls (Fugate, Zentall, & Gentry, 2013).

In fascinating and ground-breaking research on creativity, researchers found that college-age adults with ADHD demonstrated more divergent thinking and a preference for idea generation over solution development (White & Shah, 2006, 2011). They also found that young adults with ADHD had significantly greater creative achievement than peers (White & Shah, 2011).

VALUABLE TEAM MEMBERS

Research on small groups containing an individual with ADHD finds that these groups outperform groups without an ADHD member by generating more creative solutions and ideas and thus being more likely to find a correct solution to a problem (Kuester & Zentall, 2012; Zentall, Kuester, & Craig, 2011). A wise person with ADHD once suggested to me that "the ability to finish things is overrated." I find that to be an interesting perspective. Not everyone has the ability conceptualize completely new ideas and get them off the ground. Because of their energy, passion, and hyperfocus, individuals with ADHD can be in a unique position to envision new ideas, get new projects started, and make things happen. Other colleagues can take the lead in finishing the project and managing details and timetables—none of which is typically the forte of individuals with ADHD.

Working collaboratively with others who do not have ADHD results in a team with a broad range of strengths because of neurodiversity. More diverse groups, especially those that are cognitively diverse, produce better results (Hong & Page, 2004; Page, 2007). A study of children with ADHD, which had been meant to document social behavior problems, found that children with ADHD were off-task more, had more negative verbalizations, and had less cooperative behavior (Zentall et al., 2011). However, the researchers were surprised to find that the problem-solving groups that included one ADHD child were dramatically more successful in novel construction and verbal tasks than groups with no ADHD children: 88% versus 17%! Another study also found greater problem-solving success for the groups with one ADHD child versus groups with none (Kuester & Zentall, 2012). In another study with different tasks, individuals with ADHD found it particularly helpful to work with at least one other person (Riccardi, 2015). Team members without ADHD provide the structure to carry a project to completion—which is often a challenge for an individual with ADHD working alone.

ENTREPRENEURIAL ZEAL

> *What do business mogul Sir Richard Branson, Ikea founder Ingvar Kamprad, and JetBlue founder David Neeleman have in common? Well, besides being monumentally successful, they all have ADHD (Attention Deficit Hyperactivity Disorder), and, like other entrepreneurs and CEOs, some will even tell you that they are successful largely because of the "diagnosis," not in spite of it. (Archer, 2014)*

New York–based angel investor and technology expert Peter Shankman, 38, has leveraged his ADHD while running his consulting firm The Geek Factory. He once confused Shanghai with Singapore when making plane reservations; on another occasion, he booked dinners on the same night on two different continents. He, too, has embraced the necessity of executive assistants who are involved in every aspect of his life—or technology that does the same: "Google Calendar is my friend," he says. (Machan, 2011)

The strengths listed so far in this chapter are high energy, passion, dedication, ability to power through a large task, creativity, and the ability to get things started. These are exactly the abilities that could be instrumental to success as an entrepreneur, like the individuals listed in the previous vignettes. The increased novelty-seeking and risk-taking in ADHD may also be advantages for an entrepreneur (Wiklund et al., 2016). Boredom with the status quo can lead to new entrepreneurial activity within an existing business (Wiklund et al., 2016). I have often heard speculation that individuals with ADHD are overrepresented among CEOs and entrepreneurs (as have Verheul et al., 2015)—although I have never seen any data about this. A qualitative study of 14 entrepreneurs with ADHD found that impatience facilitates looking for new entrepreneurial activities; hyperfocusing on their businesses means that they may do few activities other than working and sleeping and that they have a higher work capacity, higher energy level, and less need for sleep than others (Wiklund, Patzelt & Dimov, 2015).

Note that the second example illustrates that the typical struggles with details and organization are still present. As a practical matter, this means they need very good executive assistants, accountants, and others to manage details for them.

ADAPTABILITY AND RESILIENCE

Troy: You act apologetic when you need to change my appointment, but I totally don't care. Whatever works for you is fine.

Adaptability is *not* an ability that comes directly from ADHD itself. In fact, the moment-to-moment attention of a person with ADHD is probably less flexible and adaptable to changing circumstances than the attention of a person without ADHD (Aguiar, Eubig, & Schantz, 2010). That phenomenon happens on an immediate, automatic, unconscious level of brain operation. However, adaptability can occur on a conscious level as well, and refer to a willingness to go with the flow, despite changing circumstances, and make the best of a situation. All their lives, adults with ADHD have had to adapt to unanticipated consequences caused by their challenges with planning and organization, and often they have become masters at it. If they have overcome significant difficulties, they can become resilient (Newark & Stieglitz, 2010; Wiklund et al., 2016). Unfortunately, no research has yet been done to evaluate this hypothesized strength (Newark & Stieglitz, 2010).

NONJUDGMENTAL

Again, this is another quality that does not come from ADHD itself but can come from maturity gained from the experience of living with ADHD. People with ADHD often struggle all their lives, because the world is not structured to meet their needs and support them. They often have experiences that they consider to be failures. Others can be very critical of them for losing track of possessions and details and because they have made promises and did not deliver. Because of these many difficult and painful experiences, people with ADHD often have a lot of sympathy for others who are struggling.

MASTERS OF USING STRENGTHS AND RESOURCES

Clara: My roommate always said I was lucky that I could write so well and still get As, even though I would always write my college papers at the very last minute.

Troy: My wife always manages our finances and pays the bills. She says it's not worth the trouble to try to get me to do it. I do most of the cooking, so it all balances out.

These are examples of adults with ADHD effectively using other strengths and resources to compensate for the challenges of ADHD. Clara is intelligent and has good writing skills, so her last-minute work did not impair her college grades. Troy and his wife divide tasks according to their strengths. Other examples could include using interpersonal charm to get lateness and disorganization excused by others, or using financial resources to hire others to do personal and business tasks that are difficult, like bookkeeping or closet organizing.

KEY POINTS

- The strengths of adults with ADHD are mostly speculative and anecdotal, due to lack of scientific attention and research.
- Some strengths may emerge due to the unique functioning of the brain of a person with ADHD: high energy level, passion, dedication, creativity, innovation, an ability to get things started, and an ability to power completely through a large task in one session.
- In some individuals, these strengths may contribute to success as a self-employed person, entrepreneur, or CEO.
- Individuals with ADHD can contribute to creative and original problem-solving as team members and help the team as a whole be more successful.
- The struggles of a life with ADHD may help a person be more willing to adapt to changing life circumstances and be less judgmental of others.
- Many individuals with ADHD are masters of using their other strengths and their interpersonal resources to get things done.

SECTION II

Assessment

5

A Framework for Assessment

Troy: Yeah, I was a handful as a kid. I was bouncing off the walls constantly and couldn't sit still in class or at home. I would sass back to the teacher in class and run around the classroom when I was supposed to sit still. I think that's why they took me to see a psychologist.

Assessment of ADHD differs significantly depending on whether the client had a childhood diagnosis. Those diagnosed with ADHD during childhood were usually referred for evaluation and treatment because they were disruptive in the classroom or had academic difficulties (Cherkasova, Sulla, Dalena, Pondé, & Hechtman, 2013). They tend to be male, white, and hyperactive and might have been given an additional diagnosis of oppositional defiant disorder. In these cases, ensure that a reliable assessment was done during childhood so that the diagnosis was accurate. Obtain copies of any assessments that were done during childhood, if they still exist, and review them to be sure that a psychologist performed the assessment. If these documents no longer exist, ask the client how the diagnosis was made and whether there was any one-on-one testing with a professional. If signs indicate that the assessment was thoroughly and carefully done by the appropriate professional, your main focus is determining whether ADHD is still present. You will focus on current adult functioning to assess this. If there is uncertainty about the accuracy of the childhood ADHD diagnosis, assess childhood ADHD retrospectively.

Individuals who are diagnosed with ADHD in adulthood differ significantly from those diagnosed in childhood (Barkley, Murphy, & Fischer, 2008). In these cases, carefully consider gender, cultural, symptomatic, stereotype, and historical issues that may have led to the individual reaching adulthood without being diagnosed. These considerations are discussed in this chapter.

A thorough clinical interview is our best tool to assess adult ADHD. The assessment should include the following:

- Determine whether ADHD symptoms are present and causing impairment, including the full range of adult ADHD symptoms, not just DSM symptoms (chapter 2).

- Assess emotional problems and psychiatric comorbidities (chapter 3).
- Ensure the client does not have a medical problem that is mimicking ADHD (chapter 6).
- Recognize strengths, including those that may be linked to ADHD itself (chapter 4).
- Assess developmental challenges, including whether ADHD symptoms were present before adulthood (chapter 7).
- Assess adaptive functioning problems (chapter 8).
- Assess cognitive challenges (chapter 10 and appendix 1).

It may be possible to begin to assess ADHD right from the first session. Alternatively, the client may present with a more urgent issue, such as severe depression or bipolar disorder, and the assessment of ADHD will need to be spread out over more time and done in a piecemeal fashion as time allows.

When asking about ADHD symptoms, consider the following (Tuckman, 2007):

- *How long has the symptom been present?* Inattentiveness and/or hyperactivity are generally present from childhood or the teen years on. However, executive functioning issues may only become obvious in adulthood.
- *Has the symptom been present consistently throughout the person's life?* Keeping in mind that ADHD symptoms can overlap with other disorders, was the symptom still present during periods when the individual was not depressed? When the client was less anxious?
- *How often does the symptom arise?* Anyone can have almost any ADHD symptom on occasion. A consistent pattern of difficulties in multiple settings, on the other hand, is indicative of ADHD.
- *What's causing the symptom?* Consider comorbid conditions, excessive stress, inadequate schooling, poor parenting, and other factors that could contribute to poor attention, executive functioning difficulties, and other symptoms that may or may not be indicative of ADHD.
- *Is the symptom impairing?*

I would also add the following question: *Does the symptom cause significant emotional distress?* The individual should display symptoms of ADHD from childhood or the teen years, consistently over time, across multiple settings, resulting in significant impairment.

ETHNIC AND CULTURAL ISSUES IN UNDIAGNOSED CHILDHOOD ADHD

Clara: My grades were good in grammar school, because I always did well on tests. I sometimes didn't do my homework, or I forgot it at home. That's why my teachers said that I wasn't trying hard enough and that I needed to be more motivated. I didn't have any behavior problems, and as a teacher myself, I think that's why no one noticed my ADHD. I just wasn't a squeaky wheel.

Achieving cultural competence is a significant challenge for the field of ADHD recognition and assessment. Much of the research on childhood ADHD continues to be done on children brought by their parents to an ADHD clinic. This group is heavily skewed toward white boys who have behavior issues and hyperactivity, and underrepresents all other groups (Barkley, 2006a; Nigg, 2006). If your client belongs to one or more of these groups, ADHD is likely to have been missed:

- First- or second-generation immigrants and ethnic, racial, and cultural minorities (Rostain, Ramsay, & Waite, 2015; Rothe, 2005; Stevens, Harman, & Kelleher, 2005).
- Any population with barriers to treatment—such as financial barriers, language barriers, low educational level, or poor access to healthcare (Able, Johnston, Adler, & Swindle, 2007; Rothe, 2005).
- Children belonging to any US ethnic minority, whereas white boys with externalizing behaviors are the most likely to have their ADHD recognized and treated (Morgan, Staff, Hillemeier, Farkas, & Maczuga, 2013).
- Black children are more likely to suffer a punishment approach taken by their school regarding behavioral problems (Asherson et al., 2012). In these cases, it is likely that ADHD can be missed (Asherson et al., 2012).

Clara's less assimilated immigrant parents may have had different conceptualizations of her behavior or barriers to healthcare. Teachers probably missed her ADHD because she did not have hyperactivity or behavior problems.

Little is known about how culture affects the interpretation and conceptualization of ADHD symptoms (Waite & Ramsay, 2010a, 2010b). Ethnic minority groups are poorly represented in studies of brain functioning and treatment (Nigg, 2006; Ramsay, 2010b). Often, the racial makeup of study participants is not even reported in ADHD research (Waite & Ramsay, 2010a). Here is what we do know:

- ADHD has found in every population worldwide that has been studied. Cross-cultural studies have not found any differences in how ADHD symptoms were expressed, and the frequency of ADHD diagnoses within different populations remains roughly the same (Franke et al., 2012).
- The stigma of having an ADHD diagnosis varies from one ethnic group to another; for example, only 5% of whites but 10% of Hispanics were very concerned about what others would think if their child were diagnosed with ADHD (Rothe, 2005). Knowledge about ADHD varies as well. A lack of information about ADHD within the cultural group may mean that parents do not know how to advocate effectively on their child's behalf.

ADHD UNDIAGNOSED IN WOMEN AND GIRLS

Undiagnosed ADHD is common in women and girls (Rucklidge & Kaplan, 1997; Wasserstein, 2005), although more boys than girls develop ADHD and no one is sure why (Nigg, 2006). Girls' brains tend to mature one to three years ahead of boys', so it is possible that the increased rate of ADHD diagnosis in young boys may be partially due to brain immaturity (Mahone, 2016). However, clearly, ADHD is being underidentified in girls. Why?

- At all ages, males with ADHD are more likely to exhibit disruptive, conduct-disordered, rule-breaking, externalizing, and antisocial behavior (Abikoff et al., 2002; Biederman, Faraone, Monuteaux, Bober, & Cadogen, 2004; Gaub & Carlons, 1997; Gershon, 2002). For these reasons, parents tend to bring boys in more often for evaluation and treatment of ADHD (Abikoff et al., 2002).
- Girls are much more likely to have primarily inattentive ADHD, which is more easily missed (Biederman, Mick, et al., 2002; Biederman & Faraone, 2004; Gaub & Carlson, 1997; Newcorn et al., 2001).
- While behavior problems are common in girls with ADHD, girls may display more relational aggression than overt physical aggression (Hinshaw & Blachman, 2005), which may be less obvious to parents and teachers than the behaviors of boys with ADHD. Relational aggression is the psychological term for so-called "mean girl" behavior. Note that this relational aggression may develop in reaction to earlier victimization (Philipsen et al., 2009).

Adult women's ADHD is also likely to be missed. Some reasons are (a) they are more likely to have inattentive type of ADHD, which is often less obvious than combined or hyperactive types; (b) they are more likely to have comorbid depression, anxiety, and/or affective instability, which may obscure the symptoms of ADHD (Robison et al., 2008); (c) if they do not have significant emotional problems, their ADHD may be excused as being simply "ditzy": or (d) the stereotypical image of a person with ADHD is not a grown woman.

FAMILIAL AND INDIVIDUAL CHARACTERISTICS OF UNDIAGNOSED ADHD

If your client was not diagnosed with ADHD as child, gather detailed information about childhood functioning and educational challenges to determine whether the client had previously undiagnosed childhood ADHD. ADHD is not recognized in many individuals. Even parents who have one child with ADHD often miss it in a second child (Biederman et al., 2005). Children are often treated for ADHD without anyone realizing that it is very likely that a parent will have ADHD as well (Waite & Ramsay, 2010a). Clients whose ADHD was missed in childhood almost always have one or more of these characteristics:

- Average to above average intelligence
- High school graduate and maybe also college graduate
- No history of disruptive behavior problems (Ramsay, 2010b; Wasserstein, 2005)
- Male with prominent conduct disorder diagnosis and comorbid ADHD was missed (Asherson, 2013).
- Males with ADHD, inattentive type, and few hyperactive symptoms (Ramsay, 2010b).
- Family provided a lot of structure and supervision, and if children were hyperactive, their families and teachers saw them as having a high energy level and their hyperactivity was effectively channeled into physical activity

SCREEN ALL CLIENTS WITH ANXIETY, DEPRESSION, OR SUBSTANCE ABUSE FOR ADHD

Because of high comorbidity rates, every client who presents with anxiety, depression, or substance abuse should be screened for ADHD. Look for ADHD especially in people who did not significantly benefit from past treatment for anxiety or depression (Barkley & Brown, 2008). Untreated ADHD symptoms, including forgetfulness and impulsiveness, probably interfered with treatment effectiveness and adherence. Also, anyone with longstanding affective instability should be evaluated for ADHD (Surman, Biederman, et al., 2013). Also check for some of the common emotional consequences of having untreated ADHD:

- Do you have low self-esteem?
- Do you feel that you have experienced a lot of failures and disappointments in life?
- Do you feel like an underachiever?
- Do you feel that you are a fraud or impostor?
- Do you tend to be a worrier?
- Do you have problems with being perfectionistic?

DO NOT USE THESE APPROACHES TO ASSESS ADULT ADHD

There is no commonly agreed-upon standard for assessing adult ADHD in clinical practice. Experts vary considerably in the extensiveness of the evaluations that they recommend. However, the following are some approaches to assessing ADHD that should definitely *not* be used:

- *DSM criteria alone*: Using the DSM seems like a reasonable solution to diagnosis, since this is the approach that we would ordinarily take with other mental illnesses. However, these criteria poorly describe adult ADHD and underestimate its prevalence (Barkley, 2006b).
- *EEGs or other brain scans*: Although EEG scans show some promise as a component in assessment of ADHD, they are not yet recommended (Ramsay, 2010).
- *One or more questionnaire(s) alone*: A thorough clinical interview that assesses ADHD symptoms longitudinally and developmentally is necessary. Other mental health conditions can produce ADHD-like symptoms.

CAN ADULTS ACCURATELY SELF-REPORT CURRENT AND CHILDHOOD ADHD?

Many experts recommend having an adult's parent fill out standardized questionnaires about childhood behavior (Surman, 2013a). They also recommend obtaining childhood school records to examine for clues of ADHD. This data-gathering has been recommended because self-report of ADHD can underestimate symptoms (Davidson, 2008; Kessler et al., 2011). However, gathering this data is time-consuming, logistically complex, and not reimbursed by insurance, plus clients can find it tedious and infantilizing. Research about adult self-report of symptoms has shown the following:

- *Very young adults who had childhood ADHD usually have limited insight.* Very young adults (around 20 years old) who had ADHD as children significantly underestimate their ADHD symptoms—only 4% of young adult reports indicated persistent ADHD versus 42% of parent reports (Barkley, 2006a).
- *Adults typically report an age of onset of ADHD four years later than their parents reported in real time* (McGough, 2014). So any age of onset reported by adult clients should more accurately be considered the age at which, in retrospect, the client recognizes that there were problems. It is likely that the client's parents and teachers identified problems years earlier. Also, adults may not be able to remember exact details of childhood symptoms (McGough & Barkley, 2004).
- *Nonetheless, most adults can provide sufficiently accurate retrospective reports of their childhood ADHD symptoms* (Barkley, 2011a; McGough, 2014; Murphy & Schachar, 2000; Ramsay, 2010b).

So in most cases, gathering information from the adult client is sufficient. However, in select cases, collateral information is helpful:

- Very young adults (late teens or early 20s) with a childhood diagnosis of ADHD usually underendorse symptoms (Barkley, 2006a)
- Clients with little insight into their own difficulties, or an oppositional approach to assessment (Roth, Isquith, & Gioia, 2005), possibly leading to underendorsing symptoms
- Clients with a high level of distress or an overly critical self-view (Roth et al., 2005), possibly leading to overendorsing symptoms

IS A COMPREHENSIVE MULTIMODAL EVALUATION NECESSARY?

Many experts recommend performing a comprehensive multimodal ADHD assessment, including:

- Review of past documentation (e.g., childhood report cards, past testing evaluations, individualized education plans, performance evaluations from jobs, college transcripts)
- Administering multiple collateral questionnaires about childhood and current behavior filled out by parents, significant others, or even employers
- Administering multiple self-report questionnaires (about ADHD symptoms, executive functioning, development, health history, employment, and social history)
- A thorough clinical interview addressing academic, work, and social histories
- Selected psychological and neuropsychological testing (e.g., Adler & Cohen, 2004; Asherson, 2005; Davidson, 2008; McGough, 2014; Murphy & Gordon, 2006; Ramsay & Rostain, 2015)

These evaluations are very thorough and are unlikely to result in diagnostic errors. And when a client has a complex history with many comorbid mental illnesses or medical conditions, a very comprehensive evaluation may be necessary. However, these evaluations can only be performed by a psychologist because other mental health professionals do not have sufficient graduate training in psychological testing.

Because of high prevalence rates, other mental health professionals need to be able to assess adult ADHD. The solution to this dilemma is learning how to administer an effective diagnostic interview (Barkley & Brown, 2008) and two simple screening instruments. The key to assessing adult ADHD is pattern recognition: certain developmental, cognitive, and functioning patterns characterize adults with ADHD (Ramsay & Rostain, 2015). These patterns are described in upcoming chapters. Nonetheless, more complex cases may still need a referral for psychological and/or neuropsychological testing to clarify the diagnosis.

A BRIEF INTRODUCTION TO PSYCHOLOGICAL ASSESSMENT

Although psychological testing instruments—often questionnaires—may seem simple, complex data analysis is necessary to devise each one. When psychologists construct a testing instrument, they are concerned with many indicators of quality. They examine whether answers to the instrument are stable from one time to another. This is called *test–retest reliability*. They examine whether answers to the instrument really measure what they want to measure. This is called *validity*. They carefully examine possible cut-off points to minimize errors. There can be both *false positives*—in our case identifying someone as having ADHD when he or she does not— and *false negatives*—identifying someone as not having ADHD when he or she does. When psychologists determine that a testing instrument is reliable and valid and that it has cut-off scores that are useful, we say that it has *good psychometric properties*.

Some questionnaires are simple to administer and in the public domain. The public domain instruments that are most relevant to assessing ADHD are the Adult ADHD Self-Report Scale Symptom Checklist (ASRS) and the Pittsburgh Sleep Quality Index (PSQI). Both of these have good psychometric properties (Kessler et al., 2007; Mollayeva et al., 2016; Taylor, Deb, & Unwin, 2011). These instruments are not complex and can be used effectively by psychotherapists who do not have graduate training in psychological assessment. (Appendix 1 provides further information on psychological assessment of ADHD and a recommended ADHD psychological testing protocol.)

SCREEN WITH THE ADULT ADHD SELF-REPORT SCALE SYMPTOM CHECKLIST

The ASRS is a one-page instrument for the client to fill out with six highly predictive items (a cut-off of four or more of these six items is considered suggestive of ADHD) and 12 additional items for clinical use. It is in the public domain, so it is free to use and easily found online. It adheres closely to DSM criteria for ADHD, with the addition of a few items assessing organization and procrastination. Clients can fill out this brief instrument in a few minutes during or before a session.

This scale has good psychometric properties (Taylor et al., 2011). However, be aware of these issues:

- The ASRS has 99% specificity, so clients without ADHD are highly unlikely to attain the cut-off score (Surman, 2013a).

- However, the ASRS has 69% sensitivity, so nearly one-third of individuals who do have ADHD will be misidentified as not having ADHD (Surman, 2013a). Specifically, this instrument may underidentify inattentive type ADHD. For that reason, I recommend further evaluating anyone who has a score of 3, especially if the client endorsed three of the first four items (the fifth and sixth items pertain to hyperactivity).

In conclusion, the ASRS is highly recommended as a screening instrument for adult ADHD. But keep in mind that *some clients who do have ADHD will score fewer than 4 points*. Never use a screening instrument alone to diagnose ADHD.

SCREEN WITH THE PITTSBURGH SLEEP QUALITY INDEX

Screen anyone who may have ADHD for sleep problems, since many sleep problems can mimic ADHD or be comorbid and thus worsen symptoms (Surman et al., 2009). The PSQI is a four-page instrument about sleep problems. It is in the public domain, so it is free for anyone to use, and it is easily found online. There is a scoring system for it, but simply reviewing the client's answers is usually sufficiently informative. Questions on the PSQI assess poor sleep hygiene, insomnia, sleep apnea, bad dreams, excessive drowsiness, periodic limb movement of sleep, and other issues. A quick review of the client's answers can help determine whether sleep hygiene training (Willer, 2014) or a referral for a sleep study is warranted. There are also multiple questionnaires to assess sleep apnea; look online for the GASP or the STOP-BANG.

SCREENING QUESTIONS FOR SLEEP DISORDERS

Sleep disorders (which are further discussed in chapter 6) can also be assessed through use of screening questions, such as the following. Sleep apnea questions include:

- Do you snore?
- Does your bed partner notice you stopping breathing during the night?
- Do you ever feel that you have stopped breathing during the night?

Questions about periodic leg movements during sleep and restless legs syndrome (National Heart, Lung and Blood Institute Working Group on Restless Legs Syndrome, 2000; Ohio Sleep Medicine Institute, 2015) include:

- Do you have creeping, crawling, or uncomfortable feelings in your legs or arms that are relieved by moving them?
- Does your bed partner complain that you kick during sleep or tell you that your legs or arms jerk during sleep?
- Are your bed sheets a mess or untidy in the morning?
- Do you feel you have had restless sleep at night?

Narcolepsy questions (Division of Sleep Medicine, Harvard Medical School, 2014) include:

- Once you have caught up on your sleep during weekends or vacation, are you still likely to fall asleep when inactive?
- Do you feel rested in the morning but then tired throughout much of the day?
- Do you doze off at inappropriate times?

SETTINGS FOR ADULT LIFE IMPAIRMENT

ADHD insidiously affects multiple domains of functioning, including "those from which people derive a sense of competence, industry, connection with others, and consequently, sense of self" (Ramsay, 2010b, p. 4). For that reason, ADHD can be highly impairing (Ramsay, 2010b). The DSM requires that symptoms cause clinically significant impairment in two or more settings. This is a reasonable criterion. Many settings and roles can be affected by ADHD:

- Work
- College or other training or trade school
- Relationship with significant other
- Parenting
- Relationships with friends and family
- Personal responsibilities such as finances, shopping, and housecleaning
- Recreational activities

It is not necessary to ask every question of every client about every setting or role. Instead, ask enough questions to gain a sense of whether the client has significant life impairment.

ADMINISTER THE WEISS FUNCTIONAL IMPAIRMENT RATING SCALE

Assessing symptoms of ADHD is different from assessing problems with functioning (Gibbins & Weiss, 2007). Assessing functioning problems in different life domains is an important aspect of assessing adult ADHD (Ramsay & Rostain, 2015). Adults with ADHD can have difficulties in many different domains of functioning. Just because an individual is having difficulties in multiple areas of functioning does not mean that ADHD is the correct diagnosis. But when the client does have ADHD, this instrument can assist with efficient assessment of functional problems.

The Weiss Functional Impairment Rating Scale (WFIRS) was developed to systematically survey most domains of adult functioning for difficulties caused by emotional distress or behavior problems. This instrument was developed by Dr. Margaret Weiss, can be readily found online by searching, and is in the public domain. Dr. Weiss asks that she be contacted, however, if you want to post a copy of this instrument online. The WFIRS is only a little over two pages long, and it can be filled out by a client in a few minutes.

BE ALERT TO THE POSSIBILITY OF MALINGERING

Savvy individuals can fake ADHD symptoms easily. Some individuals malinger ADHD to obtain stimulant medication. Four groups are of special concern:

- *College students* may fake or exaggerate ADHD symptoms to obtain stimulants (McGough, 2014; Upadhyaya, 2007), or they may get them from a friend with a prescription (Upadhyaya, 2007). They use stimulants recreationally or to improve cognitive performance when studying (Weyandt & DuPaul, 2008). One study found that half of the college students presenting for ADHD evaluation exaggerated their symptoms (Rabiner, 2013).
- *White-collar workers in high-intensity, high-achieving professions* may misuse stimulants for improved cognitive and work performance (Schwarz, 2014). Multiple anecdotal reports exist of adults misusing stimulants to "get ahead."
- *Athletes* may be hoping to improve their academic or athletic performances with medication (Lakhan & Kirchgessner, 2012).
- *People with substance abuse problems.*

College students easily fake ADHD on commonly administered questionnaires (Harrison, Edwards, & Parker, 2007; Jachimowicz & Geiselman, 2004). If you suspect malingering, consider taking one or more of the following steps:

- Gather collateral information from the client's parents, employers, spouses, and friends, as well as past school and medical records (McGough, 2014).
- Refer to a psychologist for administration of ADHD questionnaires and additional testing, such as the Minnesota Multiphasic Personality Inventory, to assess distress, symptoms, and validity of responses.
- Make a referral for neuropsychological testing. Alert the neuropsychologist to your concerns. Neuropsychologist have instruments that help determine whether malingering is present (Davidson, 2008; Sollman, Ranseen, & Berry, 2010).

A RECOMMENDED ADHD ASSESSMENT PROTOCOL

In summary, I propose the following procedure for evaluating ADHD.

1. *Observe the client* for behavioral clues that ADHD may be a problem.
2. *Screen the client for ADHD and sleep symptoms*: When ADHD is suspected, administer the ASRS and the PSQI. The ASRS can be easily administered in a few minutes in the office. Then, if the ASRS suggests ADHD is likely, do a thorough clinical interview.
3. *Conduct a clinical interview*. This interview may take one or two entire sessions or sometimes more. Once you think ADHD is probable, administer the WFIRS and then use the answers to guide further questioning about adaptive functioning.
4. Refer for medical and sleep evaluations as needed.
5. Integrate the findings of your interview and any evaluations to determine whether client has ADHD.
6. If you remain uncertain about an ADHD diagnosis, refer to a psychologist for psychological testing and/or a neuropsychologist for neuropsychological testing.
7. Document your findings thoroughly in the client's chart.

WHEN TO REFER FOR PSYCHOLOGICAL TESTING

Sometimes a client's life situation is chaotic and difficult. People who are under a very high level of stress will not be able to concentrate well. So if your client is going through a period of crisis, you may need to help the client through the crisis and then refer for psychological testing for ADHD.

Since substance abuse is very common among adults who have ADHD, screening for substance abuse should be done before a referral for psychological testing is made. Active substance abuse has a negative impact on mood and cognition. Separating the influences of ADHD and substance abuse in testing is not an easy task. It is more informative to do psychological testing once the client is abstinent.

If the client is having a significant episode of mental illness, such as a severe major depressive episode, this will also have an impact on cognition. Depression and anxiety can cause inattentiveness and can result in an erroneous ADHD diagnosis on psychological testing (Kooij et al., 2008). It can be difficult to disentangle the influences of ADHD versus depression and/or other mental disorders, so again it may be best to wait. When the client is in a more stable emotional state, testing will be more informative regarding actual ADHD symptomatology. Whether or not testing is postponed, comorbid anxiety, depression, and substance abuse should be thoroughly assessed through testing or clinical interview, and the client should be screened for other mental illnesses as well. Further information on psychological testing for ADHD is in Appendix 1.

HOW NEUROPSYCHOLOGICAL TESTING CAN HELP WITH ADHD DIAGNOSIS

Neuropsychologists are the one group of mental health professionals who have been consistently trained to assess adult ADHD through testing and behavioral observation. Even if all scores are in the normal range or above, a neuropsychologist can identify patterns that are suggestive of ADHD. For example, high IQ adults with ADHD performed, on average, less well on neuropsychological tests of executive functioning than control high IQ adults (Antshel et al., 2010). Also, neuropsychologists are highly trained to recognize ADHD behaviors that may be exhibited during the testing session and to interview for cognitive symptoms and problems with daily functioning. Often, behavior and functioning are the determining factors in diagnosing ADHD.

Scores on neuropsychological testing should not be used as the only information to diagnose adult ADHD (Barkley et al., 2008; McGough & Barkley, 2004). About 60% of adults with ADHD have normal neuropsychological test results but also have clear behavioral signs of ADHD (Biederman, Mick, et al., 2011; Brown, 2006; Halperin & Schulz, 2006). These normal test results are due to a *ceiling effect* (Barkley et al., 2008; Seidman, 2006), in other words, life problems are much more complicated than neuropsychological tests are (Biederman, Mick, et al., 2011). Also, the testing stimuli are novel and there is an examiner present to encourage active participation, both of which tend to encourage improved performance in individuals with ADHD. For these reasons, *neuropsychological test scores should not be used in isolation to diagnose ADHD*, although they can be helpful in understanding the deficits of an individual on a case-by-case basis (Barkley et al., 2008; Seidman, 2006).

Neuropsychological testing is particularly helpful when:

- There is concern about the client's intellectual functioning or about a potential learning disability.
- There is a suspicion that the client may be malingering. Neuropsychologists excel at detecting malingering. Some neuropsychological tests are very difficult to malinger (Tuckman, 2007).
- The client's educational institution or other organization specifically requires neuropsychological testing to document ADHD.
- The client is a young adult and has limited insight.
- The behavioral observations of a highly trained neuropsychologist would be helpful.
- You cannot determine whether the client has ADHD due to various diagnostic complexities. Neuropsychological testing may clarify the diagnostic picture.

HOW TO CHOOSE A QUALIFIED NEUROPSYCHOLOGIST

Be aware that the title of "neuropsychologist" is not regulated by law, so individuals without adequate training can and do advertise themselves as neuropsychologists.

Most psychologists have some exposure to neuropsychological testing in their training. However, only a small minority of psychologists have the necessary coursework, training, and experience to be fully trained neuropsychologists. Neuropsychologists always have doctoral degrees (Ph.D. or Psy.D.). To find a well-qualified neuropsychologist, look for a psychologist with at least one of the following:

- The initials ABPP-CN after the psychologist's name, indicating board certification in neuropsychology and/or
- Postdoctoral fellowship in neuropsychology. Do not refer to a younger psychologist for neuropsychological testing without evidence of board certification or a postdoctoral fellowship in neuropsychology.
- However, note that postdoctoral fellowships in neuropsychology were not available when late-middle-aged psychologists (and older) were in training. In those cases, look for internship training in neuropsychology and a long-standing neuropsychology practice.

Do not hesitate to ask about these qualifications. Referral to someone who is not adequately trained will result in an expensive evaluation that is not clinically or diagnostically useful.

KEY POINTS

- ADHD is often not the presenting problem.
- Always screen adults with depression, anxiety, or substance abuse for ADHD, *especially* those who have not benefitted from treatment in the past.
- Individuals from ethnic minority or immigrant groups may not been diagnosed with ADHD as children, even if symptoms were prominent. Also, nonwhite groups are understudied by researchers.
- ADHD is underdiagnosed in women and girls.
- Often, ADHD is diagnosed in children who behavior problems. Well-behaved children with predominantly inattentive type ADHD are easily be missed by teachers and parents. This is especially true for girls.
- Most adults with ADHD have good insight and can be sufficiently accurate reporters of childhood symptoms, but very young adults with a history of behavior problems and childhood ADHD usually have limited insight into their current symptoms.
- Use the ASRS to screen for adult ADHD; however, be aware that people who obtain a score less than the cut-off of 4 might still have ADHD.

6

Medical Problems, Sleep Disorders, and ADHD

Physical illnesses can mimic ADHD. Does the client have ADHD, another diagnosis, or both? Careful clinical interviewing, with medical assessments as indicated, will answer this question.

MEDICAL DIAGNOSES THAT MIMIC ADHD

Many medical problems have cognitive symptoms that can look like ADHD, including neurological and endocrine problems (Surman, 2013a). Here is only a partial list:

- Hyperthyroidism and hypothyroidism (Adler, Barkley, Wilens, & Ginsberg, 2006; Wilens, 2006)
- Seizure disorder (Sobanski, Paslakis, Schredl, Daffner, & Alm, 2013; Wilens, 2006)
- Brain trauma (Sobanski, Paslakis, Schredl, Daffner, & Alm, 2013)
- Lead toxicity (Sobanski et al., 2013)
- Dementia (Surman, 2013a)
- Neurotoxicity (Surman, 2013a)
- Medication effects (Adler et al., 2006), especially antipsychotics, anticonvulsants, and lithium
- Diabetes (Adler et al., 2006)
- Cognitive changes due to menopause (Epperson et al., 2011; Epperson et al., 2015)
- Other neurological disorders, including cerebral vascular accidents (Barkley & Brown, 2008)

Many ADHD clients have untreated or undertreated medical problems because of disorganization. So, if your client has not seen a physician within the last year, ask your client to discuss any medical, cognitive, or psychological issues with the physician (Weiss & Murray, 2003). Medical issues that might cause or contribute to the client's symptoms can then be treated. If the cognitive or executive functioning issues are of recent or sudden onset, a physician's evaluation should be obtained, even if depression or anxiety is present and may seem like an obvious explanation for the symptoms. Anyone who has ADHD-like symptoms that appeared in adulthood but denies similar symptoms in childhood and earlier adulthood should be referred for medical evaluation.

SLEEP PROBLEMS CAN BE COMORBID OR AN ADHD MIMIC

Children with ADHD often have sleep problems: difficulty with morning awakening, daytime sleepiness, delayed sleep onset, nighttime awakenings, sleep-disordered breathing, and bedtime resistance (Barkley, 2014b; Cortese, Faraone, Konofal, & Lecendreux, 2009). About two-thirds of adults with ADHD have significant sleep problems (Yoon, Jain, & Shapiro, 2012): delayed sleep onset, variable bedtimes, difficulty going to sleep, difficulty awakening, daytime sleepiness, and/or a lack of restorative sleep (Surman et al., 2009). Some of the areas of the brain that are affected in ADHD also are involved in regulating sleep (Yoon et al., 2012).

Poor sleep worsens attention and concentration problems. Additionally, sleep disorders can *coexist* with ADHD, exacerbating ADHD symptoms, or they can *mimic* ADHD. Good sleep is important for quality of life. So quality of sleep, sleep hygiene, and the possibility of sleep disorders must be evaluated.

Relationships between ADHD, sleep problems, and sleep disorders are complex and multifaceted:

1. The sleep and wake patterns of many individuals with ADHD are often disorganized and irregular. They may not have a regular bedtime and take irregular naps of varying lengths when tired. Adults with ADHD sometimes have difficulty getting to sleep because their thoughts are overly active (Brown, 2013). They may get hyperfocused on video games or other pursuits and lose track of time (Ramsay & Rostain, 2008b). They have shorter sleep durations and more frequent awakenings (Voinescu, Szentagotai, & David, 2012). Poor sleep habits make concentration problems worse. In this case, employ sleep hygiene training (Willer, 2014).
2. Individuals with ADHD tend to be "night owls," probably due to underlying differences in hormones and other biological factors that regulate sleep (Baird, Coogan, Siddiqui, Donev, & Thome, 2012). Morning bright-light therapy may be of assistance to shift this circadian rhythm (Rybak, McNeeley, Mackenzie, Jain & Levitan, 2006), or use sleep hygiene training.
3. In a few clients, stimulant medication interferes with sleep onset and sound sleep. Discuss this with the client's psychiatrist. Interestingly,

research shows that most individuals taking a stimulant have improved sleep quality and decreased nighttime awakenings (Boonstra et al., 2007; Sobanski, Schredl, Kettler, & Alm, 2008).

4. A client may have an undiagnosed sleep disorder, in addition to ADHD, which worsens ADHD symptoms further (Nigg, 2006). This issue is further discussed later in the chapter.
5. A person may have an undiagnosed sleep disorder and the symptoms mimic ADHD (Nigg, 2006; Yoon et al., 2012). This issue is also further discussed later.

Researchers have examined how poor sleep impacts cognitive functioning. They have found deficits in attention, memory, vigilance, and executive functioning (Beebe & Gozal, 2002; Durmer & Dinges, 2005; Fulda & Schulz, 2001; Naumann, Bellebaum, & Daum, 2006). There is also a negative impact on mood, response time, and physical performance (Durmer & Dinges, 2005). *Note that these deficits closely resemble ADHD.* When sleep disorders are treated, these cognitive deficits improve considerably (Engleman & Douglas, 2004; Ferini-Strambi et al., 2003). Three sleep disorders are particularly pertinent to the discussion of ADHD and sleep: obstructive sleep apnea, periodic limb movement of sleep, and narcolepsy. Each of these is discussed in a separate section of this chapter. Information on assessing sleep appeared in chapter 5.

If you think a sleep disorder is unlikely, treat the sleep hygiene, anxiety, and depression first. If these have resolved and the client still does not have restful sleep, then refer to a sleep clinic for further evaluation. When a co-occurring sleep disorder is treated, this improves attention and concentration, as well as quality of life.

SLEEP APNEA

Jose complained to his psychotherapist that he thinks he has ADHD. The psychotherapist asked about his sleep. He said that he is so sleepy that he often takes naps in the afternoon. His wife has been complaining for years about his snoring. Jose is a heavyset middle-aged man. Upon closer questioning by the psychotherapist, he admitted that he occasionally wakes up in the middle of the night gasping for breath. When the psychotherapist mentioned the possibility of sleep apnea, he said that his wife and his physician had also suggested this was a possibility, but he has been putting off getting a sleep study. The psychotherapist educated Jose about the relationship between sleep and cognitive functioning. They also discussed the health risks of untreated sleep apnea. Jose made an appointment for a sleep study, and sleep apnea was found. Once it was treated, his cognitive functioning improved. He did not have ADHD.

Obstructive sleep apnea (OSA) is a sleep disorder in which the person's airway becomes obstructed intermittently during sleep, interfering with breathing and sound sleep. Persons most at risk are male, middle-aged and older, obese, and/or have a broad neck. But even an individual with none of these qualities can have OSA due to the structure of the mouth, tongue, and throat. Sleep partners often notice heavy snoring and may notice intermittant breathing problems. The individual may or may not be aware of the breathing problems but feels unrested in the morning and tired throughout the day. In the general population, up to 5% of adults have OSA (Young, Peppard, & Gottlieb, 2002).

Adults with ADHD *are not yet known* to have OSA any more frequently than anyone else, but this issue is understudied (Yoon et al., 2012). It is quite possible that OSA is more common in adults with ADHD because children with ADHD have been found to have more sleep-disordered breathing (Yoon et al., 2012). Both children and adults with OSA can be misdiagnosed with ADHD (Beebe & Gozal, 2002; Naseem, Chaudhary, & Collop, 2001). OSA is diagnosed by a sleep study. OSA is most effectively treated with a device that blows air into the nose during sleep to keep airways open, but other treatments are available.

PERIODIC LIMB MOVEMENTS OF SLEEP AND RESTLESS LEGS SYNDROME

Shanice and her psychotherapist talked about her sleep as part of a clinical interview for ADHD. Shanice stated that she never has restful sleep. Upon closer questioning it appeared that she had symptoms of restless legs and that her husband complained that she would kick him during sleep. She was referred for a sleep study. She was found to have restless legs syndrome (RLS) and periodic limb movements of sleep (PLMS). The PLMS was effectively treated with medication. This helped her quality of sleep and her concentration and cognitive functioning. However, she still had ADHD as well.

Periodic limb movements in sleep (PLMS) is a sleep disorder in which the brain does not fully go to sleep. Individuals with PLMS do not sleep deeply enough, and sleep is not restful. They have frequent movements of the body during sleep, especially kicking, that are often noticed by sleep partners. PLMS often, but not always, co-occurs with RLS. In the general population, about 4% of adults have PLMS (Ohayon & Roth, 2002).

When a person has *restless legs syndrome* (RLS), there are uncomfortable sensations in the legs that are relieved by movement; sometimes these uncomfortable sensations can be experienced in other body parts as well (Walters, Silvestri, Zucconi, Chandrashekariah, & Konofal, 2008). These sensations tend to be worse in the evening and can be so troubling that they interfere with sleep onset. There is a high degree of overlap between RLS and PLMS: about 80% of individuals with RLS will also have PLMS (Walters et al., 2008).

Individuals with ADHD *do* have PLMS and RLS at a higher rate than people in the general population (Cortese et al., 2005; Walters et al., 2008). Both ADHD and PLMS are lifelong problems and cause similar cognitive problems. Differential diagnosis requires a sleep study. Both PLMS and RLS can be treated effectively with a variety of medications.

NARCOLEPSY

In passing, Hannah mentioned during her psychotherapy appointment that she was visiting Washington, DC, sat down on a bench, then found herself lying down and napping in the middle of an organized tour. Hannah's psychotherapist asked her whether she is often drowsy and easily falls asleep in other situations. She talked about multiple occasions of falling asleep in situations when few others would do so. She admitted that she often feels drowsy when driving and thinks that she has almost nodded off a few times. Hannah's psychotherapist referred her for a sleep study. She was found to have narcolepsy. She was treated with a high dose of a stimulant for narcolepsy but also continues to have ongoing symptoms of ADHD.

Individuals with narcolepsy have excessive daytime drowsiness, and they may or may not also have (a) *cataplexy*—a sudden reduction or loss of muscle tone under conditions of excitement or strong emotion, (b) *hypnagogic hallucinations*—seeing or hearing things that are not actually there during the transition from wakefulness to sleep, and (c) *sleep paralysis*—an inability to move the body when awakening or falling asleep—despite being awake and conscious (Naumann & Daum, 2003; Walters et al., 2008). Cognitive deficits associated with narcolepsy include problems with attention and executive functioning (Naumann et al., 2006; Rieger, Mayer, & Gauggel, 2003). Like ADHD, narcolepsy is treated with stimulant medications (Schwartz, Nelson, Schwartz, & Hughes, 2004). Almost one-fifth of patients with narcolepsy meet diagnostic criteria for ADHD as well (Walters et al., 2008).

The exact nature of the comorbidity of narcolepsy and ADHD symptoms is unclear. Are these overlapping conditions? Does narcolepsy cause ADHD-like cognitive deficits? We do not yet fully understand this. However, both conditions are generally treated with stimulant medications, and I have found that narcolepsy patients with ADHD symptoms benefit from skills training, as do others with ADHD. Narcolepsy is much rarer than OSA or PLMS. However, it is common enough that awareness of the symptoms will sooner or later help you identify an untreated individual and make a huge difference in that person's quality of life.

CONCLUSIONS ABOUT SLEEP

As mental health professionals, we are usually the only healthcare professionals that have extended, detailed, and regular conversations with clients about their health. Most physicians see their patients on an occasional basis, are pressed for time, and do not inquire in detail about functioning and sleep. For these reasons, we are the most likely healthcare professionals to hear about sleep problems and sleep disorders. Knowing about sleep is important for any psychotherapist but is especially important for anyone who wants to treat adult ADHD. Personally, I have referred dozens of people for sleep studies, and most of them have been found to have a sleep disorder that needed treatment. If all mental health professionals were well educated about sleep, millions of people would feel better every day.

KEY POINTS

- Clients with ADHD often have poor follow-through in many areas of their lives; this includes medical care. If your client has not seen a physician in the past year, be sure that the client gets a checkup. This is especially important because many medical problems, especially neurological ones, can mimic ADHD symptoms.
- All clients who present with symptoms of ADHD should be evaluated for poor sleep hygiene and screened for sleep disorders.
- Sleep and ADHD have a very complicated relationship. Most clients with ADHD will be as disorganized with sleep as they are in other areas of their lives. There is significant comorbidity between sleep disorders and ADHD as well. Also, sleep disorders that are uncomplicated by ADHD still result in very similar cognitive symptoms to ADHD.
- Accurate diagnosis and treatment of all comorbid disorders will result in improved treatment compliance and functioning.

7

Assessing Family History, Childhood, and Adult Development

Symptoms of ADHD emerge when the environmental demands exceed the resources that the person can bring to bear. A person's internal and external resources change with circumstances, developmental level, age, and maturity. Internal resources can include cognitive abilities, maturity, coping skills, self-understanding, self-acceptance, and willingness to seek and accept help. External resources include "people (e.g., parents, siblings, physicians, teachers, friends) and objects (e.g., alarm clocks, medication, calendars, reminders)" (Turgay et al., 2012, p. 193). Childhood psychosocial adversity is a sign that fewer external resources were available. At any age, a dramatic increase in environmental demands can cause an individual with underlying ADHD to "hit the wall" and be unable to cope, because demands now exceed the available resources.

Note that an individual's internal resources *can* be modified with treatment at any age. Medication can improve the individual's cognitive functioning. Psychotherapy can help the individual develop executive functioning skills and coping skills, again increasing internal resources.

ADULT ADHD IS HIGHLY HERITABLE

Troy: My wife always says that the apple doesn't fall far from the tree and that my daughter is just like me. We're both scatter-brained. She complains that she has to tell both of us to do things over and over, and still we sometimes don't get them done.

Psychotherapist: You told me that your daughter had been diagnosed with ADHD by the school psychologist, right?

T: Right. That made us wonder whether I still had it too. When I was in school, the teachers always said that I should apply myself more, and my mom said that I was just lazy.

P: Unfortunately, a lot of adults with ADHD got that kind of feedback as a kid. Would you call anyone else in your family "scatter-brained"?

T: Well, you know I was raised mostly by my mom. My dad is nothing like me, but my mom has always referred to herself as scatterbrained, and I guess I get that from her. She did a great job raising us, but she could be pretty disorganized. Even though she could afford it, we sometimes didn't have bread or milk in the house, just because she'd forget to get them when she was at the store. When my sister was old enough, she would make grocery lists for my mom so she wouldn't forget. My sister has always been kind of hyper, the way I am, but my other brothers take after Dad more. She always did better in school than I did and didn't get into trouble though.

P: Well, obviously I don't know your mom, so I can't diagnose her. But I can say that there's strong scientific evidence that ADHD often runs in families and is strongly genetically influenced. So it's not surprising that you're seeing similar problems in your mom, yourself, and your daughter.

The likelihood of developing ADHD depends on both genetic and environmental factors, as is the case for all mental illnesses. However, the heritability of ADHD is comparable to that of schizophrenia and bipolar disorder; these are the three mental disorders with the highest heritability. On rare occasions, ADHD is caused by a single gene (Akutagava-Martins, Salantino-Oliveira, Kieling, Rohde, & Hutz, 2013; Neale et al., 2010; Nigg, 2006). However, in most cases, ADHD is a *complex trait*, which means that many genes each contribute a small amount to the overall risk of developing ADHD (Gizer, Ficks, & Waldman, 2009).

ADHD often runs strongly in families, like Troy's (Coghill & Banaschewski, 2009). The following findings illustrate this:

- About one-half of children who have one parent with ADHD will develop ADHD themselves (Coghill & Banaschewski, 2009).
- The siblings of adults with ADHD have a 41% risk of ADHD (Franke et al., 2012).
- Among adoptees with ADHD, their biological parents were much more likely to have ADHD than their adoptive parents (Wallis, Russell, & Muenke, 2008). So nature (genetics) is more important in developing ADHD than nurture (environment).

Given these findings, if a client has ADHD, *there is about a 50% chance that any given first-degree relative (parent, child, full sibling) will have ADHD* as well. Also, some relatives might have mild symptoms of ADHD without the full diagnosis. During the clinical interview, ask these questions (Ramsay & Rostain, 2008b):

- Does anyone in your family have some similar problems to yours?
- Has anyone in your family ever been diagnosed with ADHD?

PRENATAL RISK FACTORS

Troy: My mom was always a heavy drinker and smoker. If you ask her, she'll always say that she didn't smoke or drink during any of her pregnancies, but my youngest brother was born when I was 8 and I remember her sneaking cigarettes and occasionally drinking when she was pregnant with him. So I'm betting that happened with all of us.

There is agreement that genetic risk for ADHD is the single most important risk factor for development of ADHD in a child (Thapar, Cooper, Eyre, & Langley, 2013). However, environmental influences can increase the likelihood of ADHD developing. The following risk factors have the most scientific support:

- *Maternal smoking while pregnant* (Banerjee, Middleton, & Faraone, 2007; Barkley, 2006a; Coghill & Banaschewski, 2009)
- *Maternal alcohol use while pregnant* (Banerjee et al., 2007; Barkley, 2006a)
- *Maternal stress and psychosocial adversity while pregnant* (Cherkasova, Sulla, Dalena, Ponde, & Hechtman, 2013)
- *Increased paternal age* (D'Onofrio et al., 2014)
- *Greater prenatal exposure to PCBs*: PCBs are manufactured compounds that have been part of paints, brake liners, electrical insulators, and more. These are stable, have extensively permeated the environment, and accumulate in the body fat of humans and in human breast milk (Banerjee et al., 2007)
- *Acetaminophen (Tylenol) use while pregnant*: (Thompson, Waldie, Wall, Murphy, Mitchell, & ABC Study Group, 2014)
- *Pregnancy and delivery complications:* low birth weight, prematurity, poor maternal health, longer labor, fetal distress, pregnancy complications, and other medical conditions during pregnancy magnify ADHD risk (Banerjee et al., 2007; Barkley, 2006a; Coghill & Banaschewski, 2009; Thapar et al., 2013)
- *Prenatal exposure to toxins, especially lead, and pesticides* (Banerjee et al., 2007)

These factors may have a negative impact on the developing fetal nervous system and activate genes for ADHD. However, it is generally not the most productive use of assessment and psychotherapy time to ask about prenatal risk factors, since most clients will not know many of the answers.

CHILDHOOD RISK FACTORS

Troy: My folks always had a bad relationship. I always remember them arguing and yelling about how much they hated each other. My mom had me when she was only 17, and they were married soon after that. There were four of us, and we were a handful for my mom. My dad's a bricklayer, and my mom stayed at home with us until I was in fifth grade. Then, my parents got divorced and I mostly lived with my mom. She was a good provider for us, but she was sometimes a heavy drinker, and sometimes she would yell. I understand that better, now that I'm a dad. Sometimes you just feel like you're going to lose it.

Not everyone who has a genetic predisposition to ADHD develops it. Adverse environment affects brain development and whether or not ADHD develops (Castellanos et al., 2003). In recent years, scientists have discovered that environmental forces can cause some genes to be turned on (active) or turned off (dormant)—this process is called *gene regulation*. ADHD genes may be turned on when a child experiences psychosocial adversity (Wallis et al., 2008).

The more psychosocial adversity a child experiences, the greater the chances that child will develop ADHD and become more impaired (Biederman, Faraone, & Monuteaux, 2002; Spencer, Biederman, & Mick, 2007). Some of the psychosocial adversity factors that increase risk of ADHD include:

- *Lower socioeconomic status of family* (Biederman, Faraone, et al., 2002)
- *Father diagnosed with antisocial personality disorder* (Biederman, Faraone, et al., 2002)
- *Mother experienced at least two psychiatric disorders* (Biederman, Faraone, et al., 2002).
- *Family conflict* (Biederman, Faraone, et al., 2002)
- *Low parental involvement and inconsistent discipline* (Ellis & Nigg, 2009)
- *Childhood maltreatment and emotional trauma* (Banerjee et al., 2007)
- *Severe institutional deprivation*: Extreme early deprivation among orphans can result in ADHD-like symptoms later, even when adopted into a family (Stevens et al., 2008; Thapar et al., 2013)

The following are some childhood environmental factors that may increase risk of ADHD:

- *Childhood exposure to toxins and pesticides, especially lead* (Banerjee et al., 2007; Bouchard, Bellinger, Wright, & Weisskopf, 2010; Nigg, 2010; Nigg, Nikolas, Knottnerus, Cavanagh, & Friderici, 2010).
- *Food additives*: About 30% of children with ADHD who were put on a diet excluding food color additives had improved symptoms, including deceased hyperactivity and improved attention; further research is warranted (Nigg, Lewis, Edinger, & Falk, 2012).
- *Environmental factors: less intensive sunlight and low altitude* (Arns, van der Heijden, Arnold, & Kenemans, 2013; Huber et al., 2015). These findings are clearly in need of further investigation.

Note that the following possible risk factors are *not* related to ADHD:

- *Television viewing*
- *Sugar*
- *Caffeine* (Nigg, 2012)

Boys are more likely to have ADHD than girls overall, but girls are more likely to have undiagnosed ADHD. When children come to mental health treatment for ADHD, the ratio of boys to girls is 10:1, yet when all children are examined from a given community for ADHD, the ratio of boys to girls is 3:1 (Biederman & Faraone, 2004; Brown, 2013) to 2:1 (Nigg, 2006).

Questions to assess family background and development include:

- Did your family have difficulty making ends meet? Were there any conflicts in the home? Did your parents have any emotional issues?
- What kinds of difficulties or stresses did your family have while you were growing up?
- Were you exposed to any physical, verbal, or emotional abuse? Were you neglected?
- Did you have any serious trauma, exposure to violence, or losses as a child?

PREVALENCE OF ADHD IN CHILDREN AND ADOLESCENTS

A prevalence rate of 6.8% for ADHD in childhood and adolescence was obtained by combining DSM diagnosis data from multiple studies (Nigg, 2006). However, the consistency of this proportion across different ages hides an important underlying phenomenon: that some children will recover from ADHD at every age, whereas others will have a newly emerged diagnosis of ADHD (Nigg, 2006). How is this possible?

- The number of children with ADHD decreases because children's brains mature and some of them "grow out of" ADHD symptoms.
- Children whose cognitive functioning might have been sufficient to cope in earlier years may struggle later on, due to increased organizational and attentional demands, and then be diagnosed with ADHD.

These two forces seem to balance each other out to maintain a prevalence of 6% to 7% of children at each age group—but note that it is not exactly the same group of children throughout all years.

CO-OCCURRING CHILDHOOD DEVELOPMENTAL, EMOTIONAL, AND BEHAVIORAL PROBLEMS

Psychotherapist: Did you have any behavior problems as a kid?

Troy: I would do anything on a dare. I remember climbing up onto the roof and then standing right by the gutter. My dad saw me up there and started yelling at me, and then I fell. Luckily, I landed in a bush and only broke my arm. I can't tell you how many things I burned in the alley behind our house, just to see what would happen. Some of them would explode. My wife says I'm lucky I survived my childhood with all my fingers, toes, and eyes intact. I argued with adults all the time when I didn't want to do things right at that moment.

P: Did you have any learning problems?

T: They told me that I had dyslexia.

Psychotherapist: Did you have any behavior problems as a kid?

Clara: No, they always said I was a good kid, despite the problems I had with school.

P: What about emotional problems? Do you think you had any depression or anxiety?

C: In retrospect, I had a lot of anxiety as a kid. I remember worrying about making people mad when I forgot things. I really wanted to do well in school, and I remember feeling depressed when I was in high school. I wanted to get straight A's like a lot of my friends, and I felt that something must be wrong with me. Or maybe everyone was right that I didn't try hard enough.

ADHD tends to co-occur with many developmental, behavioral, emotional, and learning problems in childhood:

- *Reading disabilities*: About 20% to 35% of children with ADHD have a reading disorder, including dyslexia (Asherson, 2013; Barkley, 2006a; Pennington et al., 2009; Sexton, Gelhorn, Bell, & Classi, 2011).
- *Autism spectrum disorders*: 20% to 50% of children with ADHD meet the criteria for an autism spectrum disorder and 30% to 80% of children with an autism spectrum disorder meet the criteria for ADHD. It is likely that there is a shared genetic risk for both disorders (Rommelse, Franke, Geurts, Hartman, & Buitelaar, 2010).
- *Tic disorders* (Spencer et al., 2007) can co-occur.
- *Oppositional defiant disorder and/or conduct disorder* (Barkley, 2006; Spencer et al., 2007) are common comorbid disorders.
- *Academic problems,* including lower grades, repeating grades, needing tutoring, and/or placement in special classes are more likely (Barkley, 2006a; Spencer et al., 2007).

- *Erratic academic performance:* Children with ADHD often perform at normal or near-normal levels in classes they are interested in, but when they are bored, they can skip homework and fail tests (Barkley, 2006a).
- *Social rejection*: About 50% experience social rejection (Barkley, 2006a), due to social skill deficits.
- *Low IQ*: Most have normal or above average IQ, but a disproportionate number have a lower than average intelligence level (Barkley, 2006a).
- *Depression*: By age 15, almost half of children with ADHD in one longitudinal study had experienced depression at some time in their lives (Spencer et al., 2007)
- *Anxiety* can be difficult to diagnose in children with ADHD, but those with anxiety tend to have worse long-term outcomes (Spencer et al., 2007).

A person's recall of elementary school functioning can be incomplete, because individuals of that age often have a limited ability to observe themselves.

ADOLESCENTS WITH ADHD

Clara: My high school was not that challenging. I still had issues with homework, but I did well on the tests. I got A's and B's. But I got a C in my honors English class because we had a large final paper and I didn't start it until the day before it was due.

Psychotherapist: Did you use alcohol or drugs?

C: Of course. Everyone in my high school did. I smoked some cigarettes, too, but only to be cool. I never really liked them much and I gave up smoking when I went to college.

Psychotherapist: Did you take your medication when you were a teen?

Troy: I stopped taking it when I was 16. I felt that there wasn't anything wrong with me, and I didn't like how it made me feel.

P: What were your grades like? How were you doing in school?

T: They were all over the place from B's to F's, but mostly C's and D's. I just barely missed having to repeat junior year. The main reason I went to school was to see my friends. Even though I did fail a couple classes, I had enough credits to graduate high school.

P: What else was going on with you when you were a teen? Did you have any other problems then?

T: Sure. I was drinking a lot every weekend. I would smoke pot every day after school behind the hedge in the back of the school. I totaled my dad's car and was grounded for two months. I started smoking when I was 14 and I still haven't quit. I was just running around being wild and my folks didn't feel that they could control me, so they finally just gave up trying. But when I was 19, my girlfriend, now my wife, got pregnant with our son. That scared me. I felt that I needed to get it together, but it took me a while.

Transitioning to adolescence can be difficult (Sibley et al., 2012a; Turgay et al., 2012) because adolescents have more complex social and academic challenges. Teens with ADHD are at risk for more problems, including delinquency, dropping out of school, and early initiation of sexual behavior (Sibley et al., 2012a). Plus, they start to have many of the problems that are typical of adults with ADHD as they are granted more independent privileges, including driving accidents and substance abuse.

Like Troy, teens who have been diagnosed with ADHD often have limited insight into their current and past functioning difficulties, and they typically think that they are more functional than their teachers and parents report (Sibley et al., 2012b). Also, teens with diagnosed ADHD underestimate their earlier childhood ADHD symptoms and impairment (Sibley et al., 2012b). Little is known about the insight and emotional functioning of teens who have undiagnosed ADHD, such as Clara, but her retrospective report of varied grades, anxiety and depression is what I typically hear from similar clients.

Adolescents can be challenging to diagnose because the diagnostic criteria were developed for children, not for adults or adolescents (Sibley et al., 2012a). Adolescents are less obviously hyperactive—they are more like adults and have problems with subjective restlessness, fidgeting, and having difficulty relaxing quietly—and less like children who are running around excessively and not sitting still (Sibley et al., 2012a). Individuals with ADHD are more often diagnosed in childhood or adulthood rather than adolescence, perhaps because other issues during that time tend to mask the symptoms (Ramsay, 2010b).

Barkley (2006a) notes that research on adolescents with ADHD has concentrated on those diagnosed with hyperactive/impulsive type and combined type. Thus few firm conclusions can be drawn about those with inattentive type (like Clara), many of whom are still "flying under the radar" and undiagnosed at this age. Adolescents with hyperactivity/impulsivity are more likely to have

- *Severe behavior problems*: 25% to 55% have oppositional or antisocial behavior or conduct disorder (Barkley, 2006a)
- *Continuing academic problems*: By adolescence, 30% to 58% have failed at least one grade (Barkley, 2006a), they were more likely to have been suspended or expelled from school or to drop out (Barkley, 2006a), and they were more likely to have lower grades or F's (Kent et al., 2011)
- *Alcohol and illegal drug use* (Barkley, 2006a)
- *Cigarette use* (Spencer et al., 2007)

- *Driving problems*, including auto accidents and speeding citations (Barkley, 2006a)
- *First sexual intercourse* about one year earlier than peers (Barkley, 2006a)

However, some adolescents with childhood ADHD diagnoses have better academic and later employment outcomes. These adolescents generally have these mitigating advantages (Barkley, 2006a):

- Higher intelligence
- Fewer ADHD symptoms
- Better peer relationships
- Few problems with aggressiveness and conduct
- Higher family socioeconomic status
- Parents without ADHD themselves
- Parents without substance abuse and antisocial behavior
- Parent–child relationships without conflict and hostility

CLINICAL INTERVIEWING FOR CHILDHOOD AND ADOLESCENT ADHD

The following questions can guide you in assessing relevant ADHD symptoms and behavior during childhood and adolescence.

ADHD Symptoms

- Growing up, did your teachers or parents say that you had difficulties concentrating or you were distractible?
- Growing up, did people say you were spacey, daydreaming, or zoning out?
- Were you described as a very active or impulsive child?
- Did you frequently lose items or forget to bring items home or to school?
- Did you need a lot of supervision from your parents to get your schoolwork done? Even as a teenager?
- At what age did you first experience the types of challenges we have been discussing?
- Was there ever a time when you did not have these problems?

Developmental, Emotional, and Behavioral Problems

- Did you have any behavior issues as a child? What were those?
- Did your parents complain that you were difficult?

- Did you have any social or emotional issues as a child?
- Do you think you were depressed or anxious as a child?

Educational and Learning Problems

- Tell me about your grades when you were in high school and grade school. Were there significant differences in your grades between classes you liked and those you thought were boring? Tell me more.
- Did you ever have psychological testing or were you ever told had a learning disability? Did you receive learning assistance or were you ever placed in a special class?
- Did you have any trouble getting homework done?
- Were you able to sit still in class and concentrate on the teacher when you were a child?
- Were you ever retained in a grade?
- Were you ever suspended or expelled from school?
- Do you feel that you have underachieved educationally? Why?
- Growing up, did your teachers or parents say that you didn't try hard enough, that you were unmotivated or lazy, or that you weren't achieving your potential?
- Did you "grow out of" any of these problems?

You do not need to ask all these questions, just enough to determine that ADHD symptoms and developmental issues were present. Individuals with ADHD may have problems recognizing their own symptoms through the high school years and sometimes even beyond. If that seems to be the case with your client, you may need to gather additional information from family members or educational documents in order to make a determination about childhood ADHD. Psychological testing can also be helpful to assess childhood or teenage ADHD symptoms (see appendix 1).

DOES ADHD DIAGNOSED IN CHILDHOOD REMIT IN ADULTHOOD?

Troy: I always thought that people outgrew ADHD by the time they reached adulthood, so I figured that I must have outgrown the ADHD that I had as a kid.

Psychotherapist: Actually, research has found that, in most cases, people still have significant ADHD symptoms once they reach adulthood.

Brad holds a position of high responsibility at a prestigious advertising firm. He admits that, when he was a child, he had typical symptoms of inattentive type ADHD, including not paying attention in classes that he considered boring, difficulty getting things done, losing track of personal possessions, and being criticized for being "lazy," "unmotivated," and "not living up to your potential." He's never been diagnosed with ADHD, nor has he ever taken any stimulant medication. He has to manage details on the job and he does that well. Nonetheless, he feels that his brain works just the same now as it did when he was a kid. When asked how he functions so well, he says that he's realized that there are some things that just need to get done, no matter how difficult they are, in order for his life to run smoothly—so he dedicates the necessary mental effort to getting them done.

Whether childhood ADHD remits in adulthood depends on how we define remission. Here are two ways that remission can be defined (Biederman, 2011):

- *Syndromatic remission:* The person no longer has enough symptoms to meet the diagnostic criteria for ADHD. Past research found that about 64% to 85% of adults diagnosed with childhood ADHD remitted according to this definition—which used earlier, more stringent diagnostic criteria of six or more symptoms of either inattention or hyperactivity/impulsivity (Biederman, Petty, Evans, Small, & Faraone, 2010; Faraone, Biederman, & Mick, 2006; Kessler et al., 2005).
- *Functional remission:* The person no longer has impairing symptoms of ADHD and the person's functioning level has normalized. Only about one-third to one-fourth of adults who were diagnosed with ADHD in childhood no longer have functional impairment from ADHD symptoms (Biederman et al., 2010; Faraone, Biederman, & Mick, 2000, 2006).

So, in most cases, the answer is no, ADHD does not remit in adulthood. *In at least two-thirds of cases, the functional impairment of ADHD lasts through adulthood, regardless of whether the individual has enough symptoms to meet a strict definition of ADHD.*

Some adults do recover from childhood ADHD, like Brad in the previous scenario. Some of them probably have brains that matured later and thus outgrew ADHD (Turgay et al., 2012). Children with ADHD are three years behind their peers in cortical maturation (Shaw et al., 2007). Also, there is a subgroup of "remitters" whose functioning improves significantly, despite still having some underlying brain differences and/or cognitive and motor symptoms of ADHD. They have "outgrown" childhood ADHD through development of skills, emotional maturity, and/or maturation of the brain. They occasionally struggle with mild ADHD symptoms, but they have sufficient compensatory skills to cope effectively. Yet, these individuals may still have persistent neurocognitive differences indicative of ADHD (Halperin, Trampush, Miller, Marks, & Newcorn, 2008). The continued cognitive deficits and brain differences found in remitters varies somewhat from study to study, and firm conclusions will need to wait for a meta-analysis or review (Cheung et al., 2016; Halperin et al., 2008; Mattfeld et al., 2014; Turgay et al., 2012). However, it appears that high IQ is a factor in remission (Cheung et al., 2016).

EMERGING ADULTS ARE HIGHLY CHALLENGED

Psychotherapist: So you had a son when you were 19 years old. What was going on in your life at that point? What happened from there?

Troy: Aimee and I moved in together in a trailer. Her mom paid the deposit because she said that she wasn't ready to have a baby in her house. Aimee was working at a fast-food place, but her mom took the baby sometimes when she was at work. I was working off and on for my aunt's moving company. She would call me when she needed another guy on a job. I hated the guy she had bossing us around, and I quit a bunch of times, but my aunt always made him take me back. I was trying to be a good dad, but I was immature. I would hang out with the guys several nights a week and come home drunk and stoned. Then Aimee and I would fight because she was mad that I left her all alone with the baby. She had an abortion the second time she got pregnant. I was mad that she didn't ask me, but now I know that I wouldn't have been able to handle another kid at that age.

P: Wow, that sounds rough.

T: It was. We were really struggling. When I was 24, Aimee got pregnant again. I really wanted another kid, because I was having a lot of fun with my son now that he was 5. She said that I had to show that I could get it together for us to have that kid. So I went by my cousin's, who has an auto repair shop. I'd been dropping in to visit with him and tinker on cars for years. I told him that I would do any job he had, but I wanted to learn to be a mechanic. He hired me to clean up the shop at night to start. Then I went over to the community college to enroll in their auto mechanic program. When I came home that day and told Aimee what I'd done, she cried. I could tell that she was skeptical that I could keep it up, but I've always loved cars, so the work and the classes weren't difficult for me. Things have improved a lot since then.

Transitioning to adulthood, especially from ages 18 to 25, is particularly challenging for individuals with ADHD (Turgay et al., 2012). The young adult no longer has daily supervision and structure from parents and has more independence and more opportunities. Also, many more things can go wrong. This is clearly a high-risk period (Turgay et al., 2012). Both work and college are more difficult than high school and require more self-organization and self-direction with each ensuing year (Manos, 2010). Meals, regular sleep, social activities, living situations, and finances may be chronically disrupted by disorganization. Treatment is very helpful during this transition period (Ramsay & Rostain, 2008b).

Unfortunately, most emerging adults who had been diagnosed with ADHD during childhood have very poor insight into their own difficulties, and many do not take their medication—in one study, none were continuing to take medication by age 21 (McCarthy et al., 2009). Multiple studies have found that the parents of these young adults see their dysfunction more accurately than they do (Barkley, Murphy, & Fischer, 2008; Sibley et al., 2012b). Other findings about young adults who had been diagnosed with combined type or hyperactive/impulsive type ADHD during childhood include the following:

- Continued impairment in executive functioning, attention, and distractibility (Barkley, 2006a)
- Increased risk for illegal drug use (Barkley, 2006a)
- Increased risk for antisocial and illegal activities (Barkley, 2006a)
- Less likely to attend college (Barkley, 2006a)
- Increased risk of adulthood interpersonal hostility, paranoia, suicide attempts, and arrests (Murphy, Barkley, & Bush, 2002)
- Increased risk for employment problems, including being fired or laid off, poor performance ratings, and changing jobs more often, as well as lower socioeconomic status (Barkley, 2006a)
- Continued peer problems, including fewer friends and acquaintances and more problems keeping friends (Barkley, 2006a)
- Significantly more likely to have a child by age 20 (Barkley, 2006a) (Many of these children were being raised by the mother's family, put up for adoption, or in foster care; Barkley, 2002)
- More likely to have contracted a sexually transmitted disease (Barkley, 2006a)
- More motor vehicle crashes, speeding tickets, traffic citations, and license suspensions (Barkley, 2006a)
- Significantly increased risk of violent behavior (although the large majority were never violent toward a partner; Wymbs et al., 2012)

Inattentive symptoms are more likely to persist to adulthood than hyperactive/impulsive symptoms (Asherson, 2013; Dias et al., 2013), although overt hyperactivity does persist in some individuals. Any type of childhood ADHD leads to increased risk of depression, substance abuse, emotional distress, and mental health treatment.

DOES ADULT ADHD EXIST WITHOUT A HISTORY OF CHILDHOOD ADHD?

A debate is currently raging about ADHD that appears to emerge in adulthood in longitudinal studies (Castellanos, 2015; Faraone, 2016; Moffitt et al., 2015). Researchers are unclear as to whether ADHD is actually emerging in adulthood with absolutely no history of childhood ADHD or whether something else is going on that may explain this apparent emergence of ADHD. Some possibilities include:

- Childhood ADHD was mild and the individual did not have behavior problems. Coping was adequate until overwhelmed by adult demands.
- Parents provided needed support and structure, so ADHD only appeared to emerge in adulthood when these supports were no longer present.

- The individual had other ways to compensate as a child that were not sufficient to the demands of adulthood (e.g., interpersonal charm, strong work ethic).
- The individual has developed a medical problem (e.g., sleep apnea) with similar cognitive symptoms to ADHD, so ADHD appears to emerge in adulthood but is an inaccurate diagnosis.
- Substance abuse is causing ADHD-like symptoms (Moffitt et al., 2015).
- Adult onset of anxiety or depression may cause ADHD symptoms to emerge (Franke et al., 2012).

An individual who had previously functioned adequately or marginally can suddenly become unable to function capably when environmental demands increase. For this reason, it may *appear* that ADHD is emerging in adulthood. Brown (2008) states that "For some affected individuals, impairments of ADHD may not be noticeable until they are challenged with increased demands for self-management typically not presented until late adolescence or early adulthood" (p. 409). Others agree that sometimes significant dysfunction is not obvious until adulthood (e.g., Attention Deficit Disorder Association, 2006; Ramsay, 2010b), although, in retrospect, mild symptoms were present during childhood or adolescence but were not significantly impairing at that time.

Clinically, I have not yet found an adult client with ADHD who did not have at least mild signs of childhood ADHD. Typically, they have had problems with concentration, distractibility, planning, and other cognitive difficulties of ADHD all along but had sufficient support, structure, cognitive resources, or coping skills to function adequately until adulthood.

ADHD AND COLLEGE

Clara: When I was a freshman and sophomore in college, my grades were all over the place, but then they improved when I was a junior and senior.

Psychotherapist: I assume you were taking mostly science and education classes as a junior and senior?

C: Yes.

P: And were they interesting to you?

C: Definitely. But some of the education classes were a bit boring and I did a haphazard job on the homework. My education class grades were mostly B's, some B-minuses. But my science class grades were all A's. I loved all my science classes. I even took the most difficult chemistry and physics classes and got A's in those.

P: Tell me more about the classes you took when you were a freshman and sophomore. I assume you had to take some required courses?

C: I took history and English classes, but they were all boring. I took French, and it wasn't too hard, since I'm bilingual in English and Spanish, but I didn't care about the homework and usually didn't do it. I still did okay on the tests. I got B-minuses and C's in those classes. I got a D in my last semester of French because I didn't ever learn all the verb conjugations.

P: Okay, you've given me a lot of information here. What you've described is a pattern that I often see in people who are intelligent but have ADHD without hyperactivity. Since you didn't have hyperactivity or behavior problems as a kid, and you managed to pull off a lot of good grades because you are smart, no one noticed that you had learning problems. Instead, they chalked it up to being lazy or unmotivated. I don't think it was that at all. I agree with you; I think it was ADHD without hyperactivity, what we call the predominantly inattentive type. Sometimes people grow out of childhood ADHD, but I see that you didn't. You've been struggling all along with concentration, distractibility, procrastination, and getting organized. The pattern of grades that you described in college is pretty typical of a person with ADHD, as are the struggles you're having at work. Your husband sees most of this, but you try to keep it hidden from everyone else, and it sounds like you mostly succeed at that. Then you feel bad about yourself.

In this example, there is a stark contrast in Clara's performance of interesting versus dull tasks. Although she might have been interested during lectures in French class, she found the homework dull and rarely did it. This is likely related to differences in the reward system of the brain of many individuals with ADHD. Clara clearly had some learning problems and her grades were uneven, but she passed all her courses and finished her degree.

Many adults with ADHD do not do as well as Clara did in college (Barkley, 2006a). In fact, 42% of ADHD adults who attended college had interruptions in their attendance (Brown, 2005). Many drop out.

However, those ADHD adults who do well in college may represent a particularly resilient group (Wilmshurst, Peele, & Wilmshurst, 2011). Overall, there is evidence that college students with ADHD are more likely to have problems with academic and psychological functioning (Rabiner, Anastopoulos, Costello, Hoyle, & Swartzwelder, 2008; Weyandt & DuPaul, 2006), as well as lower self-rated social skills and self-esteem (Shaw-Zirt, Popali-Lehan, Chaplin, & Bergman, 2005). Those who attend college sometimes have insight into their need for support and seek out student counseling centers and student support centers (J. Kolar, personal communication, 2015; M. Peitrus, personal communication, 2015). Those who have insight can learn effective study and coping skills and do well at college. Those who do not seek support will probably drop out. Remind your college student clients with ADHD to report the diagnosis to the office of disability services as soon as possible; this provides the option of accommodations if needed (Ramsay, 2010b).

Whether or not extended time on tests is helpful for college students with ADHD is debatable and controversial. Research suggests that they do not use the extended time effectively (Lovett & Leja, 2013), they answer as many items as other students within the normal time period, and their proportion correct does not differ (Miller, Lewandowski, & Antshel, 2015). If your client attended college, ask about educational functioning during that period:

- Did you graduate?
- Did you have any problems in college?
- How long did it take you to finish?

ADHD DIAGNOSED IN ADULTHOOD

Clara: Once I graduated from college, I started working at my high school. The school isn't large, so I'm the only chemistry teacher. I talked to the biology teacher a lot about how she managed labs during class time. I was always having problems getting through everything during class, especially in my first year. I would feel like a failure for having these problems. Then I would be exhausted and have to go home and grade papers and then work up the next day's lesson plan. I was tired all the time and so depressed. I felt like I would never get a handle on teaching, and I thought about quitting every single day. I knew I was a fraud and it was only a matter of time before my colleagues figured it out. Sometimes I would spend most of Saturday in bed, until I had to get up on Sunday to grade and prepare for the week. But my kids kept me going; I couldn't drop out in the middle of the year and leave their education in even more of a mess.

Psychotherapist: That sounds really hard. I can see that you were having all of the typical struggles that a first-year teacher has, plus you were having problems with organizing yourself and the kids due to your ADHD. No wonder you were so depressed during that time.

In college and the workplace, Clara's challenges with managing and organizing herself created functional problems and contributed to emotional distress. Adults whose ADHD is diagnosed in adulthood are significantly different from adults whose ADHD was diagnosed in childhood (Barkley, 2006a). Logically, we know these facts about them:

- Their classroom behavior was never so impaired that teachers referred them for evaluation for ADHD.
- Their parents did not consider them impaired enough to request or seek out an evaluation.

Most of the demographic factors that contribute to ADHD being missed in childhood were discussed previously. Other characteristics common in adults who have ADHD that was missed in childhood but was diagnosed in adulthood are:

- Effective parenting: Parents provided a lot of structure (Murphy & Gordon, 2006)

- No hyperactivity, or parents channeled the hyperactivity through lots of physical activity
- Inattentive type (Ramsay, 2010b; Wasserstein, 2005)
- No history of disruptive behavior problems (Ramsay, 2010b; Wasserstein, 2005) or male with conduct disorder diagnosis, but comorbid ADHD was missed (Asherson, 2013)
- At least average intelligence, so less attention to schoolwork is not as obvious (Barkley, 2006a; Barkley et al., 2008)
- If client is middle-aged or older, ADHD was probably not recognized during the time period when the client was a child. These individuals could have been quite academically impaired, but at that time in history, teachers and parents usually would have considered their problems to be due to be laziness, lack of motivation, or lack of effort.

Those diagnosed with ADHD in adulthood are usually *much less* impaired in life functioning than those diagnosed with ADHD in childhood. However, they are still more likely to have adaptive functioning challenges than the average individual (Barkley et al., 2008). And they are *more* likely to have depression, anxiety, and low self-esteem than adults diagnosed with ADHD during childhood.

LATER ADULTHOOD

Later adulthood is defined as ages 25 and up (Turgay et al., 2012). As an adult grows older, life demands continue to increase. The individual may be married and need to develop communication and problem-solving skills. The individual may have children who need structure and guidance. Work, academic, and community responsibilities tend to increase in complexity over time. Even milder symptoms can be quite disruptive to functioning and relationships:

- Difficulty sitting through meetings
- Impatience or rude impulsive remarks when waiting in lines or dealing with salespeople
- Blurting out tactless remarks before thinking
- Not following through with requests from spouse
- Inconsistent and disorganized parenting
- Forgetting appointments and obligations
- Procrastinating on tasks
- Missing deadlines
- Temper outbursts
- Speeding while driving (Barkley & Cox, 2007; Turgay et al., 2012)

Studies of adults with ADHD have not found significant gender differences in psychopathology, addiction, social functioning, or cognition (Biederman & Faraone, 2004; Biederman, Faraone, Monuteaux, Bober, & Cadogen, 2004). The only significant differences were fewer diagnoses of conduct disorder and antisocial personality disorder in women (Biederman et al., 2004).

OLDER ADULTS

Little is known about late middle-age and elderly adults with ADHD. When discussing this population, keep in mind some crucial historical markers in the history of ADHD diagnosis (Holland & Higuera, 2015; Wender, 1995):

- Prior to 1968: ADHD unrecognized as a disorder
- 1968 to 1986: "Hyperkinetic disorder" in the DSM-II
- 1987 to 1999: No inattentive subtype recognized in DSM-III
- 1992: Ground-breaking study by Ratey, Greenberg, Bemporad, and Lindem on psychological treatment of adult ADHD in clients who had previously been considered treatment failures
- 1994: Original publication of *Driven to Distraction* by Hallowell and Ratey, bringing adult ADHD to public attention
- 1995: Significant research published indicating that ADHD often lasts into adulthood
- 2000: Faraone et al. publish an article in *Biological Psychiatry* summarizing current research evidence that adult ADHD is a valid diagnosis

As this timeline indicates, elderly and middle-age individuals were children and young adults when the concept of ADHD, as we currently understand it, was essentially unknown—much less did anyone realize that those neurocognitive difficulties could persist to adulthood (Goodman, Mitchell, Rhodewalt, & Surman, 2016).

Adult ADHD clearly does last through old age (Michielsen et al., 2012). Older adults who have ADHD have indicated that they are financially less well-off and have lower educational achievement, greater social isolation, and a history of job performance problems (Brod, Schmitt, Goodwin, Hodgkins, & Niebler, 2012). These are essentially the same problems that younger adults have. Older people can be diagnosed in a chain reaction from recognition of ADHD in a grandchild, then in the parent, then in the grandparent. Others self-identify (Michielsen et al., 2012). ADHD is easily missed in older adults. Even most memory clinics do not routinely screen for it (Fischer, Gunter-Hunt, Steinhafel, & Howell, 2012).

Cognitive changes that frequently occur due to aging can be difficult to differentiate from ADHD (Berck, 2015), as can many medical problems (Goodman, Mitchell, Rhodewalt, & Surman, 2016). Researchers caution that ADHD symptoms can be mistaken for signs of dementia in the elderly (Brod, Schmitt, et al., 2012). A careful examination of life difficulties over time will often clarify the diagnosis. Unless they have medical reasons not to take medications to treat ADHD, a person of any age can benefit (David Goodman as quoted in Berck,

2015). However, careful attention should be paid to comorbid medical conditions that could be exacerbated by stimulants (Goodman et al., 2016). A pilot study found that similar doses of stimulant medications were needed in the elderly as in younger adults (Manor, 2016).

KEY POINTS

- ADHD is highly heritable and often runs in families. A good rule of thumb is: *About half of first-degree relatives of an adult with ADHD will have ADHD as.well.*
- Researchers agree that there are many genetic pathways to developing ADHD, so any two people with ADHD are likely to have different combinations of genes that predisposed them to develop the disorder. In other words, individuals with ADHD are genetically *heterogeneous.*
- Only about one-third of children with ADHD later have normal adult functioning (Cherkasova et al., 2013).
- For most people, ADHD is a lifelong condition that can impact functioning at every age.
- Environmental demands increase dramatically as people age. This is especially true for emerging adults. Resources and strengths such as supportive families or high intelligence may no longer be able to compensate sufficiently for ADHD. Thus ADHD may appear to have emerged in adulthood. However, closer questioning will elicit earlier childhood symptoms such as frequently losing items, daydreaming, distractibility, disorganization, and needing intensive supervision to complete tasks.
- Adults diagnosed with ADHD in adulthood are a different population from those who had been diagnosed in childhood. Those diagnosed in adulthood tend to be more often female, inattentive type, more highly educated, and higher functioning—although they are at greater risk for depression, anxiety, and low self-esteem.
- Carefully evaluate middle-aged and older adults for ADHD, since ADHD as we now understand it, was unknown when they were children.

8

Assessing Adaptive Functioning

Adults have many complex roles and responsibilities. Adults have to plan, organize, manage, and prioritize constantly (Weiss et al., 2008). Adults with ADHD are constantly struggling with these issues and have an increased risk of the following adaptive functioning problems (Barkley, Fischer, Smallish, & Fletcher, 2006):

- Academic problems and lack of achievement
- Work problems and lack of achievement
- Driving problems
- Financial and paperwork problems
- Self-management problems
- Poor health behaviors and adverse health outcomes
- Suicide risk and self-harm
- Criminality, violence, and psychopathy
- Social problems with friends and family

Adults with ADHD vary considerably in their functioning levels (Asherson, 2013; Kuriyan et al., 2013), however, certain behavior patterns are particularly indicative of adult ADHD. Adults can have either obvious or subtle signs of dysfunction—or obvious signs in some areas of functioning and subtle signs in others. This chapter provides descriptions of ADHD behavior patterns in both their subtle and obvious forms to help you recognize ADHD and assess adaptive functioning.

OBVIOUS DEFICITS: AN OVERVIEW

The lowest functioning individuals with ADHD are very dysfunctional (Asherson, 2013). They are likely to have comorbid learning disabilities and/or psychiatric diagnoses. They have a difficult time maintaining functional relationships, performing necessary everyday tasks, and holding down a job. They may be incarcerated. They may be irritable, overly angry, antisocial, and/or have substance abuse problems. Clients with these characteristics are challenging, and a focus on these issues may miss underlying ADHD. Often, but not always, these individuals were diagnosed with ADHD as children. They are likely to have had clear adaptive functioning or behavior problems throughout their entire lives. Troy has some of these characteristics. Once the clinician realizes the importance of assessing ADHD in this individual, the symptoms are usually readily apparent.

SUBTLE DEFICITS: AN OVERVIEW

The highest functioning adults with ADHD (such as Clara) may appear to be functioning normally to others. Subtle functioning deficits due to symptoms of ADHD are most observable to clients and their families. Clients try to hide these deficits, with varying degrees of success. Usually, these individuals were not diagnosed with ADHD as children.

Many of these clients with subtle functioning deficits have recognized their problems with accuracy, paying attention to others, making progress on projects, and other work-related skills. Because of this insight, they exert a lot of mental effort and do their very best to be sure that these things are done right. This effort often leads to perfectionism. Surman (2013) wisely points out the importance of assessing whether the person is making a special and concerted effort to do well. Many people who have ADHD can perform adequately or well at work by employing considerably more mental energy and effort than the average person. Others often do not notice subtle signs of ADHD such as getting their work done at the last minute. However, they are unlikely to be able to maintain this level of effort throughout all of their life demands. Other areas, such as home functioning, will usually suffer and show greater ADHD-related deficits.

They may have made some progress with coping and executive functioning skills. Some of the progress they have made may even be well integrated into ongoing habits. For example, you may ask client whether he often loses track of his cell phone or other important objects. The client replies, "No, I used to have that problem, but now I always make a habit to check and see that I have my cell phone, wallet, and keys before I leave the house." In this example, you can see that the client determined that there was a problem and made a significant effort to establish a new habit. Therefore, his answer could still be still suggestive of adult ADHD, depending on findings about the larger context of his life.

Thus higher functioning clients may have made progress in some areas. However, when questioned, continued problems become clear: disorganization, procrastination, concentration, poor time management, and lack of achievement of long-term goals. They feel that they are not living up to their potential; they are self-critical and have low self-esteem. They usually have considerable angst, comorbid depression, and/or anxiety. Substance abuse may be present. They may not have enough DSM-5 symptoms for a diagnosis of ADHD, but applying our knowledge from chapter 2 about current research into additional ADHD symptoms, it is clear that they do have ADHD.

ACADEMIC PROBLEMS

The college-age adult's obvious ADHD symptoms were described in a previous chapter: poor or uneven grades, dropping out of school, interruptions in attendance, and emotional distress during college. These individuals often blame themselves for not finishing college. They may ruminate about it, wondering why others could complete college and they could not. They likely know others of similar intelligence who did not have problems in college. They wonder what is wrong with them. Alternatively, they may not have enrolled in college in the first place (Barkley et al., 2006) or might be high school drop-outs (Biederman et al., 2006).

Subtle problems are less impairing but remain distressing to the individual. Adult students with ADHD are usually pushing up against deadlines. They will stay up all night to start an English paper they have known about for weeks. Maybe they tell themselves that this is okay because they do their best work at the last minute. Or maybe they get upset at themselves for putting it off for so long. Maybe the English paper will be turned in after the deadline. They can lose track of when assignments are due, and they may constantly be begging for extensions. They will have difficulty doing larger projects without considerable structure from their professors. Their grades during the first two years may be extremely varied, while their grades during junior and senior years are likely to be better, since they are focusing on their areas of interest, their majors. They often need extra time to finish their degrees. They may notice that they spend more time studying than other students do in order to get the same grades. They chronically feel like underachievers. They wonder how others can be so much more organized. If these students go to graduate school and have not already sought professional help, they are likely to have significant problems with keeping up with the work and will be forced to recognize their learning problems at that time. Interview questions to assess educational history and academic problems were presented in chapter 7.

Adults with ADHD who effectively manage college often have a high level of intelligence and motivation toward academic pursuits. Also, some of them effectively seek out and use appropriate support services. They still have occasional subtle problems as described earlier, but they learn to work effectively around them.

WORK PROBLEMS

Adults with ADHD are more likely to have obvious work problems. They are disorganized and sporadic in their efforts to find work, and their job applications may be incomplete (Adamou et al., 2013). They are more likely to be fired, have poor work evaluations, be unemployed, and move frequently from one job to another (Barkley et al., 2006; Barkley, Murphy, & Fischer, 2008; Biederman et al., 2006; Küpper et al., 2012). They may have increased days out of work and problems with work quantity and quality (de Graff et al., 2008; Kessler et al., 2005). They may have more workplace accidents or injuries (Kessler, Lane, Stang, & Van Brunt, 2009). If the individual has mood problems, these can have a negative impact (Küpper et al., 2012). They can have difficulties with time management and keeping on top of their workloads (Adamou et al., 2013). Alternatively, if they enjoy their work, or derive rewards from it, they can become hyperfocused on the job and have poor work–life balance (Adamou et al., 2013). They may quit a job from boredom or because they are irritated without having another job to go to. Overall, their work histories can be spotty (Barkley et al., 2008).

Subtle work problems are also a possibility. The adult may have a seemingly ordinary work history. Jobs that can work out well for adults with ADHD often involve a lot of movement, intellectual or creative stimuli, and/or demands that work is done immediately. For these reasons, younger adults with ADHD often do surprisingly well in the restaurant industry. Also, when adults with ADHD find an interesting career, they can be highly motivated. However, they may still struggle with being bored at work, at least sometimes, because all jobs have some boring elements. They may overcommit and have difficulties with follow-through (Nadeau, 2005). Because of memory deficits, they may not remember things that others ask them to do (Nadeau, 2005). Their bosses may need to repeatedly nag them to get paperwork done. If they have a desk or workspace, it is likely to be disorganized (Nadeau, 2005). They may also have interpersonal issues because they may tend to blurt out tactless remarks. Coworkers may respect their work but also say that they are disorganized, "all over the place," or "a loose cannon." Some questions to assess work problems include:

- How often have you changed jobs?
- What was the reason for the job change?
- Has it been hard to get along with bosses?
- Have people complained that you make too many mistakes at work?
- Do you feel that you have underachieved in the workforce?
- Do you have any problems with organizing or prioritizing your work?

There are reports that adults with ADHD are more likely to be self-employed (Mannuzza, Klein, Bessler, Malloy, & LaPudula, 1993). Barkley (2010a) hypothesizes that perhaps the flexibility of being self-employed is helpful, and the immediacy of needing to work to get paid provides incentive to be productive. I might also wonder whether these self-employed adults with ADHD have found something that they are passionate about and this helps keep them motivated.

Adults with ADHD who do well on the job often have good interpersonal skills. They have found a career that is interesting to them and they are very passionate about it. When they struggle with disorganization, they either have developed the skills to get back on track or they get help from coworkers, assistants, or employees.

DRIVING PROBLEMS

Driving problems are more common in individuals with ADHD. These include accidents, tickets for reckless driving, driving without a license, hit-and-run crashes, and license suspensions (Barkley & Cox, 2007; Bernardi et al., 2012; Fischer, Barkley, Smallish, & Fletcher, 2007). Adults who have emotional dysregulation as a symptom of ADHD may express their anger and poor frustration tolerance through aggressive, unsafe driving (Oliver et al., 2012; Richards, Deffenbacher, Rosén, Barkley, & Rodricks, 2006). Stimulant medication improves driving performance (Jerome, Segal, & Habinski, 2006). Questions to assess driving problems include:

- Do you like to drive your car faster than others drive? Are you especially impatient when you drive?
- Have you ever been in a car accident? Had any tickets? Had your license suspended?

Be sure to ask specific behavioral questions about driving problems. Many individuals with ADHD unrealistically overestimate their driving abilities (Jerome et al., 2006), so general questions such as "Are you a safe driver?" or "Are you a good driver?" may not be informative.

The driving problems noted here are more likely within the ADHD population but are not applicable to everyone. It is also possible that the individual with ADHD does not have driving problems. However, even a safe driver with ADHD is likely to occasionally struggle with being overstimulated while driving. If your client has a history of driving problems, jointly consider the following interventions:

- Installing an app so that the phone cannot be used when driving
- Putting the phone in the trunk so it cannot be used when driving
- Selling the car and taking ride services or public transportation
- Not driving unless medication has been taken that day

FINANCIAL AND PAPERWORK PROBLEMS

Financial mismanagement can be a major problem for adults who have ADHD. Not having any savings, credit cards, or retirement accounts are signs of obvious financial dysfunction (Barkley et al., 2006). When these accounts exist, they may drain them sporadically for things that seem important in the present, overspend, make impulse purchases, have high credit card balances, exceed credit limits, make late bill payments or miss payments, have cars repossessed, have a lower credit rating, bounce checks, fail to save documents for income taxes, and lose friends from borrowing money without repaying it (Barkley & Benton, 2010; Bernardi et al., 2012; Kessler et al., 2005). They often have difficulty getting their federal and state income taxes done in a timely manner, and they may need to ask for multiple extensions. If the taxes are done on time, they may be running to the post office on the evening of April 15 to mail them.

Even for higher functioning individuals, paying the bills on time can be a problem. Generally, mail piles up in multiple places in the home. Since paperwork is boring, important documents cannot be found because they are buried in piles with unopened mail, old receipts, and other unimportant pieces of paper.

Questions to assess financial and paperwork problems include:

- Do you get your income taxes paid on time?
- Have you ever had problems with getting bills paid on time? Tell me more about that.
- Do you have difficulties keeping track of and organizing your personal paperwork?
- Do you have difficulties managing money or credit cards?

Individuals with ADHD whose finances and paperwork are not a problem have put many of their bills on auto pay, or their spouse takes care of the financial paperwork. They may hire an accountant, office assistant, or bookkeeper if they are self-employed. Or they may have developed self-management skills to regularly address finances.

HOUSEHOLD MANAGEMENT PROBLEMS

Regular housework can be a challenge. Individuals with ADHD may completely run out of clothes, stay up till 3 AM getting all the laundry done, and then feel sleepy at work all the next day. They have difficulty maintaining a consistently clean home. Roommates and partners may complain that the home has not been cleaned for many days, there is clutter all around, the bathrooms are filthy, and the sink is full of crusty dirty dishes. They may go into a frenzy of cleaning and clean the whole place top to bottom. Then the home regresses to its dirty state again. Roommates and partners get tired of reminding them to do housework.

They get excited about new projects but then often move on to other interests. The remains of multiple projects may be sitting around the house in a disorganized fashion, with an intention to complete them some day, a day which often never comes. Over time, this creates so much clutter. In more severe cases, ADHD may lead to hoarding (Frost, Steketee, & Tolin, 2011). This difficulty prioritizing, sorting, and organizing can easily lead to too many possessions. Questions to assess this include:

- Do you have problems being organized with shopping or cleaning?
- What does your closet look like? Your bedroom?
- Do you have any conflicts with your roommate/spouse regarding housework?

- Do you have any issues with clutter?
- When do you do your laundry?

Household management problems are nearly universal among most ADHD adults. There is always something more interesting to do at home than housework. Nonetheless, a disorganized, cluttered, and messy home is as aversive to themselves as it is to others—and perhaps even more so. Individuals with ADHD are distracted whenever they see the mess, and it contributes to anxiety, negative self-talk and overstimulation. When they do rid themselves of clutter, they often feel considerably better.

Some adults with ADHD have figured out ways cope with these issues more effectively. If they can afford it, they hire a housekeeper. Maybe their spouse cleans up after them. Some are highly motivated to keep their roommate or partner from being distressed about a messy home, and that provides sufficient motivation to clean up. Others do their best to keep their possessions at an absolute minimum so they have less to organize. Some may keep possessions organized on the surface, but, inside the drawers and closets, disorganization is obvious.

Once clients progress in therapy, they develop habits to get things done regularly. Stimulant medication often helps significantly with getting housework done. Also, they realize that they need to develop routines to accomplish household tasks. Even though it does not come naturally, when their homes are organized and clean, individuals with ADHD say that they have a feeling of peace and calm.

ADVERSE HEALTH OUTCOMES AND POOR HEALTH BEHAVIORS

Psychotherapist: Please tell me about your eating habits. . . . I am concerned that you are often missing breakfast and lunch. This probably contributes to difficulties concentrating in the morning. What is your usual sleep pattern like? . . . These challenges that you are having with setting a regular bedtime and awakening time are probably contributing to your concentration problems. What do you think? Do you notice having more problems concentrating when you haven't gotten enough sleep? . . . I'm thinking that these problems are worth addressing and that you don't need these sleep and eating issues contributing to your concentration problems. Is this a good time to work on these issues?

Obvious health habit dysfunction and physical health problems are more likely in adults with ADHD (Brook, Brook, Zhang, Seltzer, & Finch, 2013):

- *Substance abuse* and other addictive behaviors (Nigg, 2013)
- *Physical injuries*—especially from auto accidents (Nigg, 2013), as well as increased risk of presenting to the emergency room with an injury, bone fractures, and head injuries (Dalsgaard, 2016)

- *Tobacco smoking* (McClernon & Kollins, 2008)—nicotine is a way to self-medicate cognitive symptoms (Nigg, 2013)
- *Sexual and reproductive health outcomes* include having sex at an earlier age (Barkley, 2002), having more sexual partners (Barkley, 2002), having more children by age 20 (Barkley, 2002), being more likely to have a sexually transmitted disease (Barkley et al., 2006; Nigg, 2013), having more unplanned pregnancies (Barkley et al., 2008), and being less likely to attend recommended prenatal checkups (Ninowski, Mash, & Benzies, 2007)
- *Increased risk of obesity and binge eating* (Pagoto et al., 2009; Pagoto, Curtin, Applehans, & Alonso-Alonso, 2012)
- *Sleep disorders*
- *Increased mortality*—mostly due to accidents (Dalsgaard, Østergaard, Leckman, Mortensen, & Pederson, 2015)

Adults with ADHD are often overdue for medical checkups. They have higher health expenses; this may be caused by increased risk of injuries, substance abuse treatment costs, or more serious illness resulting from nonadherence to treatment, among other possible causes (Harpin, 2005). Be aware that many of these findings are from longitudinal studies of primarily males with diagnosed hyperactive or combined type ADHD (Barkley, 2002), usually the most impaired subgroup of ADHD adults.

Higher functioning adults with ADHD may not have these more severe health problems. Multiple health behaviors are still likely be problematic, however, due to executive functioning problems and difficulties adhering to long-term goals:

- *Sleep* may be disorganized, with varying bedtimes, times to awaken, and occasional naps. Clearly, this has a negative impact on cognition.
- *Eating* may also be problematic, including problems with eating impulsively, eating foods with lower nutritional density, and eating higher fat foods (Nigg, 2013). Meals may be skipped, which has a negative impact on cognition. Trips to the grocery store may be occasional, impulsive, and done without a shopping list.
- *Exercise*: Adhering to a regular exercise program can be a challenge, and adults with ADHD often get less exercise (Nigg, 2013). It is well known that exercise improves cognition in the general population, and experts hypothesize that it may be even more useful for people with ADHD (Nigg, 2013).
- *Being overdue for appointments and checkups* at the dentist or doctor is also common.

Questions to assess health habits include:

- When was the last time you saw a physician? Had a pap smear? Saw a dentist?

- What medical problems do you have? Do you have any pain? Have you discussed these with your physician?
- Is your sleep regular? Do you take naps?
- Is your eating regular? Are you skipping meals? Which ones?

Good daily health habits are essential for optimal functioning, especially with people with ADHD. Motivated clients will work collaboratively in therapy to improve these health habits.

SUICIDE AND SELF-HARM RISK

Most people with ADHD do not have suicidal ideation or suicide risk (Nigg, 2013). Nonetheless, adults with ADHD can be at increased risk of suicidal ideation and suicide attempts (Barbaresi et al., 2013; Chen et al., 2014; Ljung, Chen, Lichtenstein, & Larsson, 2014). The greatest risk of completed suicides is when ADHD co-occurs with depression, antisocial behavior, or substance abuse (Nigg, 2013). Current hyperactivity considerably increased risk of self-injury and suicide attempts in young women with ADHD (Hinshaw et al., 2012).

All clients with acute distress should be screened for suicidal ideation (Ramsay & Rostain, 2008b), and, when necessary, a full suicide risk assessment should be completed (Willer, 2014). As with any distressed population, in most cases, suicidal ideation *does not* lead to self-injury, suicide attempts, or completed suicides (Willer, 2014).

PERPETRATORS AND VICTIMS OF CRIMINALITY AND VIOLENCE

Only a very small proportion of adults who have ADHD have problems of criminality, violence, or psychopathy. That said, these difficulties are more commonly found in the ADHD population than in the general population. Greater risk was found for antisocial activities and arrests—primarily for illegal drug possession, use, and sale (Barkley, Fischer, Smallish, & Fletcher, 2004). About 20% of prison inmates have ADHD (Westmoreland et al., 2010). While an overlap between psychopathy and ADHD has been proposed, a recent study found that the connection is through shared behavior (nonconforming, nonplanful, impulsive, rebellious) and not the emotional aspects of psychopathy, such as cold-heartedness (Eisenbarth et al., 2008). Childhood ADHD plus adolescent antisocial behavior and/or substance abuse led to greater criminality; childhood ADHD without these risk factors did not (Mannuzza, Klein, & Moulton, 2008). In a few individuals, adult hyperactivity coupled with substance abuse increased the risk of injurious violence towards intimate partners, family and friends (Gonzalez, Kallis, & Coid, 2013; Gudjonsson, Sigurdsson, Sugfusdottir, & Young, 2012).

Young women with ADHD were found to be more likely to be the victims of rape, attempted rape, and other nonconsensual sexual experiences (White & Buehler, 2012). No one knows why. These problems appear to get their start in childhood, since males with ADHD may be more prone to bullying and females with ADHD may be more prone to be victims of bullying (Bacchini, Affuso, & Trotta, 2008).

WHY SOCIAL PROBLEMS?

On average, adults, mostly men, who had been diagnosed with childhood ADHD, were found to have the same number of social acquaintances but fewer close friends and more trouble keeping friends (Barkley et al., 2006). Individuals with ADHD can have social problems for many reasons:

- *Fluctuating attention*, leading to intermittently listening to people and missing social cues (Ramsay, 2010b). This lack of information getting through becomes frustrating to friends and family. The friends and family get aggravated: "I already told you about that; you weren't paying attention again!"
- *Easily bored*: Even though the individual intends to pay attention and be supportive, it is easy to get bored when others are talking about their workplace or interpersonal struggles. Friends and family notice the individual's boredom and wandering attention. Understandably, they can feel emotionally disconnected, hurt, or angry.
- *Easily distracted*: No one likes talking to someone who ignores them and starts looking at or listening to something else.
- *Forgetfulness*: They may forget to thank others, say goodbye (Ramsay, 2010b), lose track of plans—leaving friends hanging, and commit other social faux pas.
- *Poor follow-through*: Because of fluctuating attention and poor executive functioning, they may not follow through on promises (Ramsay, 2010b).
- *Tactlessness*: They may blurt out tactless remarks due to impulsiveness (Ramsay, 2010b).
- *Impatience and restlessness*: which often appears rude (Ramsay, 2010b).
- *Lateness* is a chronic problem for many adults with ADHD, and many people find this offensive.

Questions to assess social functioning include:

- Do you have difficulty paying attention when someone is talking about subjects you are not interested in?
- Do you forget to respond to text messages, phone calls, or emails?

ADHD is often misunderstood. Others can be judgmental and stigmatize people with ADHD. Individuals with ADHD behave in ways that can upset others and

ADHD symptoms are erroneously perceived as controllable, and (Canu, Newman, Morrow, & Pope, 2008).

Regardless, many adults with ADHD do not have significant social problems. They may be very interested in hearing about other people and have few problems paying attention. Also, other people may find their passions, enthusiasm, and creativity to be appealing and forgive any minor social lapses that may occur.

SPOUSE/PARTNER PROBLEMS

Most partners of adults with ADHD get frustrated at times. In more severe cases, partners of adults with ADHD can feel ignored and neglected (Ramsay, 2010b). Common family problems with money, routines, homework, and child behavior can be magnified by having a spouse with ADHD, who may make impulsive decisions and may parent inconsistently (Ramsay, 2010b). The partner may be embarrassed by the spouse's social errors. The partner may be fed up with the emotional ups and downs of the spouse with ADHD and concerned about the impact of emotional dysregulation on their children (Eakin et al., 2004). The partner may be tired of the spouse not following through on commitments and responsibilities and not remembering what he or she has been told. The partner may be tired of having to clean up messes and clutter or shouldering most of the organizational burden for the family. The partner may be tired of the spouse "zoning out" when listening and not responding when spoken to. The spouse may be overly involved in online gaming or other "screen time" activities (Roberts, 2016). The partner may be frustrated by sexual issues, which vary from one individual to the next. Common sexual issues are no apparent interest in sex, being overly demanding of sex, and being interested in pornography and masturbation rather than sex with the partner (Pera, 2016). Because of all this, the partner may draw the conclusion that the spouse does not care (Robin, 2002). In more severe cases, the adult with ADHD is more likely to be separated or divorced (Biederman et al., 2006).

Clinically, I often find that adults with ADHD are often attracted to partners who can provide organization and structure to their lives. The partners, in turn, may appreciate the enthusiasm and spontaneity of the individual with ADHD or other positive qualities that this individual possesses. However, the differing coping strategies of one partner with ADHD and one without does cause inevitable challenges. The partner without ADHD can become frustrated with doing most of the organizing, structuring, and planning. The partner may start to wonder why the spouse is not stepping up. When the ADHD is undiagnosed, this can create significant relationship problems. Even when the ADHD is diagnosed, these difficulties need to be recognized, understood, negotiated, and resolved. Good communication and mutual understanding is essential when one spouse has ADHD and the other does not. Psychoeducation of the spouse without ADHD can be extremely helpful. Some questions to assess problems with the client's relationship to partner/spouse include:

- Does your spouse get upset with you because of anger or irritability on your part?
- Does your spouse get upset with you because you say you will do things and you don't follow through?
- Does your spouse get upset and complain that you are not listening?
- Does your spouse complain that you leave tasks partly done? That you lose track of possessions and appointments? Or that you are disorganized and messy?
- Does your spouse complain that you don't do your share of planning and organizing for the family?

When the spouse with ADHD and the partner have a healthy and functional relationship, they display good mutual understanding, including an understanding of how ADHD impacts family functioning. They often divide family tasks according to personal strengths, with the partner taking on more of the household organization (Eakin et al., 2004) and the spouse with ADHD performing other household tasks.

PARENTING PROBLEMS

Parenting is challenging for adults with ADHD. Additionally, since ADHD is so strongly heritable, there are often both adults and children with ADHD in the household. In fact, in one study, 84% of adults with ADHD had at least one child with ADHD and 50% had at least two children with ADHD (Biederman et al., 1995). When the adult with ADHD is a single parent, managing children and a household alone may be extremely difficult (Ramsay, 2010b). Also, adults with ADHD are more likely to be parents at a younger age (Barkley et al., 2006), so they can have less maturity and life experience to bring to parenting.

Research has found that parents with ADHD report difficulty sustaining attention while supervising their children, procrastinating about parenting tasks such as bath time, have fewer routines, and have more difficulty remembering their children's activities and homework (Johnston, Mash, Miller, & Ninowski, 2012). There was also less consistency, with both more lax and more overreactive parenting, as well as more arguments with their children and less effective problem-solving (Johnston et al., 2012; Murray & Johnston, 2006). Children with ADHD are more vulnerable to these family problems, while children without ADHD can be emotionally protected by having one non-ADHD parent (Minde et al., 2003). Questions to assess parenting include:

- Do you have difficulty with maintaining routines with your kids?
- Do you struggle with being a consistent parent?
- Do you argue with your kids? Do they have tantrums? (Tantrums are more likely when parenting is inconsistent and parents give in to tantrums at times.)

Little is known about positive parental functioning of adults with ADHD. However, no consistent differences were found between parents with ADHD and controls regarding emotional responsiveness to their children (Johnston et al., 2012).

SUBTLE DEFICITS VERSUS OVERDIAGNOSIS

Throughout this chapter, I have emphasized that sometimes ADHD causes obvious dysfunction and other times it does not. When obvious dysfunction is absent, individuals with ADHD can still be struggling with self-management. They win this struggle often enough that their difficulties may not be obvious to most people. However, their families, close friends, and roommates realize there is a problem. Adults with ADHD experience considerable angst, comorbid depression, anxiety, or substance abuse. They feel that they are underachievers and that something is terribly wrong.

Many adults have wondered about whether they have ADHD for years, but others may have disparaged this idea. In some cases, teachers may have suggested to their parents that they should be evaluated when they were children, but the parents insisted nothing was wrong and did not follow through. Some families are negatively predisposed to mental health treatment and stigmatize seeking help.

I have met many of these clients through my private practice. In private practice, clients tend to be higher functioning. Many have had some successes in life, which may include graduating from college, finding a career that is a good fit, or finding a loving partner. However, they continue to struggle with emotional pain from untreated ADHD. Should these individuals be diagnosed with ADHD? We cannot say that they are highly dysfunctional. They are not. However, they are exerting considerable effort not to be dysfunctional with their daily, even minute-by-minute, struggles against their cognitive deficits. Because they are coping somewhat effectively with these cognitive deficits, does this mean they should be denied medication? Do individuals who have angst about cognitive dysfunction and ADHD symptoms have a valid disorder, even if they are relatively high functioning? I would argue yes. However, we must be cautious about the risk of overdiagnosis. So we must ensure the following:

- Attention and concentration issues were present during childhood and were not explained by comorbid distress, mental illnesses, or any other factors than ADHD.
- At least subtle dysfunction is apparent in many areas of functioning throughout the lifespan and is not explained by comorbid mental illnesses or any other factors than ADHD
- If the adult functions effectively in some areas, it is clear that considerable sustained effort and practice was necessary to develop these coping skills.

Also, ensure that current dysfunction is not explained by a lack of skill development over time. Adults who grew up in dysfunctional homes often did not learn effective organizational and coping skills. These individuals may appear as if they have executive functioning difficulties and ADHD, but they simply have a skills deficit instead.

MEDICATION IMPROVES FUNCTIONING

Stimulant medications improve these areas of functioning (Surman, Hammerness, Pion, & Faraone, 2013):

- Academics, self-esteem, and social functioning (Arnold, Hodgkins, Caci, Kahle, & Young, 2015)
- Health (Surman, Hammerness, et al., 2013)
- Parenting: increased maternal involvement, improvements in supervision, and consistent discipline (Chronis-Tuscano et al., 2008)

Some functional improvements have also been seen with atomoxetine but apparently to a lesser degree (Adler et al., 2008; Durell et al., 2013). The combination of medication and psychotherapy is the most effective treatment for ADHD (Brown, 2013; Safren, Perlman, Sprich & Otto, 2005; Ramsay & Rostain, 2008a).

KEY POINTS

- Adults with ADHD vary considerably in their functioning levels. For some, the functioning deficits will be obvious and quite impairing. For others, functioning deficits are subtler and will be most apparent to them and their families, close friends, and roommates.
- Functioning problems occur in most areas of functioning, including academic problems, work problems, driving problems, financial and paperwork problems, household management problems, poor health behaviors, adverse health outcomes, and social problems with friends and family.
- An individual's internal resources *can* be modified with treatment at any age. Medication can improve the individual's cognitive functioning. Psychotherapy adapted to adult ADHD can help the individual develop executive functioning skills and coping skills, again increasing internal resources.

SECTION III

Treatment

9

Psychotherapy Goals, Structure, and Challenges

"Pills do not teach skills" (Ramsay, 2010b, p. 5). Despite significant cognitive improvement from stimulant medication, often the coping skills of adults with ADHD remain suboptimal. Psychotherapy focuses on improving coping skills to effectively address cognitive and emotional challenges. We also help the client process the emotional fallout from years of untreated ADHD and perceived failures. Adults with ADHD vary considerably in their symptoms, problems, functioning levels, and comorbidities, so treatment needs to be carefully tailored to the individual's needs (Ramsay, 2010b). The most important aspects of cognitive-behavioral psychotherapy (CBT) with adults who have ADHD are (Knouse & Safren, 2010):

- Educating the client about psychotherapy, addressing treatment-interfering behaviors, encouraging medication adherence, and referring to additional resources as needed (this chapter)
- Psychoeducation to understand their cognitive differences and how these have led to current life problems (chapter 10)
- Acquiring healthy habits and effective coping skills (chapter 11)
- Examining maladaptive cognitions that naturally develop from living with ADHD but decrease motivation, increase avoidance, and contribute to depression and anxiety (chapter 12)

Challenges to working with adults who have ADHD include (Ramsay & Rostain, 2005):

- Tangential speech resulting in difficulty concentrating on one theme
- Forgetting to discuss the most relevant life problems because they have not thought about what to talk about in advance
- Often being late to session
- Forgetting to cancel sessions until the last minute

These behaviors are not resistance (Ramsay & Rostain, 2005). Instead, they are symptoms of underlying cognitive dysfunction. Adults with ADHD also have challenges with motivation and feeling discouraged quickly.

CULTURAL COMPETENCE IN TREATMENT

Cultural competence remains an understudied topic in ADHD treatment. Most research has been done with adults who are employed and finished high school, so effective interventions with other adults with ADHD are unclear (Ramsay, 2010b). Here is what we do know:

- Many white families tend to be at a cultural extreme of independence. Other cultural groups are more normative and exhibit greater interdependence with family members. If appropriate, consider involving other family members—besides just the spouse—in assessment, psychoeducation, or treatment (Rostain, Ramsay, & Waite, 2015). The family can be often a powerful source of support and an important resource.
- As always, attending to the client's cultural values helps facilitate effective treatment (Rothe, 2005).

Some speculate that ADHD may not be as disabling in more community-oriented cultures (Meyer, 2010). The family and community may provide more structure, more immediate feedback, and clearer expectations for behavior to the ADHD adult than they receive in an individualistic society.

IS CBT EFFECTIVE?

While treatment programs vary, all CBT approaches to ADHD treatment provide skills training. Among nonmedication interventions, the CBT approach to psychotherapy of ADHD:

- Has the most empirical support (Ramsay, 2010a; Ramsay & Rostain, 2007; Vidal-Estrada, Bosch-Munso, Nogueira-Morais, Casas-Brugue, & Ramos-Quiroga, 2012; Weiss et al., 2008)
- Is an effective combination treatment with medication (Knouse & Safren, 2010; Ramsay, 2007)
- Improves symptom relief over medication alone (Philipsen, 2012; Safren et al., 2010; Solanto et al., 2010)
- Alleviates anxiety and depression (Safren et al., 2005)
- Improves quality of life (Philipsen et al., 2015)

- Has enduring efficacy when treatment is over (Philipsen et al., 2015; Salakari et al., 2010; Stevenson, Whitmont, Bornholt, Livesey, & Stevenson, 2002)

Most of the psychotherapy research has been conducted on group therapy (Vidal-Estrada et al., 2012), but individual psychotherapy by informed practitioners may be equally or possibly even more effective (Philipsen et al., 2015; Weiss et al., 2012).

Some adults with ADHD can benefit from CBT without medications (Ramsay & Rostain, 2011). Some people cannot take stimulant medication because of cardiac conditions or other medical reasons. A small minority struggles with unpleasant side effects. A few do not receive therapeutic benefit from stimulant medication. Others may have relatively mild symptoms of ADHD. Some just do not want to take medication. All of these individuals are candidates for CBT alone (Ramsay, 2012; Ramsay & Rostain, 2011).

THE COURSE OF PSYCHOTHERAPY

I prefer to initially meet with individuals who have ADHD on a weekly basis. This allows me to obtain a good understanding of that person's ADHD symptoms, life challenges, history, and functioning. Early on, there is a strong emphasis on psychoeducation (chapter 10). Since I have a private practice, many of my clients are high functioning. Often, within relatively short order, maybe three months or so, many will transition to biweekly sessions. Later, they may prefer to attend as needed or schedule once a month. In the majority of cases, long-term continuous and intensive treatment is unnecessary (Murphy, 2005). Nonetheless, as with any population, there will be some individuals with trauma, relationship, or mood issues who need more long-term treatment.

The need for weekly psychotherapy will fluctuate over time. A return to weekly sessions is sometimes essential for further skill development when role demands increase, a crisis has occurred, there is significant life change, or the individual has long-term goals to achieve (Murphy, 2005). At other times, an occasional check-in session is helpful for support, stress management, and tune-up of skills. Since ADHD is a lifelong condition and life demands vary considerably over time, the client's need for psychotherapy will vary as well. Once significant progress is made, many prefer to have monthly or bimonthly check-in sessions. Many appreciate an occasional session as an opportunity for self-assessment and reflection on recent progress with life goals and stressors.

I never really say goodbye to any client who has ADHD. While it is possible that I may not see the client again, it is just as likely that the client will return some day. Stresses and new responsibilities can arise in the future that overwhelm the individual's ability to cope (Rosenfield, Ramsay, & Rostain, 2008). So I welcome the client to come back on a one-time, as-needed, or regular basis at any time.

BE COLLABORATIVE AND ENCOURAGING

Psychotherapist: I see that you're only 5 minutes late to your session today. This is a lot of progress, because you've usually been 10 to 15 minutes late in the past. What did you do today that helped you get here in a more timely manner? . . . Were you less anxious and stressed when you were driving here today? . . . Given how things went today, what are your thoughts about continuing to make progress on lateness? . . . Yes, things didn't go perfectly this morning either, but you made a lot of progress. I hear that you underestimated how long it would take to stop at the bank on the way here. But we've figured out what to work on for next time. What did you learn about how long the bank errand really takes?

An active, collaborative psychotherapy approach with effective teaching and plenty of encouragement is essential (Ramsay, 2010a; Solanto, 2011). Recognize and celebrate incremental progress as in the previous vignette. When the client comes in after making efforts on the homework, even if it is partial progress, emphasize that progress has been made. Recognizing progress builds self-efficacy. Only after you reinforced the progress, move on to asking how to continue to work on the issue. Maintaining effort on a problem over time will help the client learn to be persistent rather than avoidant; persistence is an extremely valuable quality for individuals with ADHD and those who are persistent tend to be more functional. Explicitly emphasize a problem-solving approach rather than self-blame. Most clients find it gratifying to have a psychotherapist who understands their difficulties and does not blame them (Tuckman, 2007). When the client verbalizes self-criticism about imperfections and errors, emphasize that errors are a normal part of the learning process. Address negative self-talk as needed.

Repetition of main psychoeducational points is especially essential for clients with ADHD. With clients who have tangential speech, you may need to redirect to the topic at hand (Tuckman, 2007). Summarize after you explain a concept: "So, it's essential to choose one type of calendar—paper or electronic—system and stick to that." Then ask the client questions to encourage application and elaboration on what you have said: "What has been your experience with paper versus electronic calendars? Have you tried to use more than one at a time? How did that go? Which do you think would work better for you?"

TREATMENT RECOMMENDATIONS AND INFORMED CONSENT

Psychotherapist: Can we talk a little more about treatment for adult ADHD?

Clara: Sure.

P: I prefer to take what I call a two-pronged approach to treating adults with ADHD. First, there are a lot of organizational skills that do not come naturally to a person who has ADHD. Let's think about your email, which you've told me, is kind of a mess. Organizational experts say that you should try to keep your inbox as empty as possible, only leaving a few items in there that need some action soon and removing everything else. If we could help you learn to do that, you wouldn't lose track of important emails. There are other organizational skills that we could work on, like how to break up a big task into manageable pieces. Overall, we'd work on time management, organization, and planning skills. How does that sound?

C: Great. I need help with all that. But what's the second prong?

P: The second prong is medication for your ADHD. Some people have negative feelings about medications. But the bottom line is that you're probably spending a lot of mental energy pushing yourself to concentrate and get things done. To many people that can be pretty exhausting.

C: True. But I'm not sure I want medication.

P: I understand that, and we can make some progress without it. But people with ADHD make more progress when they have both medication and therapy. I've had a lot of clients take medication for ADHD, and they rarely are bothered by side effects. If they are having any, they work together with their psychiatrists to find a medicine that works better for them. Once they try medication, it's often a big relief. They find that it's much easier to concentrate and they can get things done in a timely manner without it being such a strain. I would suggest that you make a consultation appointment with a psychiatrist that I know and get some more information before you make up your mind about medication. A psychiatrist is the best person to answer your questions about medications. You don't have to make a commitment to take medication in order to have a consultation meeting. How does that sound?

C: Okay, I can go with that.

P: Even if you try medication, it's not a lifetime commitment. You can see what you think about it for a month or two and if you feel that medication is not for you, you can work with the psychiatrist to discontinue it, no big deal.

C: But if I do find it helpful, then it is a lifetime thing, right?

P: Basically yes. The medication only helps when you're taking it, so if you decide that it's helping, you will probably want to continue it indefinitely. But it's entirely up to you.

In this scenario the psychotherapist is making treatment recommendations and ascertaining the client's agreement to treatment, which is an important part of the informed consent process. The psychotherapist is respectful of Clara's concerns and her autonomy to make decisions about medication, while also urging Clara to obtain more information before making a decision. The psychotherapist also educates Clara further about psychotherapy. Informed consent is an ongoing process of continuing to educate the client about treatment approaches over time and ascertaining the client's understanding and agreement.

OVERVIEW OF TREATMENT GOALS

Once you are seeing the client regularly, and you have determined that ADHD is present, the following can serve as a suggested hierarchy of treatment goals:

- Address treatment-interfering behaviors such as lateness, missed appointments, and late cancellations (addressed in this chapter).
- Provide psychoeducation about ADHD and its treatment. Educate the client about the benefits of using a combination of medication and psychotherapy for cognitive symptoms. Psychoeducation is a key step in reinstilling hope for the future in the ADHD client (Ramsay, 2010a).
- Refer the client for a psychiatric evaluation to obtain medication to treat ADHD and comorbid conditions. Problem-solve about medication adherence as needed. Even substance abuse recovery can be helped with medication for ADHD (Wilens, 2011).
- Address alcohol and drug abuse or problematic use, as appropriate, given the client's readiness. Depending on the client, this may involve monitoring, psychoeducation, motivational interviewing, harm reduction, or referral to self-help programs or structured treatment programs.
- If the client has an extremely impairing mental illnesses, such as severe major depression or untreated bipolar disorder, treat that first (Sobanski et al., 2013). If the comorbid condition is less impairing, treat ADHD and the other condition simultaneously.
- Refer clients for medical and dental evaluations if they have not seen a doctor in the past 6 to 12 months. Be sure clients follow up regarding any medical and dental problems and problem-solve about any follow-up issues. Many adults with ADHD have untreated medical problems because their life disorganization extends into health-related self-care and follow-up.
- Educate the client about the negative impact of irregular sleep and eating on cognition. Assist client healthy eating and good sleep hygiene habits. (see chapter 11 for further discussion of these issues).
- Educate the client about how exercise improves cognition. If the client is motivated, assist the client in establishing and meeting exercise goals (chapter 11).
- Help the client learn to recognize and articulate dysfunctional negative and positive cognitions and replace these with more helpful self-talk (chapter 12).
- Assist the client with the self-management skills that are most related to areas of impairment or that he or she is most motivated to address (chapter 11).

As the client progresses with ADHD treatment, low self-esteem typically lifts and depression often diminishes. As clients are able to manage their lives in a more organized and predictable way, anxiety also tends to lessen. Often, additional medications are not needed for depression or anxiety when these are treated jointly with ADHD.

Be careful not to work on too many goals at once. Between one to three clearly defined goals of treatment are plenty at any point in time (Knouse & Safren, 2011). For example, you and the client may set two goals for the client for the next week: to attend one Alcoholics Anonymous (AA) group and to write down all appointments in the calendar over the next week. Over subsequent sessions, you will follow up regarding attendance at AA and calendar use, and these will be a focus of treatment until they are solidly established. At that point, additional goals can be considered.

LATENESS AND TIME AWARENESS

Psychotherapist: I've noticed that you're often running 5 to 10 minutes late for your appointment.

Troy: I'm sorry. My wife is always mad at me because it seems like I'm late for everything. My boss gets on my case too—I'm usually only 5 minutes late though.

P: Lateness is a common problem among people with ADHD. Do you lose track of time or have a hard time estimating how long it will take to get out of the door?

T: Yes, both of those things. Aimee tells me to get ready because we have to leave in 10 minutes, and I think I'll just finish up one more thing, but then she's saying we have to walk out the door and I'm not ready.

P: That's a related problem—sometimes having difficulty tearing yourself away from something can make you late leaving the house.

T: That happens a lot.

P: How do you feel emotionally when you are running late?

T: Anxious and stressed. Always looking at the clock in the car. Worried I'll be late again.

P: Let's start with working on your time awareness—keeping track of what time it is and actually measuring how long things will take. How would you feel about wearing a watch, so you always have the time right available in front of you?

T: Well, I have my phone, but I'm not always looking at it, so that's probably a good idea. I do have a watch at home.

P: Okay, so if you could start wearing it, that would be a good first step. I also notice that folks with ADHD not only lose track of time but have a tendency to leave at the last possible moment and not build in any extra time for traffic and other things that may slow you down. So there's a need to build in some padding to your time estimate. I'd recommend that you build in enough padding that you are on time or early 90% of the time. How does that sound?

T: I can try to do that.

P: Try to keep track of exactly how long these trips take, from door to door, so you build in time to park, deal with traffic, and so on. Let your wife know that you are working on that and taking her concerns seriously, okay?

T: Okay.

P: Finally, a lot of people find it helpful to enter alarms and notifications into their phones. So if you know you need to leave the house 30 minutes ahead of time to make it to your appointment, you might want to put an alarm in for 45 minutes before your appointment so you have 15 minutes to wind up whatever you are doing and get out the door. How does that sound?

T: That might help a lot.

P: Let me know how this goes next week, okay?

Often clients with ADHD can be extremely late, so this must be the first therapeutic priority. If your client is not present, even the best treatment will not help. Some clients need intensive work on time awareness and estimation. They tend to allow—at most—the best-case amount of time to travel, so they always run late.

The client undoubtedly has had many negative experiences regarding lateness. Friends and family have been nagging the client about these difficulties for years, so addressing lateness will be a sensitive issue. The client can feel criticized and defensive. Often, carefully targeted psychoeducation can help to defuse this. The psychotherapist in the previous scenario starts out with bringing up Troy's lateness as matter-of-factly and as tactfully as possible. The psychotherapist and Troy discuss the life problems that this lateness causes, as well as how Troy feels when he arrives late. Addressing these issues demonstrates that a different, more empathetic approach is being taken to these problems and that he is not being criticized. Also, exploring Troy's dissatisfaction with his lateness helps increase his motivation to address it. At that point, the psychotherapist provides carefully targeted psychoeducation about lateness and ADHD.

There are many reasons why a client with ADHD runs late, and it is necessary to undertake a careful behavioral analysis for each client (Ramsay & Rostain, 2005). ADHD can contribute to lateness in many different ways:

- Dislike of waiting and being early: "I hate to be early; it's a waste of time."
- Inaccurate time estimations: "It won't take a minute to stop at the bank on the way." "I can fit in one more task at home before I leave."
- Difficulties with planning: The client may only allow enough time to drive to the office in good traffic and does not account for possible delays, time to gather possessions and leave the house, walking to the car, parking, road construction, and so on.

- Difficulties with set-shifting or hyperfocus: The client may have difficulty disengaging from a previous activity to leave on time or be so engaged in the previous activity that all sense of time is lost.
- Losing track of possessions: The client often cannot find his or her bag, keys, phone, and so on, and departure is delayed.
- Sleep dysfunction: The client hits the snooze button too many times and ends up running late.

Careful follow-up questioning is needed to determine which factors contribute to lateness for a particular client. Each of these difficulties requires a different targeted intervention, many of which are discussed in subsequent sections. Once the psychotherapist and Troy determine what his specific problems are, they can move on to problem-solving.

Solanto (2011, p. 108) provides a chart listing many common activities, including commuting, preparing dinner, and so on. The client is asked to estimate how long the activity will take and then is asked to time the activity and compare the estimate to the actual time taken. Additional tips to help with time estimation and time management include (National Resource Center on AD/HD, 2003; Solanto, 2011; Tucker, 2007):

- Wear a watch.
- Put up plenty of clocks in home and work areas, so they are clearly visible at all times.
- Work in a team with a coworker who manages time well.
- Address overly positive cognitions, such as "this will only take a minute."

Since most adults carry smartphones, these can be used to help manage time, contacts, schedules, and reminders (McGough, 2014). The client could set alarms for appointments, for leaving the house in a timely manner, and for taking medications (Knouse & Safren, 2011).

Sometimes your client will not be motivated to address something you consider a problem. Motivation can be an issue because of the extra mental energy necessary to activate the executive functioning pathways of the ADHD brain. I have had psychotherapy clients who attend regularly, but are often 5 to 15 minutes late, and are not yet motivated to address this. I will point out the lateness as a chronic problem occasionally and wait for a time when the client is motivated to address it. The client is at least attending regularly and for enough of the session to make some progress. Choose your battles wisely so that you and the client do not get frustrated.

MISSED APPOINTMENTS AND LATE CANCELLATIONS

Psychotherapist: So, Clara, how have you been since I saw you last? . . . I wanted to talk for a few minutes about last week. You emailed me two hours before your scheduled appointment to cancel it. As you probably remember, I have a 24-hour cancellation policy, and I generally charge $100 when a session is missed or *canceled late. Because this was the first time that you did this, I will lower the fee to $20, but if this happens again I will have to charge the entire amount. I'm wondering what the struggles are that led to this late cancellation. It sounds like you knew about the staff meeting in advance. . . . Okay, so I'm hearing that you often double-schedule yourself and don't realize it until the last minute and then you feel bad about yourself. These kinds of scheduling problems often happen with adults who have ADHD. This is because of the difficulties they have with organization. Do you think that this is something that you want to work on? . . . Tell me about your calendar. What kind of calendar do you use?*

Some clients with ADHD attend their psychotherapy appointments regularly and cancel in a timely manner. These individuals have generally worked hard to develop this skill. However, others miss appointments or cancel at the last minute (Ramsay & Rostain, 2005) or show up at the wrong appointment time or day. Also, they may often text, call, or email, saying that they have lost track of their appointment times.

No-shows are very frustrating for the psychotherapist. However, with clients who have ADHD, no-shows are not usually about resistance—although, as with other clients, that is a possibility. Have a clear policy of charging a fee for missed appointments and late cancellations. However, flexibility is encouraged as to whether to charge this entire fee, or a fee at all, for the first time a session is missed or the first time there is a late cancellation. If you decide to be flexible, be clear that you will not excuse the fee (or part of the fee) next time. This helps provide motivation to address this problem.

Contact the client after a no-show or late cancellation and determine what happened. For the ADHD client, no-shows and late cancellations are usually a sign of ineffective calendar use. Often clients with ADHD get excited about trying a new calendar or organizational system. Then, after a week or two, it becomes boring and they stop using it. The client may have multiple calendars and not consistently use any of them. The client may be occasionally using a calendar but often forgetting to include events, meetings and appointments. Or the client may not even be using a calendar and is trying to keep track of everything without one. Effective use of calendars is addressed in chapter 11.

TANGENTIALITY

Psychotherapist: I've noticed that you can move from one topic to another pretty quickly. Is this something you notice in yourself? . . . Some topics are so complicated that it really helps to talk about just one topic in a lot of detail for a while. Would it be okay if I help focus our conversation when I notice that this is happening?

Psychotherapist: I'm noticing that you've brought up a lot of important topics in just a few minutes: your relationship with your partner, anger management issues, and some challenges you're having on the job. Let's focus in on just one of these at a time. Which one would you prefer to start with?

The two interventions above can be used with clients who are tangential during the session. Not all adults with ADHD are obviously tangential, but many are. You will almost certainly not be the first person who has noticed tangentiality, and usually the client is well aware of this tendency.

WHY DO ADHD CLIENTS HAVE MOTIVATION PROBLEMS?

Russell Barkley often says that people who have ADHD know *what* they need to do. The problem is with *doing what they know*. I agree with this completely. People who have ADHD know that they need to keep track of their calendars, that it would be helpful if they kept track of what they need to do, and that having one's paperwork organized is a good idea. The problem is that they often have difficulty with motivation and with knowing *how* to do these things effectively.

- Because of executive functioning difficulties, they often have difficulty choosing among a multitude of ways to solve a particular problem and have tried many methods without settling on one. For example, they may have an organizer, a wall calendar, and an online calendar, all of which are used in spurts of brief enthusiasm but none of which is used consistently.
- There is almost always a lag between organizational difficulties and the negative consequences of these organizational difficulties. Because of differences with the reward system of the brain, these negative consequences may be discounted, resulting in lack of current motivation to address the organizational problems.
- Because of difficulties maintaining motivation and consistency, important behaviors have never become habitual. For example, when they learn of new appointments, they often just think they will remember them and will put them in their calendars later, instead of taking a moment to add them to the calendar immediately. This does not work, and has never worked, but they have never have developed the habit of immediately putting appointments in their calendars.
- They think that they should be able to do things in the same manner as everyone else. They repeatedly try this, which does not work because their brain functioning is different. Then they become demoralized and stop trying for a while. Psychoeducation is key to encouraging the client to be open to different strategies: "I see that one thing you have been struggling with for a long time is that you think you should be able to do this in the same way that everyone else does. Clearly that is not working. It just makes you upset and angry at yourself. As we've been talking

about, your brain works in a different way than most other people's. This does not mean that you cannot get things done like everyone else can, but it does mean that you often will need to use a different strategy that works for *your* brain. Let's work together to try to figure out a strategy that will work effectively for you."

PSYCHOTHERAPY HOMEWORK CHALLENGES

People who have ADHD have a hard time getting their homework done. They may forget about it or procrastinate, as with so many other tasks in their lives. Then they may be tempted to avoid their sessions so that they do not have to face feelings of failure and inadequacy. To avoid all this, I prefer to assign "no-fail homework." The first part of the no-fail homework is the actual homework assignment. The second part is: "Now, I know you've struggled with getting this kind of thing done in the past. So if you notice that you're putting it off or you're not getting around to it, try to pay attention to whatever feelings or thoughts you're having at the time. That way, we can gain more understanding of what is getting in the way of you accomplishing your goals. So either you do it or we gain more insight into the kinds of problems that you are having with getting things done."

Before the client leaves the session, develop a very specific plan for accomplishing the homework. Ask the client when would be a good time during the week to do the homework. Consider asking the client to calendar it in during the session. If the client has made progress on calendar skills (chapter 11), this may help make the task happen.

While psychotherapists traditionally use the term "homework," this may bring back negative associations with school for many clients, especially those with ADHD. For that reason, "action plan" has been suggested as an alternative (Beck & Broder, 2016).

MOTIVATION AND THERAPEUTIC PRIORITIES

When treating a client with ADHD, keep in mind how the reward system of the client's brain works. It is most important that the client is interested and engaged—and therefore motivated and working hard in psychotherapy. It is less important that the client learns psychoeducational material or skills in any particular order. When your client brings up a life problem, use that as an opportunity to educate about applicable aspects of ADHD and work on associated self-management skills. Follow up on the client's use of that skill for the next several sessions until it can be applied fairly consistently.

Motivation to change can be provided by emotional maturity, concerns for how ADHD affects loved ones, and dissatisfaction with one's current situation. Developing skills to address difficulties in motivation appear to be an important ingredient in effective CBT treatment of ADHD (Knouse & Safren, 2010). Ask about the negative emotional, career, and interpersonal consequences of ADHD behaviors such as showing up late or procrastinating on projects. Emphasize the connection between managing symptoms and the client's long-term goals: for example, improving forgetfulness and lateness will lead to improved relationships and work performance evaluations (Knouse & Safren, 2011). Ask the client whether this issue is problematic enough to be a focus of therapy. If the client is not particularly concerned, let it go. The client will not be motivated to work on it, no progress will be made, and everyone will be frustrated.

Here are two strategies for choosing what life skills to work on. First, consider starting with the easiest issues, then move to the most difficult (e.g., teach effective calendar use before planning out larger projects). The client will be less intimidated by starting with easier issues, so that can be productive and give early successes. Second, consider starting with whatever the client considers to be the most immediately problematic: "I usually don't respond to my girlfriend's text messages, and she's mad at me" or "I keep forgetting appointments, and my husband is at the end of his rope." Clients with ADHD are especially motivated to address immediate problems, and that motivation can contribute to progress.

For many people who have ADHD, long-term rewards are difficult to use for motivation. For that reason, vividly imagining all the positive things that will occur when the long-term goal is achieved may be a helpful motivator (Solanto, Marks, & Wasserstein, 2011). Time can be spent in the psychotherapy session assisting the client with thoroughly discussing, imagining, or visualizing the positive effects of achieving the long-term goals. The client can then use this vision of the future when choosing between distractions versus tasks that leads toward the long-term goal.

MEDICATION: PSYCHOEDUCATION AND ADHERENCE

Provide psychoeducation about what medication can do: for example, "get around to, stick with and finish tasks" (Surman, 2013a, p. 40) and "maintain focus, be at physical rest, and control impulsive behavior" (Surman, 2013b, p. 47). Medication is helpful in improving concentration and reducing distractibility. If the client has made partial progress toward life skills without medication, taking medication will usually facilitate further progress. Also, provide psychoeducation about what medication cannot do. Medication does not solve deficits in organizational and life skills that impede effective functioning (Surman, 2013b).

Adherence to medication is a problem for almost all medical and psychiatric patients (Willer, 2014). Forgetting to take medication can be a problem with ADHD clients as well (Knouse & Safren, 2011). On the other hand, since individuals with ADHD are especially responsive to immediate rewards, and stimulant medication begins to work very quickly, this can help with adherence. In any event, adherence should be carefully assessed and addressed effectively. For further information on medication adherence see Willer (2014).

Clients with ADHD will often also forget to obtain prescriptions or get their refills in a timely manner (Ramsay & Rostain, 2005). Since stimulants are a controlled substance, it is difficult to obtain prescriptions at the last minute. Help the client problem-solve about reminders.

OCCUPATIONAL COUNSELING

Adults with ADHD often struggle with finding a good match between their skills and a profession. A good fit is crucially important for individuals with ADHD to do well at work (Murphy, 2005). A good fit ensures interest in their work, therefore maximizing motivation and work performance. They may do better if they are self-employed with a flexible work schedule, or if they have high levels of physical activity (restaurant server) and/or high levels of stimulation (stock market) (McGough, 2014; Weiss et al., 2008). Jobs that provide plenty of novel stimulation, new challenges, and new things to learn can often be a good fit. In some jobs, it is an advantage to hyperfocus (surgeon) or to be able to talk at length (telemarketing or radio announcer) (Weiss et al., 2008). But any job that the client finds interesting can be a good fit. Rarely are career counselors trained to understand these needs of adults with ADHD, so you will often need to assist in this area (Ramsay, 2010b).

Discussing the client's occupational history in detail will help provide clues about occupational fit (Ramsay, 2010b). Other considerations include (Ramsay, 2010b):

- Find a good match with the individual's cognitive strengths and weaknesses.
- Carefully consider the issue of distractibility in the workplace.
- Remember that positions requiring immediate response (law enforcement, construction, food service) may be a better fit.
- Consider whether flexibility or structure is more important for that particular individual.
- Note that workplace safety issues can be more of a challenge for adults with ADHD.

SOCIAL ISSUES AT WORK

People with ADHD can do well in a collaborative work environment. They can provide energy, enthusiasm, and innovative ideas. However, it is most beneficial for them to work with colleagues who have good planning and project management skills. Working with others helps provide accountability and structure.

Clients may need to advocate for themselves at work (Murphy, 2005). Most individuals with ADHD struggle with what, if anything, to tell bosses and colleagues. They may not wish to share their diagnosis of ADHD, and this is usually not necessary (Tuckman, 2007). However, it can be helpful to share insights about how they work effectively: "One of my strengths is generating ideas for how to accomplish the project, but I work best in a team environment with someone who is good at working out a timetable for the project" or "Sometimes I get really wound up in my work and don't hear when people are talking to me. If you need to interrupt me, can you call my name first and be sure that I'm looking at you, so you've got my attention?" On the other hand, it might be wise to disclose the diagnosis of ADHD if the client fears losing a job because accommodations are needed to succeed or if the client is likely to be fired because of performance issues; Americans with Disabilities Act protections may apply (National Resource Center on AD/HD, 2003).

SOCIAL ISSUES AT HOME

Psychotherapist: So tell me about your relationship with your husband.

Clara: He's a great guy. He's an accountant, and he works at a legal firm downtown. He's an only child, and he grew up in this really WASPy family, but he does great with my big family and everyone loves him. He's super-supportive.

P: Does he ever complain that you're not listening to him?

C: Yes, he has to remind me of social events two or three times, and he gets irritated at me that I forget, even after he's already reminded me once. And sometimes I don't remember other things he's told me.

P: A lot of people with ADHD have problems concentrating on and listening to conversations at times. Like other people with ADHD, you don't always process the information he tells you. It sounds like this frustrates your husband. That's a common dynamic in relationships where one partner has ADHD.

Assess your client's relationship problems on an individualized basis. Research indicates that relationship issues are common with adults who have ADHD. Spouses and partners complain about forgetfulness, messiness, disorganization, lateness, unreliability, not listening, and not finishing tasks (Murphy, 2005). They are often frustrated that their spouse functions better at work than at home (Murphy, 2005). Psychoeducation is especially important for spouses of individuals with ADHD (Murphy, 2005); this can be accomplished in a joint session. Couples therapy might be a helpful adjunctive treatment.

To improve relationship skills, you might need to employ assertiveness or anger management training, or teach the client active listening skills. Other interventions that can be helpful include:

- Learning to not engage in long monologues about topics of personal interest. For some individuals, the "three-sentence rule" about any topic of interest is recommended (Rosenfield et al., 2008).

- Developing a system to keep track of invitations, appointments, social engagements, and so on.
- Developing a system to respond to email, phone, and text messages.
- Learning to pause and think about how to communicate tactfully.

To have a healthy relationship, the client's partner needs to maintain a balance between expecting appropriate adult behavior and tolerating minor issues that cannot be completely changed by an individual with ADHD (Wymbs & Molina, 2015). Tolerating minor annoyances could include accepting that the partner will always be more prone to errors, that the partner will occasionally be distractible, and that occasionally the partner will complete household tasks, such as laundry or cleaning the kitchen, to an 80% or 90% level. These principles can be applied in joint psychoeducational sessions with the individual's psychotherapist. Parenting interventions may be helpful as well, since there are often both adults and children with ADHD in a family. For a detailed discussion of this, see Chronis-Tuscano and Stein (2012).

ENCOURAGE ASKING FOR SUPPORT AND COLLABORATION

Many adults with ADHD find that it is easier to work on projects collaboratively with others (Surman, 2013b). Also, many people with ADHD report that just the simple presence of supportive others nearby helps them get things done. Somehow, the presence of other people apparently makes it easier to focus on the task at hand. They may make plans with a friend (who may have ADHD as well) to get together to do work. Some people will even keep a phone line open between themselves and the other person. Some call this "body doubling" (see Riccardi [2015] for more information on the practice). I have not seen any research articles on body doubling. However, if your client is having a lot of problems with procrastination and motivation, ask if a partner, friend, or relative can help with the project or even just be present when the client is working on the project. This support and structure often helps.

GROUP THERAPY OR A SUPPORT GROUP

Research suggests that sharing experiences with other adults who have ADHD may be helpful because of the affirming experience of meeting others who have similar challenges and can understand them (Bramham et al., 2009). CHADD (Children and Adults with Attention-Deficit Hyperactivity Disorder) organizes many support groups for adults who have ADHD nationwide; check with the local CHADD chapter (see the Recommended Reading at the end of this book). Group therapy can also provide a structured review of adaptive skills.

REFER FOR ADJUNCTIVE TREATMENTS AS NEEDED

Adults with ADHD often have a multitude of life problems. Experts in many fields can be helpful to them in addressing these issues. Referrals may also be needed for assistance with job skills, parenting skills, financial management, or home organization (Knouse & Safren, 2011).

KEY POINTS

- CBT is an effective treatment for adult ADHD.
- Often, the combination of stimulant medication and CBT provides the most improvement, but CBT can be effective alone as well.
- Frequent encouragement is essential when working with adult ADHD clients.
- Many aspects of ADHD contribute to being late for the therapy session. A careful behavioral analysis is necessary.
- Disorganization about appointments is common. Effective calendar use helps.
- Try "no-fail" homework: either do it or report what happened emotionally, cognitively, or logistically so it did not get done.
- Watch medication adherence.
- Good career fit is essential for people with ADHD.
- Partner psychoeducation can help.
- Group therapy, a support group, or other adjunctive treatments may be helpful.

10

Psychoeducation about Cognitive Differences

Psychotherapist: You've said that you've been struggling with organization and planning your entire life. We've recognized that your strengths include conceptualizing the big picture and coming up with new ideas, rather than detail-oriented skills. In the past, it's been hard for you to learn how to plan and organize because of your problems with attention and concentration and also because these things just don't come naturally to adults who have ADHD. While detail-oriented skills may never be your forte, now that you are taking medication, you can concentrate a lot better. And, even though organizing and planning never came naturally to you, you can learn how to do these things effectively by learning it as a skill. Once you have these skills down, you can organize and plan when you need to. We will work on this together. How does that sound?

Clara: But everyone else can do it. Why can't I? I still think that I should just try harder.

Psychotherapist: I hear you, but remember what your friend Whitney, the school psychologist, said to you. There is a lot of evidence that the brain of a person with ADHD is different in many ways from the brain of a person without ADHD. Please keep in mind that the way that your brain naturally operates is not your fault. ADHD is very common. But the world isn't built for people who have an ADHD brain; it's built for everyone else. So people who have ADHD are constantly running into challenges.

Psychoeducation is probably the most powerful and effective intervention for ADHD, and experts universally agree that psychoeducation is essential for effective treatment (Knouse & Safren, 2011; Ramsay & Rostain, 2008b; Safren, Perlman, Sprich & Otto, 2005; Solanto, 2011).

Clients learn to understand how their brains function differently and how this contributes to their difficulties. Psychoeducation helps clients stop telling themselves that they "should" be able to use their brains the same way everyone else does. These insights empower the client to learn, develop, and deploy effective individualized coping strategies (Vidal et al., 2013).

Group psychoeducation for adults with ADHD and their family members improves the quality of their relationships and their psychological well-being, as well as anxiety, depression, and ADHD symptoms (Hirvikoski, Waaler, Lindström, Bölte, & Jokinen, 2015; Vidal et al., 2014). Individual psychoeducation can provide the same benefits.

Individuals with ADHD are *heterogeneous;* in other words, any two people who have ADHD usually differ from each other considerably. This heterogeneity applies to cognitive differences as well. One person may be late all the time but has only moderate problems with reading challenging materials. Another may always be prompt but can barely concentrate to read at all, despite a high level of interest in the book's subject. Most clients will have significant EF problems and, if any hyperactivity remains, it is only subjective restless feelings. However, certain rare clients will have very problematic hyperactivity and few EF problems. Research findings usually only highlight *group* differences, between those with ADHD and those without, and don't accurately describe the *individual* cognitive challenges of any one person with ADHD. So your client will usually have most of the cognitive differences described in this chapter, but not necessarily all, therefore personalize your client's psychoeducation.

REDUCED ALERTNESS TO NEW STIMULI

Troy: Sometimes my wife has to ask me a question two or three times before she gets my attention.

Psychotherapist: A lot of people with ADHD have problems refocusing their attention on a new stimulus, like your wife talking to you. This is caused by differences in brain functioning. Can you explain this to her and ask your wife to call your name until she is sure that she has your attention, before asking you a question?

Adults with ADHD have been found to have reduced *alertness* or *arousal,* meaning they have difficulty staying alert to relevant new information and stimuli (Aguiar, Eubig, & Schantz, 2010). This is associated with underactivity in related portions of the brain (Nigg, 2006).

SUSTAINED ATTENTION TAKES MORE EFFORT

Clara: I get my grading done, mostly in a timely manner. But I always feel that it's easier for other teachers. It takes me so much effort.

Psychotherapist: This is a very astute observation. Research has found that adults with ADHD can often do as well as other adults on attention tasks. But they've found evidence that the brains of the people with ADHD are working a lot harder to get the task done to the same level.

Like Clara, most adults with ADHD report that they have to exert more effort to accomplish tasks than others seem to. This is mentally exhausting. In one study, adults with ADHD did as well as controls on an attention task, but, in order to do so, they had to maintain an increased level of frontal cortex activation throughout the task (Loo et al., 2009). So adults with ADHD may have to maintain high levels of frontal cortex activation (in other words, *cognitive effort*) to sustain attention and perform as well as controls. Stimulant medication helps improve concentration, so it reduces the amount of cognitive effort needed to accomplish attention tasks.

INCREASED ERRORS AND MORE DIFFICULTY DETECTING THEM

Brad is a classical musician. He has been striving for years to get a position with a major orchestra. At the urging of his girlfriend, he was evaluated for adult ADHD and treated with stimulant medication and psychotherapy. He observed that, since being on medication, his ability to detect and correct errors in his playing has increased dramatically.

Troy: My boss gets on me because sometimes he says I'm his best worker and other times I make sloppy mistakes. He says I'm a flake. He always assigns me the cars that are difficult to diagnose, and I like figuring those out. One time, he called me into the office and then when I came back, I forgot to put the cap back on a radiator. Luckily, not much damage was done, but he was really mad about that one.

Individuals with ADHD have these problems:

- *More errors*, resulting in variability in performance on school, job, and home tasks (Castellanos & Tannock, 2002).
- *Decreased ability to detect errors* (Chang, Davies, & Gavin, 2009; McLoughlin et al., 2009), resulting in overrating their competence.
- *Overestimating their competence:* Adults with ADHD usually rate themselves as competent drivers, but they have more driving errors, as measured by collisions, speeding tickets, and driving citations (Knouse, Bagwell, Barkley, & Murphy, 2005).

WORKING MEMORY DEFICITS

Ellen is a graduate student taking German reading comprehension. She has been diagnosed with adult ADHD. She has noticed that it is difficult for her to hold all the necessary information about a sentence that she is translating in her mind at the same time. Her psychotherapist educated her about the challenges of decreased working memory in adults with ADHD.

Jamal is a physical therapy graduate student. He complains that he has difficulty remembering everything that his patients tell him when he needs to chart. The psychotherapist educated him about decreased working memory and encouraged him to take extensive notes when meeting with a patient so he can use these when he is documenting the interaction later.

Psychotherapist: Many adults with ADHD have problems with working memory. Working memory involves holding information in mind and using that information to do something. Working memory also involves keeping that information in mind while you are temporarily doing something else. When people have problems with working memory, the best solution is to develop a system to write everything down. I know this sounds simple, but having an understanding about how your own brain works, and using that information effectively, rather than comparing yourself to others, is not the easiest thing to do.

Working memory is "the ability to hold something in mind momentarily while doing something else or while using the information to perform an action" (Aguiar et al., 2010, p. 1649). Working memory is a crucial cognitive function in planning, reasoning, reading comprehension, math, and problem-solving.

An individual with working memory problems will more easily lose track of information when attempting to hold that information in mind during a task or when switching from one task to another., Components of working memory are (Aguiar et al., 2010; Fried, 2016):

- *Nonverbal or spatial working memory*, for example:
  - Looking at a map, then keeping in mind the essential spatial information of the route to travel to a destination.
  - Watching someone demonstrating a new piece of sporting equipment and then using the equipment to duplicate what was shown.
- *Verbal working memory*, for example:
  - Translating a sentence from one language into another. One must keep many words from the sentence in mind in order to rearrange the sentence into a new one that makes sense in the second language.
  - Listening to someone describe a route to a destination verbally. In order to arrive at that destination, one must remember the verbal directions and apply them.
  - Holding a phone number or web address in mind while looking for a pen and paper.
  - Remembering the unfamiliar name of someone before introducing that person to someone else.
  - Remembering which groceries to buy at the store.

Some, but not all, individuals with ADHD have deficits in working memory, both verbal and visuospatial (Aguiar et al., 2010; Seidman, 2006; Theiling & Petermann, 2014); however, visuospatial working memory is usually more impaired (Nigg, 2006).

EXTERNAL DISTRACTIBILITY, ESPECIALLY REGARDING NOISE

Clara: Small noises will distract me from my work. I've never understood how people can work in a coffee house. All that noise makes it impossible for me to focus.

Psychotherapist: A lot of adults with ADHD find distracting noises to be particularly problematic.

Adults with ADHD have difficulty staying on task in the presence of distracting noises (Corbett & Stanczak, 1999). This is may be due to an *auditory selective attention deficit* (e.g., difficulties selectively paying attention to one auditory stimulus among many; Nigg, 2006).

INTERNAL DISTRACTIBILITY

Clara: When I am grading papers, I am often distracted by my own thoughts and I have a hard time concentrating.

Psychotherapist: What you're noticing is an important brain difference in ADHD related to a network of connectivity in the brain called the default mode network. This network involves daydreaming and thinking about yourself and others in your life—in other words, things you think about when you are just sitting around without anything in particular to do. This network is overly active in ADHD, even when the brain is supposed to be concentrating on other tasks. People often experience this as being distracted by their own thoughts.

Gina, a psychologist with ADHD: Interestingly, I finally got diagnosed with inattentive-type ADHD this summer. I've had my suspicions for a long time but recently had a patient who was so very like me that I diagnosed with the condition that I thought I'd better get assessed. Too hard to diagnose yourself. I'm on Adderall, and I cannot even express how much easier it is to focus on work now. It was like I had 27 browsers open all the time, and the pop-up blocker was broken, so no one ever could interrupt me, because I was already internally interrupted. Now I can take one of the 27 things out, work on it until it is finished (Imagine that!!!), put it back, and take another one. Driving is SOOO much easier and less scary; I am never driving without medication again. Most importantly, with all that noise in my head ordered, I feel a great sense of peace. That's the best part of it. In three months on the medication, I accomplished more than I did the previous YEAR. Downside: there is a big crash six hours after I take my medication. I want to take a nap and/or my heart thumps. It passes in 15 minutes.

Individuals with ADHD tend to have wandering minds, and they frequently are interrupted by their own thoughts. This symptom of *internal distractibility* is highly predictive of an ADHD diagnosis (Barkley, Murphy, & Fischer, 2008). This phenomenon has a basis in brain functioning. The *default mode network* is a network of brain regions that is active when an individual is awake but resting and not focused on a task. When the default network is active, people are contemplating what others are feeling and thinking, thinking about their own lives and relationships, and thinking about their past and future (Buckner, Andrews-Hanna, & Schachter, 2008). Structurally, the default network consists of portions of the frontal lobes and other cerebral cortex areas. In adults with ADHD, the default mode network tends to be overactive. Also, in most people, the default network is suppressed when an individual is working on tasks but less so for individuals with ADHD. This results in a decrease in concentration and more mistakes (Raichle, 2010). Adults with ADHD describe this phenomenon subjectively as being distracted by their own thoughts (Castellanos & Proal, 2012; Shaw, Stringaris, Nigg, & Leibenluft, 2014), as described in the previous two vignettes. Stimulant medication helps to suppress this overactivation, so that the individual can more effectively complete cognitive tasks (Castellanos & Proal, 2012).

Greater activity in the default mode network is also associated with:

- *Major depression* (Guo et al., 2014; Sheline et al. 2008; Zhu et al., 2012), which may be related to the comorbidity between ADHD and depression.
- *Negative cognitions*: specifically, being overly focused on self, overly ruminative, and having negative emotions and negative self-perceptions (Berman et al., 2010; Guo et al., 2014; Hamilton et al., 2011). These problems are commonly found in adults who have ADHD.
- *Creativity* also involves differences in the default network (Beaty et al., 2014; Kühn et al., 2014). Interestingly, this is one of the hypothesized strengths that might come with a diagnosis of ADHD, as discussed in chapter 4.

HYPERACTIVITY

Many adults with ADHD have an increased level of physical activity. One study used an infrared motion tracking system on a headband to measure small movements while adults with ADHD did a cognitive task (Lis et al., 2010). Adults with ADHD showed about *three times* as many movements. In a naturalistic study of ADHD adults, a wrist device was used to measure activity level (Boonstra et al., 2007). Individuals with ADHD have a higher level of physical activity, even when the demands of their occupations were controlled for statistically. Some clients will notice that they have particularly high activity levels, whereas in others, it may not be present or problematic.

How brain differences may cause hyperactivity are currently unclear. Several studies have found evidence of underactivity in areas of the brain that control physical activity in ADHD children, and it is likely that this is related to hyperactivity (Castellanos & Proal, 2012).

PHYSICAL COORDINATION PROBLEMS

Clara: I've always been klutzy and not very good at sports.

Psychotherapist: Coordination problems are actually very common among people who have ADHD.

About half of children with ADHD have significant problems with physical coordination (Mostofsky, 2016). Coordination problems seem to persist through adolescence (Fliers et al. 2007). Whether these problems persist to adulthood is poorly documented, but one study did find that adults with ADHD had significantly more motor problems than controls (Stray et al., 2013). The *motor control network* of the brain, which controls intentional physical movements and the timing of behavior, tends to be underactive in people with ADHD (Castellanos & Proal, 2012).

TIME ESTIMATION PROBLEMS

Psychotherapist: A lot of people who have ADHD have problems with estimating and managing time, which often leads to chronic lateness. Interestingly, research about brain functioning has found that many adults with ADHD have more difficulty estimating how much time has passed than people who don't have ADHD.

Many individuals with ADHD have decreased accuracy in estimating the length of time intervals (Aguiar et al., 2010; Barkley, Murphy, & Bush, 2001; Barkley et al., 2008; Seidman, 2006). Timing difficulties are consistent with brain imaging studies indicating abnormalities of the cerebellum (Nigg, 2006). Most individuals with ADHD underestimate how long tasks will take.

EMOTIONAL DYSREGULATION

Psychotherapist: About half of people with ADHD have problems managing their emotions. Problematic emotions often include anger, frustration, and irritability.

Emotional dysregulation, present in about half of adults with ADHD, is clearly rooted in differences in brain functioning (Shaw et al., 2014). Multiple brain differences have been observed that can contribute to increased irritability, reactive aggression, and temper outbursts (Shaw et al., 2014).

ATYPICAL REWARD SENSITIVITY

Troy: It drives my wife crazy that I have never turned in our federal or state income taxes on time on my own. I just can't concentrate on them, and I always need an extension. Even then, I do them at the last minute. She says she can't understand how I can concentrate for hours on video games, but I can't spend an hour to finish the taxes. I don't know what's wrong with me. This year my wife had to sit down with me in order to get the taxes done on time. We worked together on the taxes until they were finished.

Clara: I can get really bored and I have a hard time paying attention. My husband won't let me pay the bills because I got them mixed up once and it took him months to figure out what I had done wrong. I just couldn't concentrate. I would get bored and walk away and then need to drag myself back to working on them. You'd think I'd have difficulties with all the complex steps in the chemistry experiments, but I do fine with that. I have no problems paying attention to the students and the experiments during class. But I've wondered so many times, what's wrong with me? Why can I do well with all the details of chemistry at school but be a complete failure when it comes to the bills?

Psychotherapist: Scientists have discovered that the brains of people with ADHD respond much differently to things that are interesting and things that are boring. This is the difference that you are noticing between how you do with the video game and the taxes [or the chemistry experiments and the bills]. Many people with ADHD have underactive reward pathways in the brain. The practical implication of this is that they have difficulty with boring tasks and they struggle with mustering the motivation and concentration to get them done. On the other hand, people with ADHD are especially passionate about things that they find interesting. They can easily spend a lot of time on interesting things, and their concentration on interesting things is fine. When people don't understand these cognitive differences, they tend to get very down on themselves, and I can see that you are struggling with that.

Most individuals with ADHD have *difficulty concentrating* on boring tasks—like doing their taxes, bills, and other paperwork—but have no problems with pursuing activities that they find to be interesting (e.g., intrinsically and immediately rewarding), like video games, favorite classes, or preferred hobbies, and they can pursue these interesting activities for hours (Brown, 2013). In other words, motivation interacts in important ways with attention (Nigg, 2006) as illustrated in the previous examples.

There is usually a stark contrast in *performance* on interesting (or immediately reinforcing) versus boring tasks. Their performance on interesting (or otherwise immediately reinforcing) tasks is often just as good as people without ADHD. And they can often work much longer on these tasks than people without ADHD. This performance differential frequently leads to the erroneous assumption that ADHD is not present and the person is just unmotivated, lazy, and does not care about certain things. *This is not true.*

In fact, the brains of at least some, and probably most, adults with ADHD have *atypical reward sensitivity* (Edel et al., 2013; Plichta et al., 2009; Plichta & Scheres, 2014; Stohle et al., 2008), in other words, their brains process rewards differently:

- *They hate to wait,* otherwise called *delay aversion:* They feel stressed and frustrated when they have to wait for things; for example, they have difficulty waiting in lines or give up when they cannot get things immediately.
- *They have difficulty working toward future rewards,* otherwise called *delay discounting*: The individual does not believe that larger future rewards are worth it; for example, the individual may have difficulty starting a retirement account, preferring to spend the money on a new large-screen TV.

These findings are consistent with recent brain research showing decreased function in the brain dopamine reward pathway in adults with ADHD (Volkow et al., 2011). The following are some of the behavioral implications of atypical reward sensitivity:

- *Very responsive to immediate rewards.* Adults with ADHD are highly responsive to immediate monetary rewards and, in the presence of monetary rewards, can even perform *better* than adults without ADHD (Mitchell, Robertson, Kimbrel, & Nelson-Gray, 2011).
- *Interesting and novel stimuli maintain attention and motivation.* Adults with ADHD are highly motivated to do activities that they find to be enjoyable, interesting, challenging, and/or inspiring, and they can do these activities for hours while sustaining attention (Ek & Isaksson, 2013). These activities are immediately and intrinsically reinforcing.
- *Understimulating, boring tasks decrease motivation and concentration.*
- *External supervision or collaboration can provide the immediate reinforcement and structure to help keep a person with ADHD on task.* Social support from a friend or relative and doing tasks together with others were helpful in getting tasks done for adults with ADHD (Ek & Isaksson, 2013). Note that Troy in the previous vignette did much better with the taxes when he worked on them collaboratively with his wife.

- *Need a deadline to get things done.* When a deadline is looming, immediate consequences focus the mind of the adult with ADHD and, generally, the task gets done.

HYPERFOCUS

Troy: My wife found me still playing a video game at 2 AM in the morning when I needed to get up at 6. She shook me by the shoulder and told me to stop and get to bed. I had just gotten lost in the game and I had no idea what time it was.

Psychotherapist: A lot of people with ADHD notice these same things. If there is something they are interested in, they can work on it for hours, and sometimes way longer than most people ever could. We call this "hyperfocus."

Clara: Usually, I just ignore cleaning the bathroom, but when guests are going to come over, I clean it up. Once I get into it, I end up scrubbing down the grout with a toothbrush and taking the grill off of the fan in the ceiling to wash it. My husband tells me not to bother with all that, but once I get started, I just want to get everything done.

Hyperfocus is a phenomenon in which the individual is so cognitively involved in a particular activity that all sense of time is lost and other stimuli from the environment are ignored. Oddly, aside from one dissertation and occasional speculations, hyperfocus is almost entirely unexamined by the scientific literature (Schecklmann et al., 2009; Sklar, 2013).

The previous clinical examples illustrate the phenomenon of hyperfocus. The first example is typical; the individual with ADHD is completely absorbed in an activity that has very high interest value. The second example illustrates that Clara can bring hyperfocus to a task that does not have high intrinsic interest value but that somehow becomes reinforcing and involving once it is started. Also, once hyperfocus starts, Clara has difficulty prioritizing how to clean the bathroom efficiently and gets "lost in the details," a common phenomenon. In fact, hyperfocus has been described as a "beneficial symptom" (Schecklmann et al., 2009). However, hyperfocus also can be seen as perseveration, causing difficulties switching tasks when necessary (Ramsay & Rostain, 2015).

Hyperfocus has some similarities to the concept of *flow* (Sklar, 2013). In flow, "a person must concentrate attention on the task at hand and momentarily forget everything else" (Csikszentmihalyi, 1990, p. 6). The flow experience is enjoyable, involves using one's skills at a high level, and provides positive feedback (Csikszentmihalyi, 1990). Usually, more challenging tasks lead to hyperfocus—consistent with the similarity to flow (Forster, Robertson, Jennings, Asherson, & Lavie, 2014). My guess is that hyperfocus involves both flow and the atypical reward sensitivity of ADHD. The individual becomes involved in an enjoyable, interesting, and/or challenging activity; flow is achieved; and the task becomes immediately reinforcing, resulting in hyperfocus.

EXECUTIVE FUNCTIONING PROBLEMS

Clara: I was having lunch with some colleagues at school. We were discussing lesson planning and I got enthusiastic about an experiment I was planning for the students. Afterwards, I realized that I had probably gone on too long and bored my colleagues. I don't know why I do these things!

Psychotherapist: You seem to be struggling with a cognitive problem called response inhibition that is common in individuals with ADHD. With this problem, people can get really into doing something and they keep on going without thinking that maybe they should stop, like you did when talking about the experiment.

Troy: I was trying to make a cake for my youngest son's birthday. But the kids kept interrupting me. It took me forever because I just don't cope so well with interruptions.

Psychotherapist: A lot of people who have ADHD have problems with what we call set-shifting. In other words, it is really difficult for them switch back and forth between two different activities or tasks, like making the cake and talking to your kids. I suspect that this is what was happening. People with ADHD usually do a lot better when they can just concentrate on one thing at a time.

Clara: Every year, I have an individual conference with each student regarding science fair projects. I tell them at the beginning of the semester about the meetings, but I rely on the kids to schedule them. I always find myself overwhelmed by dozens of appointments at the end of the semester, just when I have to grade finals. I asked my colleague what she does. She schedules these conferences over four weeks in the month before finals. I need to try that.

Psychotherapist: Planning problems are common among adults with ADHD. This is related to underactivation in a network of connectivity in the brain that is called the executive control circuit and involves the frontal lobes of the brain and other areas. These brain areas plan, make decisions, organize, prioritize, and perform other executive functions.

Executive functioning (EF) refers to "deliberate or goal-oriented control of behavior" (Nigg, 2006, p. 67). Executive functions take mental effort to accomplish (Nigg, 2006). All the major researchers and theorists agree that, for a large majority adults with ADHD, EF deficits are a major problem. The *executive control circuit* is a network of brain connectivity that involves EF, specifically, motivation, decision-making, planning, and flexibly responding to the changing environment (Castellanos & Proal, 2012). In ADHD subjects, the *control circuit is underactivated* (Castellanos & Proal, 2012). This is consistent with clients' reports that it takes a lot of mental effort to make plans and get organized.

Russell Barkley (2006b) is the chief proponent of a model of ADHD that considers EF difficulties to be *the* hallmark of adult ADHD. He asserts that all adults with ADHD have EF difficulties. He has a wide conceptualization of EF, which includes emotional dysregulation and problems managing time (Barkley, 2011b). Others consider this definition of EF to be overly broad (Willcutt, Doyle, Nigg, Faraone, & Pennington, 2005). I respect Barkley's desire to include all the factors that are involved in self-direction and self-control. However, for simplicity's sake, I use the narrower definition of EF here.

Executive functions include (Attention Deficit Disorder Association, 2006; Aguiar et al., 2010; Brown, 2006; Jurado & Rosselli, 2007; Shiels & Hawk, 2010) the following:

- *Starting a task in a timely manner*
- *Prioritizing* goals and work
- *Planning and problem-solving*
- *Paying attention to important information and ignoring task-irrelevant information*
- *Refraining from behaving inappropriately, otherwise known as response inhibition.* A common example of a deficit in *response inhibition* is the complaint among loved ones that the ADHD individual "doesn't have a filter"; in other words, blurting out whatever comes to mind, without stopping to think whether it may be inappropriate.
- *Adapting to changing circumstances and switching between tasks, otherwise known as set-shifting*
- *Self-monitoring of progress*, including using self-talk to guide behavior, monitoring for errors, and self-correcting errors
- *Sustaining attention and effort* until the task is completed

Problems with all of these aspects of EF are associated with adult ADHD (Willcutt et al., 2005).

Both EF difficulties and abnormal reward sensitivity are probably related to planning difficulties. For example, if an individual has EF problems, these deficits will make it difficult for the planning process to occur. On the other hand, if an individual has abnormal reward sensitivity, the lack of reinforcement around long-term goals will lead to a lack of planning for them.

You will see problems with planning in almost all adults who have ADHD. When talking to clients with ADHD, they will often agree that they "jump into the middle" of large tasks without formulating a plan of attack ahead of time, which has a negative impact on their performance (Young, Morris, Toone, & Tyson, 2007). It does not cross their minds to construct a timetable or prioritize which aspects of the task are most important. All structured skills training programs for adults with ADHD include planning skills (e.g. Safren et al., 2005; Solanto, 2011).

IMPULSIVITY

Troy: My boss, Mitch, came up to me on Friday and told me that in order to stay on track with our current workload, I'd need to work this Saturday. I'd been looking forward to playing volleyball with the guys at the beach. I cussed Mitch out for scheduling me to work. I've lost jobs for cussing people out in the past. Luckily, Mitch and I are cousins and he knows I don't really mean it.

Psychotherapist: Impulsivity is a major problem for a lot of people with ADHD. Let's work on building in a moment to think about how you are going to respond when you are angry or irritated.

Impulsivity is generally considered a core symptom of ADHD. When we think of impulsivity, we think of someone acting quickly, without thinking through the consequences of that action or whether that action is helpful in achieving his goals. This does not sound too complicated, but breaking this down into measurable cognitive activities is actually more complex than it would initially look. Some experts suggest that impulsivity has three parts: (a) inattention to the task at hand; (b) lack of planning, in other words, thinking only of the present and not thinking through the consequences; and (c) not inhibiting the immediate behavioral response (Malloy-Diniz, Fuentes, Leite, Correa, & Bechara, 2007). Impulsivity in ADHD also appears to be connected to abnormal reward processing in the brain (Plichta & Scheres, 2014). In this chapter, we have already talked about these components of impulsivity, all of which can be impaired in ADHD.

MOST ADULTS WITH ADHD HAVE NORMAL INTELLIGENCE

Here are some key research findings about ADHD, intelligence, and learning:

- *Most people with ADHD have normal IQs* (Biederman, Fried, Petty, Henin, et al., 2012; Biederman, Fried, Petty, Mahoney, & Faraone, 2012; Gimpel et al., 2005; Tsai et al., 2013; Zhang, Jin, & Zhan, 2011).
- *People with ADHD are more likely to have low IQ.* (Biederman, Fried, Petty, Mahoney, et al., 2012; Bridgett & Walker, 2006; Brown, 2013; Frazier, Demaree, & Youngstrom, 2004).
- *Some people with ADHD have high IQ.* But, despite their high IQs, these individuals still often have significant deficits in EF, relationship problems, occupational functioning problems, and comorbid mental illness (Antshel et al., 2009; Brown, Reichel, & Quinlan, 2009).

- *People with ADHD are more likely to have lower academic achievement or learning disabilities.* On average, adults with ADHD have been found to have lower achievements in spelling, reading, and arithmetic (Biederman, Fried, et al., 2011; Frazier et al., 2004); reading or arithmetic learning disabilities are also common (Seidman, 2006).

In conclusion, individuals of all intellectual levels can and do struggle with the challenges of ADHD.

Clinically, I often find that individuals with average to high IQ and ADHD—who did *not* have childhood behavior problems—often "coast" through grade school, and maybe high school as well, without doing much reading or studying and doing their assignments at the last minute. Many of these individuals have parents who provided them with structure. Since these individuals did not have behavior problems, any unevenness in their academic performance from one class to the next was not considered a significant problem by parents or teachers. Then, later in life, perhaps as parents, on the job or in college at the undergraduate or graduate level, they "hit the wall" and are faced with tasks or self-management challenges that are beyond their abilities to concentrate or organize. At that point, they are likely to come for treatment. Many of them had been wondering for years if they had ADHD but had not done anything about it.

STIMULANTS HELP COGNITIVE DEFICITS IN ADHD

Clara: Sorry for missing my last appointment. My medicine is helping, and I thought I'd remember the new appointment time, but I forgot to make a note of it in my calendar.

Troy: Mitch says I'm a lot more together at work since I started taking the medication. I do feel much more focused and less scattered.

Most clients consider their improvement on stimulants to be significant and extremely helpful. Stimulant medications help cognitive functioning in ADHD significantly. Stimulants improve attention, response inhibition, processing speed, reaction time, vigilance, distractibility, EF, and short-term memory, all of which result in improved on-task performance and fewer errors (Brown & Landgraf, 2010; Brown, Brams, Gao, Gasior, & Childress, 2010; Boonstra, Oosterlaan, Sergeant, & Buitelaar, 2005; Seidman, 2006). There is also evidence that stimulant use can help with emotional dysregulation (Reimherr et al., 2007; Rösler et al., 2013; Shaw et al., 2014) and social functioning (Faraone & Glatt, 2010) and can decrease suicidal behavior (Chen et al. 2014) and hyperactivity (Faraone & Glatt, 2010). Stimulants can help normalize reward processing networks (Rubia et al., 2009). Stimulants do not help as much with working memory (Spencer, 2016). However, keep in mind that "pills do not teach skills," as is illustrated by the previous example. Clara still has not developed the skill of consistent and effective calendar use.

Stimulants have a powerful "normalizing" effect on brain functioning. In general, medication improves ADHD symptoms about 50% (McGough, 2014). There is evidence that over time medication can begin to normalize some of the structural and functional brain deficits of ADHD in children (Hart, Radua, Nakao, Mataix-Cols, & Rubia, 2013; Spencer et al., 2013). It is not yet clear whether this finding applies to adults. Clearly, further research is needed.

Research on whether atomoxetine (Strattera) helps cognitive functioning is more limited. However, one randomized, double-blind, placebo-controlled study found that EF scores improved significantly on atomoxetine (Adler, Clemow, Williams, & Durell, 2014).

HOW TO USE PSYCHOEDUCATION

Troy: My dad always said that ADHD was just an excuse for me being lazy and unmotivated.

Psychotherapist: I don't want to disrespect your dad, but I think that he might not have been well-informed about ADHD. It turns out that the brains of people with ADHD actually do work quite differently from the average brain in many ways. These differences make it more difficult for people with ADHD to be organized, concentrate on boring tasks, and achieve their long-term goals.

Research has repeatedly shown that psychotherapy clients have a very poor memory for professional advice, and rarely do they remember more than a third of what they have been told (Harvey et al., 2014). For this reason, repetition is crucially important (Knouse & Safren, 2010). Refer clients to reliable information sources to reinforce psychoeducation you provide (Knouse & Safren, 2011). See the recommended books and resources for clients at the end of this volume.

Avoid providing a massive "information dump" about cognitive functioning in ADHD. Your client will be bored and will remember very little of it. Psychoeducation is most effective when it is targeted to the client's current concerns so it will be interesting and immediately reinforcing, and therefore strongly attended to. A timely intervention is the most effective intervention (Barkley et al., 2008). Then immediately move into problem-solving and skills-building. Once clients understand their problems, they will often devise their own novel solutions. Asking clients to summarize what they have learned during the session can help encode information into long-term memory (Harvey et al., 2014).

PSYCHOEDUCATION: SELF-EFFICACY, SELF-COMPASSION, AND HOPE

Psychotherapist: I see that you are getting overwhelmed with the idea of putting together your website and then you are procrastinating about it. This dynamic of feeling overwhelmed and then procrastinating is a common one for people who have ADHD. Can you take this pad and pen and make a list of all the tasks you would need to do in order to put the website together? [Client takes about 10 minutes to put together a list of tasks, with the assistance of only a few questions from the psychotherapist.] How does that list look? . . . So now that you have the list, I can see that you are feeling much less overwhelmed by the website. I can also see that you are thinking about where to start and what preparatory work you need to do. This is an important illustration of a couple things. First, remember how we were talking about people with ADHD often having reduced working memory? This means it isn't workable to plan out complicated tasks like putting a website together in your head. When you tried to do that, you just felt overwhelmed, and you procrastinated. However, you were able to make an excellent list. Then, when you have the list, you can figure out what to do when. So getting things down on paper and out of your head and then working with that information is a key skill for people who have ADHD. Also, notice that when you do that, you feel capable of making this website happen. I think this illustrates the point that a person who has ADHD can often do a task as well as a person who doesn't have it but that you have to know how your brain works and use a strategy that is effective for you. If you try to use your brain the way everybody else uses theirs, you will often be frustrated. A brain that has ADHD is a different tool and has to be used differently in many situations. Remember, for any project, planning is always the first step.

Disappointment, failure, and underachievement are common experiences among adults with ADHD. They have had many years of struggle without understanding what they are up against. They wonder what is wrong because they cannot get things done in the same way others do. They feel powerless and incompetent.

Instilling hope that treatment can be effective and life can improve is an essential aspect of psychotherapy for adult ADHD (Murphy, 2005). Hope is necessary to engage in and persist in treatment (Murphy, 2005). It is important to provide psychoeducation about ADHD and clarify that it is highly treatable (Murphy, 2005). Feeling understood by the psychotherapist will provide a profound corrective experience after a lifetime of feeling inexplicably different and inferior.

In the previous example, the psychotherapist helps the client realize that she is capable of making a plan to put together her own website. They use time in the session to illustrate an effective coping skill for challenges with working memory. Like most other people with ADHD, this client has at least an average level of intelligence. She has experience in this area and knows what to do but has been procrastinating. The psychotherapist educates the client again about working memory and places the emphasis on empowering the client to utilize skills that will help her accomplish her goals despite working memory problems.

Research has shown that psychoeducation emphasizing biological mechanisms can reduce self-stigma and self-blame but also can make a person feel pessimistic about recovery (Deacon & Baird, 2009; Kemp, Lickel, & Deacon, 2014; Kvaale, Haslam, & Gottdiener, 2013). Psychoeducational messages that emphasize the malleability of the brain and the ability of the client's efforts in treatment to help result in greater optimism and self-efficacy (Farrell, Lee, & Deacon, 2015). In the previous example, the psychotherapist reminds the client of the biological bases of the difficulties that she is having but also shows her experientially that she can learn different ways of addressing the task that are effective, leading to a greater sense of self-efficacy and hopefulness in the client.

An important part of psychotherapy is improving the client's sense of self-efficacy (Manos, 2010). Watch carefully for all-or-none thinking. Identify and complement the client's progress, especially when the progress is partial. Clients with ADHD are usually impatient and want complete change immediately. Educate the client that change is usually gradual, and it is often most effective to work on one or two changes at a time.

COMMON EMOTIONAL REACTIONS TO PSYCHOEDUCATION

Throughout their lives, people who have ADHD usually have a profound sense of being different from other people in ways that cannot be fully articulated (Young, Bramham, Gray, & Rose, 2008). If the ADHD was not understood during childhood, the individual was often criticized by parents and teachers. Criticisms from parents and teachers impact their self-worth and self-image. Common criticisms include being told that they were lazy, unmotivated, and did not apply themselves, or maybe that they were "bad kids" and "just acting out for attention" (Young et al., 2008).

Internalizing these negative ideas about oneself leads to considerable emotional pain. Educating clients about ADHD helps them to reconceptualize these past difficulties and to realize that they may not have been "bad kids," "lazy," or "unmotivated" after all. When clients have difficulty being empathetic toward themselves, consider talking to them about either a real or hypothetical other person who has ADHD. Ask them whether they would say some of the things that they say to themselves to that other person and if not why. This exercise can help most people recognize that they are less critical and more empathetic toward others than they are toward themselves.

Common emotional reactions to a diagnosis of adult ADHD include relief and elation, confusion and emotional turmoil, anger, sadness and grief, anxiety, and acceptance (Young et al., 2008). Some clients are relieved to receive a diagnosis of ADHD and to learn that they can understand their problems and something can be done. This relief can segue into anger, regret, and emotional pain as they think about how many years they struggled with ADHD (Turgay et al., 2012). Grief can also be a reaction, as the person thinks about lost opportunities and how ADHD has had a negative impact throughout the life span (Ramsay & Rostain, 2005). Many complicated emotions arise about self, family, the past, and the educational system. Clients will reassess past experiences in light of the ADHD diagnosis (Turgay et al., 2012). Many struggle with the stigma of having a diagnosis. They have heard uninformed people make negative remarks about ADHD and claim it is just an excuse for people who are lazy and unmotivated. With effective psychotherapy, the client can develop self-understanding, self-compassion, and hope for the future.

KEY POINTS

- Psychoeducation about brain differences in ADHD is essential for self-understanding, self-compassion, hope, and effective problem-solving.
- Psychoeducation should be carefully calibrated to the interests and attention of each particular client.
- Effective psychoeducation for ADHD involves an explanation of why a problem exists and a roadmap to its solution.
- Many strong emotional reactions to learning about ADHD are common, including anger, grief, mourning, confusion, anxiety, feeling stigmatized, and ultimately relief and acceptance.
- Some or all adults with ADHD are:
    - Impaired in the alerting function (being ready to respond to new stimuli), which results in slow and variable responses, greater errors, and more difficulty detecting errors.
    - Able to sustain attention adequately, at least for brief periods, but it is much more difficult for them to do so.
    - Highly distracted by noise.
    - Highly distracted by their own thoughts, due to increased default mode network activity.
    - Often still at least mildly hyperactive, as measured by moving around much more during a sitting task and more physical activity during daily life.
    - Physically uncoordinated and/or have difficulty estimating time.
    - Emotionally dysregulated, which appears rooted in brain differences. This affects about half of adults with ADHD.
    - More motivated in these situations: when immediate rewards are involved, when others closely support and collaborate on their work, when the task is more novel and stimulating, and when there is time pressure to complete the task.
    - Impaired in EF, including motivation, decision-making, planning, choosing what to attend to, and flexibly responding to the changing environment.
    - Of average or high intelligence. However, a somewhat larger proportion of individuals with ADHD have a lower IQ than the proportion in the general population.

11

Skills Training

Effective organizing and planning skills improve functioning, and are therefore an essential element of effective treatment of ADHD (Knouse & Safren, 2010; Weiss et al., 2008). People without ADHD learn organization and planning skills naturally as they go through life. Because of cognitive differences, these skills do not come naturally to most people with ADHD, so they have to be learned. Clients with ADHD do not typically think through their problems systematically, prioritize, and make plans. Instead, they tend to react impulsively or avoid. A different way of addressing problems can be modeled in the session: taking time to reflect carefully about a current situation, considering options, planning a course of action, and then deciding how to implement this (Ramsay, 2010). These behaviors model executive functioning skills.

Listen carefully to clients talk about their problems with ADHD and then address whatever problems that they find to be of greatest concern first. When they identify a problem, clients with ADHD are more motivated, which means that the likelihood of follow-up with homework is greater. When clients make progress, confidence is built.

The information in this chapter draws heavily on two manualized treatments, one for individual therapy (Safren, Perlman, Sprich, & Otto, 2005) and one for group therapy (Solanto, 2011). Almost everyone with ADHD has some deficits in organizational skills. But not all clients will have every one of the organizational problems addressed in this chapter. Evaluate each area to see if assistance is needed. Since using a calendar and a task list effectively are considered to be foundational skills (Sprich, Knouse, Cooper-Vince, Burbridge, & Safren, 2012), these two skills have longer vignettes.

WHAT PEOPLE WITH ADHD KNOW AND DON'T KNOW

> ADHD is a performance disorder. You can't perform the things you know how to do. It is not a knowledge disorder. Most people with ADHD know about as much as anyone else from their neighborhood, with their education, in that school, at that age, but they can't use it. Not to anywhere near

> the degree of effectiveness of others. So people with ADHD know what to do, but they can't do what they know.
>
> —Russell Barkley

In the this quote, Dr. Barkley wisely points out that individuals with ADHD often know *what* to do. For example, they know that life would be more manageable if they kept track of their appointments. Many of them just cannot seem to do it. Why is that? The following shows how a new habit of keeping better track of appointments is implemented for people who do *not* have ADHD:

- Individual recognizes that not keeping track of appointments is creating problems in life.
- Individual decides on a calendar system and begins putting all appointments in calendar.
- She maintains keeping track of appointments consistently for a long enough time period.
- Her new calendar-use behavior eventually becomes a new habit, which then requires little mental energy to maintain.

To make effective coping skills habitual, the first step is *recognizing* the problem, the second step is making a concerted effort to *solve* the problem, and the third step is doing it *consistently* until it becomes a new habit. In contrast, the following is the usual sequence of events for an individual with ADHD:

- Individual with ADHD recognizes he needs to keep track of appointments, so he gets a new calendar app. He gets excited about being organized and puts all his appointments in the app, color coding them according to the type of activity. This excitement lasts for a week or two.
- After that, continuing to consistently calendar in appointments is a problem because
  - Maintaining the calendar crosses over to being a tedious chore instead of new and exciting.
  - Working toward the long-term goal of habit development is understimulating and boring.
  - The individual gets distracted by something more interesting, thinking "I'll do that later," but does not.
  - The individual forgets to use the calendar app.
  - His fluctuating attention makes consistency difficult to achieve.
  - The heightened mental energy necessary to continue the habit requires consistency of self-management that is difficult to achieve.
  - The client is pessimistic because of past frustrations with similar tasks (Ramsay & Rostain, 2016).
  - Client observes own struggles with maintaining behavior, prematurely assumes "I've failed again," gets discouraged, and gives up efforts.
- Soon, the calendar app is no longer used and his schedule becomes chaotic again. So the behavior never reaches the new habit stage where it

requires little mental energy to maintain. This pattern generally repeats multiple times for the same problem.
- As "failures" add up over time, the individual feels incompetent and asks himself why everyone else can manage their schedules and he can't.

So people with ADHD know ***what*** *to do, they just haven't figured out* ***how*** *to implement it in a way that works for them.* Figuring out *how* is not obvious or they would have done it already. What works for people without ADHD often does not work for them the same way. Psychoeducation about brain functioning in ADHD helps the client understand this problem. Clearly, the individual does know that using a calendar is a good idea. Here is what the individual may not know or recognize:

- Starting a new organizational system will be easier at first because it is novel, but then it will be very difficult for a while—when it feels like a tedious task—and then it will later become easy again as it turns into a habit.
- Establishing new habits is extra difficult for people with ADHD because of cognitive differences, specifically, their fluctuating attention and their differences in the reward system of the brain, which contribute to difficulty persisting with tedious tasks.

Thus, effective habit acquisition is especially difficult for individuals with ADHD. Solanto and colleagues (2008) wisely assert that "development of new, more adaptive habits and functional routines in adults with ADHD demands a certain degree of unambiguous emphasis and repetition so that desired behaviors (e.g., checking a planner every day) ultimately become automatic and no longer dependent on the individual's active executive or decision-making functions" (p. 4). So when you teach a skill, emphasize the importance of converting that skill to a habit (Knouse & Safren, 2011; Ramsay, 2010a) and continue emphasizing the skill in therapy until it is acquired as a habit.

ESTABLISH NEW HABITS

Psychotherapist: I'm noticing that you lost track of your appointment last week after you asked me to move it to a different time.

Clara: That kind of thing happens to me all the time.

P: Was the changed appointment in your calendar?

C: Yes, I just didn't look at it.

P: You've been working on regularly getting your appointments into your calendar, and I can see that you've made a lot of progress in that area, but I can also see that you've discovered that if you don't look at the calendar, it doesn't do any good.

C: True.

P: Do you want to fine-tune your calendar use so that this kind of thing doesn't happen so much in the future?

C: Yes, I'm totally ready to do this. I'm tired of all these mix-ups. It's stressing me out.

P: I recommend that you develop new habits to look at your calendar regularly. First, it's important to look at it in the evening to review what you have going on the next day. It's also important to look at it again in the morning before you leave, to refresh your memory of what you have scheduled that day. Then you can check the calendar for details as needed throughout the day. Can you work on developing those habits over the next week and let me know how it goes?

C: I think that would help.

P: I understand that it's been difficult to develop these calendar habits, but I'm here to help you if there are any problems. If you realize that you didn't check your calendar at one of these times, make a mental or physical note about what happened that particular day and we'll problem-solve about it next week, okay?

C: Okay.

Clients with ADHD are usually impatient. They want to solve all their problems immediately. They can be excited about solving a problem and get overly ambitious with their solutions. But their cognitive differences make it difficult for them to be consistent and persist (Ramsay & Rostain, 2016), as discussed in the last section. They become discouraged when difficulties arise and slide back into avoidance.

Here are some strategies to assist with habit development:

- Educate the client about conscious versus automatic behaviors and the need to practice a new behavior over and over until it becomes an automatic habit and, therefore, not so effortful (Lally, Wardle, & Gardner, 2011). Educate the client that people vary considerably in how long it takes to develop new habits, but at least a three weeks of consistent effort will probably be necessary—and, quite possibly, much more time than that (Lally, Van Jaarsveld, Potts, & Wardle, 2010).
- Ascertain whether the client is motivated to work on a goal that is connected to the new habit; the psychotherapist in the previous example explicitly asks Clara whether she is motivated—she says she is and volunteers her own reasons for this motivation. Goals encourage learning new habits (Wood & Neal, 2007). If the client is not yet motivated, it may be better to move on to a different topic, rather than risk another failure experience—especially in the context of psychotherapy. If she is unmotivated now, let the client know that this issue can be revisited in the future.
- Discuss the cues that need to trigger the habit (Wood & Neal, 2007); in the example, the psychotherapist suggests that Clara check her calendar every evening and morning. It might even be helpful to link calendar-checking with a pre-existing habit, such as making or drinking her morning coffee.

- Assure the client that you will be available to help support her efforts. Make it clear that you understand that difficulties will arise but that you will work together to problem-solve about them. Your consistent support and encouragement provides scaffolding that will help the client maintain the effort necessary to convert this behavior to a habit over time.
- Ask the client: "What will happen after you leave here today that could get in the way of putting this plan into action?" (Ramsay & Rostain, 2016, p. 43).
- When a client comes in after a week of (at least occasionally) successfully practicing a skill, spend some time talking about how use of this skill has affected his or her life over the last week. Often, skill use will lead to more calm, less worry, less rushing, and less distress. Recognizing the absence of these aversive experiences will reinforce maintenance of the skill.
- Help the client define partial or incomplete efforts as making significant progress toward the goal and being an improvement over not working on the goal at all. Clients with ADHD can sometimes be perfectionistic, which can lead to prematurely abandoning efforts, rather than building on partial successes.
- Continue to check in with the client at following sessions to see how she is doing with implementing the skill routinely and problem-solve as needed.

The best strategy for a person with ADHD is usually the simplest effective strategy so there are fewer impediments to following through on them regularly (Knouse & Safren, 2013). We must help them establish specific, doable solutions instead of idealized, ambitious solutions. Elaborate strategies are novel and appealing and may be exciting to implement, but they will rarely be maintained. Complicated systems are not sustainable for adults with ADHD because they are easily overwhelmed by complexity and then resume procrastination.

We provide encouragement and problem-solving to help them stick with a solution until it develops into a habit. This provides an experience of success, which helps to build confidence. It also provides a model for how to address their difficulties that they may be able to eventually internalize and implement on their own.

I often advise ADHD clients to work on no more than one or two new habits at once, until they feel that these are well-established, then move on to developing the next healthy habit. By the time they get to psychotherapy, they are likely to understand that their desire to solve everything all at once has not been effective, but we often need to reinforce that point.

DECREASE AVOIDANCE AND PROCRASTINATION

Most people with ADHD have problems with procrastination, sometimes known as avoidance (Ramsay, 2007). Larger, multistep projects are particularly problematic. Procrastinating on complex long-term tasks leads to feelings of distress, incompetence, failure, and underachievement (Ramsay, 2007; Ramsay & Rostain, 2005). These difficulties have their roots in very real cognitive differences, specifically executive functioning problems and differences in the reward system of the brain—which makes it difficult to complete tasks that are not due immediately or that are not intrinsically interesting.

When your client brings up a pending project or expresses concern about a long-standing pattern of procrastination, use this opportunity to explore the problems that have stemmed from procrastination in the past. These problems have usually included stress, "pulling all-nighters," being late with projects, and, most importantly, a chronic feeling of not living up to one's potential by doing things in a rushed manner. Discussion of these aversive consequences of procrastination will help cement the client's motivation to address the issue.

Discuss and assess factors that can contribute to procrastination:

- A lack of problem-solving and planning skills (Knouse & Safren, 2011) due to executive functioning problems.
- Underestimating the amount of time and effort needed.
- Feeling stressed, overwhelmed, and anxious when thinking about the project, then using avoidance to relieve the stress—so it is reinforced in the short term (Ramsay & Rostain, 2008b). Because of cognitive differences, most people with ADHD are highly responsive to short-term rewards, such as the relief they obtain by avoidance, which helps maintain procrastination.
- Many projects are not immediately reinforcing or punishing until very close to the deadline.
- Unrealistic positive cognitions: they may say to themselves that they do a good job doing things at the last minute, but when they have completed the task, they will say that they could have done a better job if they had more time.

Educate the client that, although working in a step-by-step manner over time is not a skill that comes naturally to people with ADHD, it is a skill that can be cultivated and improved over time and an essential life skill to accomplish significant goals.

Exposing clients to situations that they would typically avoid helps them learn how to use effective coping skills (Ramsay, 2007). When difficulties are encountered, behavioral alternatives can be developed to help clients push through and achieve their desired goals (Ramsay, 2007). For example, if a client cannot concentrate to read, the client may avoid the reading assignment completely. The client may engage in self-criticism due to the inability to concentrate and read as long as classmates can. Some possible for solutions that may work include:

- Read for 25 minutes, then take a 10-minute break, and then return to reading. A timer can be helpful in returning to work in a timely manner.

- Work on the reading assignment in the morning after taking medication and while the client's energy level has not been depleted by other tasks during the day.
- Get together with a classmate and sit and do the reading together. It is commonly observed that working together with someone else, even if they are working on separate tasks, helps a person with ADHD concentrate and get things done.
- Use the "10-minute rule," which entails asking the client to do the aversive task for 10 minutes, then reassess whether it is possible to continue. Often once the client starts the task, further progress is not as difficult (Ramsay & Rostain, 2008b).
- Schedule the task into the client's calendar with specific beginning and end times.
- Discuss emotions, thoughts, and events that might interfere with the plan to complete the task and discuss how to manage these effectively (for more details on this approach, see Ramsay & Rostain, 2015).
- Address the importance of learning to tolerate some anxiety, frustration, or other emotional discomfort in order to achieve goals (Ramsay & Rostain, 2015).
- Help the client recognize the feeling of satisfaction from completing a task (Ramsay & Rostain, 2015). Being able to make progress on the reading assignment will help the client feel more confident and competent (Ramsay, 2007).

The accountability that the client has to the psychotherapist can also be a helpful motivator (Ramsay & Rostain, 2015).

When clients feel overwhelmed with responsibilities, they will often be resistant to your efforts to help them make a plan to effectively manage their lives. Remind clients that when their lives feel more manageable, they will feel less overwhelmed and stressed. Talk the client through a plan and timetable to address these responsibilities effectively. Once a plan is in place, how does the client feel? Probably the client feels relieved. Note with the client that relief can come from effective coping—avoidance is not necessary for relief. Clients with ADHD will rarely adhere strictly to the plan made in the session, but the plan will often help them make incremental improvements, which should be recognized and celebrated.

DEVELOP SKILLS FOR REGULAR AND SUFFICIENT SLEEP

Poor sleep impairs cognition in anyone. As a reminder, I recommend screening for both poor sleep hygiene and potential symptoms of a sleep disorder (chapters 5 and 6). Also consider whether anxiety or depressive symptoms are interfering with sleep. If there are sleep hygiene issues and the client is motivated to address them, work on this early in treatment. (For basic instructions in sleep hygiene, see Willer, 2014).

Discuss the tendency for adults with ADHD to be night owls. If the client is a night owl, and personal or work schedules are not compatible with staying up late, careful attention to sleep hygiene will be needed. Engaging in a discussion of the negative consequences of an erratic sleep schedule (tiredness, lateness, susceptibility to illness, worse attention and concentration) can help engage the client in addressing this issue (Solanto, 2011).

Often adults who have ADHD have difficulty getting to sleep in a timely manner (Solanto, 2011). Reasons for this include:

- The individual is having difficulty stopping what he is doing in order to go to bed. Engaging activities include playing video games, watching movies, and reading articles or using social media on the phone. These activities are immediately reinforcing, which makes them especially difficult to disengage with. Sometimes setting an alert for a time to stop activities and start gearing down for bed can be helpful.
- Many of these activities involve engaging with LED screens. As has recently been discovered, screens put out a blue light that tends to activate sensors in the eye, alerting the brain that it is daytime. Educating the client that light from screens is problematic near bedtime can be helpful.
- Erratic wake–sleep times from the previous day may result in the individual not being sleepy at bedtime.

Discuss activities, such as reading, doing crossword puzzles, playing relaxing music, or taking a warm bath that will help the client relax and get ready for sleep (Solanto, 2011). Continue to problem-solve about sleep as needed. With clients who have ADHD, it is often unrealistic to expect adherence to firm bedtimes and wake times as one might prescribe for other clients who have sleep hygiene issues, but narrowing the windows for each of these can still improve sleep quality significantly.

People with ADHD often have difficulty with sleep onset because their minds are so active. Carefully chosen noise can help. Sounds that might be overly stimulating for someone without ADHD (e.g., podcasts, soundtracks) can be helpful sleep aids for a person with ADHD.

ESTABLISH REGULAR AND HEALTHY EATING HABITS

Clients with ADHD often skip meals and eat erratically, echoing the disorganization found in other areas of life. They may eat too much junk food or take-out because it is easy and does not require planning.

Poor eating habits negatively affect cognition, so assess your clients' eating habits. Are they eating healthy food? Or are they eating too much junk food from either disorganization or impulsiveness? Be sure your client is informed about a healthy diet (plenty of vegetables, fruits, whole grains, beans and nuts, with minimal processed food, sugar, and meat). Educate about the helpfulness of supplementing with omega-3 fatty acids (see chapter 14 and appendix 3).

Often clients with ADHD aspire to prepare healthy meals for themselves but then don't get around to it and end up eating fast food or skipping meals. So they know *what* to do; they just have not figured out *how* to do it in a way that works for them. Remind the client that "perfect is the enemy of the good." Brainstorm with the client about simple ways to have healthy food readily available at home, in the car, or at the office. Grab-and-go foods are especially useful: dried fruit, bananas, individual yogurt tubs, nutrition bars, nuts, prepackaged baby carrots, and so on. Refer to a dietician if further education is warranted.

When the client is a parent, organizing food and meals may be a challenging family issue. Food is purchased that is not used and is then thrown away. Meal plans may not exist, or too many meals may be delivered. Apps can help. An individual I know who has ADHD swears by the Pepper Plate app. It allows her to plan menus in advance, and the app uses the recipes to generate a shopping list. The menus and shopping list can be shared between family members who can then share shopping and cooking responsibilities. Other apps exist that can perform the same functions.

ESTABLISH AN EXERCISE ROUTINE

Psychotherapist: Sounds like you're feeling ready to start exercising regularly. I think that's a great idea, because I suspect it will help take the edge off of that restless feeling you have at work. What have you enjoyed doing in the past? . . . What goals would you like to set for yourself over the next week? . . . Okay, let me know how it goes. If you don't end up doing what you've planned, make a note of what happened—how you were thinking or feeling, or what happened—then we can problem-solve about it next time.

Exercise improves health (Eijsvogles & Thompson, 2015) and cognitive functioning (Chang, Labban, Gapin, & Etnier, 2012; Hillman, Erickson, & Kramer, 2008). Since exercise helps with cognition in the general population, it is likely that individuals with ADHD will have similar benefits. However, so far, research in this area has been very limited (Archer & Kostrzewa, 2012; Gapin, Labban, & Etnier, 2011). Recent studies have found improvements in hyperactivity, executive functioning, response inhibition, motor skills, moodiness, oppositional behavior, and inattention among children with ADHD who participated in a regular exercise program (Hillman et al., 2014; Hoza et al., 2015; Smith et al., 2013; Verret, Guay, Berthiaume, Gardiner, & Béliveau, 2012). A correlational study found that adults with ADHD who engaged in frequent aerobic exercise reported less impulsivity and worry (Abramovitch, Goldzweig, & Schweiger, 2013). Adult clients with ADHD tell me that aerobic exercise "takes the edge off" restlessness and helps concentration. It also may help with irritability and emotional lability. One of the foremost experts on ADHD recommends moderate to vigorous physical exercise as an intervention for ADHD (Nigg, 2013).

I prefer to provide very brief psychoeducation about exercise early in treatment. With ADHD clients, it is best to "strike while the iron is hot." So if the client does not verbalize an interest in exercise at that time, I wait. When the client expresses an interest or verbalizes a problem that could be helped by exercise, then utilize an intervention.

HYPERACTIVITY

A small minority of adults have obvious hyperactivity, and this symptom is challenging for them. They often choose jobs that keep them on the go, and they keep busy during their personal time. Their high energy levels can help some of them accomplish a lot but can also contribute to relationship struggles: "You can never sit still and just relax!" Interestingly, stimulants do help take the edge off of hyperactivity. But it is still there. Some will self-medicate with marijuana, which helps them sit still in the evenings. Psychoeducation for the client and partner can be helpful in fostering mutual understanding.

Here are some tips to help with hyperactivity in the workplace (National Resource Center on AD/HD, 2003):

- Get regular exercise.
- Take breaks from computer work to walk around, get a little exercise, or do physical tasks.
- Take notes in meetings.
- Bring lunch and use the lunch hour for exercise.
- Take a brisk walk around the block if feeling agitated.

Some find that they can sit still more easily in the evening if they have the stimulation of looking at both their phone and TV or if they have something to do with their hands (like knitting).

KEEP TRACK OF POSSESSIONS

Most people with ADHD have difficulties keeping track of possessions (Safren, Perlman, et al., 2005). Sometimes the item will be sitting around the house but the client forgets where it is—such as keys, phones, incoming mail, and so on. Other times the client may lose items permanently—such as leaving a laptop on the bus, leaving a phone in a restaurant, or losing scarves, hats, and glasses. The following are some principles to apply (Safren, Perlman, et al., 2005):

- Each commonly used item should have a one standard storage place that is easily accessible (e.g., keys go onto key rack when entering home or into a purse or bag).

- Develop a new habit of putting things in their place *immediately* when entering the home (e.g., the incoming mail goes into a basket near the door, the coat goes in the closet [with the mittens in the pockets], the purse goes on a table by front door).
- Develop new habits of returning items that are easily lost to their place *immediately* after use (e.g., after using the phone, the client either puts it back into her purse or on a table to charge)
- Others in the household can be advised of this plan so they can help with reminders if important items are out of place.
- Schedule a time at least once a week to go through the home and put away anything that is not in its place.
- Keep duplicates of important items, such as keys and glasses (Murphy, 2005; Tuckman, 2007). Consider hiding one set of keys outside the house or on the body of the car.
- Prepare all needed materials for the next day (lunch, keys, paperwork) the night before to reduce chaos in the morning (Murphy, 2005).

REDUCE ENVIRONMENTAL DISTRACTIONS

Managing the environment to reduce distractions can be helpful (National Resource Center on AD/HD, 2003; Safren, Perlman, et al., 2005; Solanto, 2011). If the client has little control over the work environment, these interventions can reduce distractions:

- Do not respond to email while working on a project that requires concentration. Close the email tab and turn off notifications of incoming email. Check email when between projects or at set times. This reduces set-shifting and increases effectiveness. If the client has difficulty accepting this recommendation, ask, "When was the last time you got an emergency email that needed to be addressed immediately?"
- Keep browser closed or, if that is not possible, only open to tabs that pertain to the project at hand. Do not have tabs open to email, social media, news, and other distractions.
- Turn off the phone when working on projects that require concentration. Instead, check and respond to messages during breaks, or address them when a project is over.
- Reduce clutter in the workspace.
- Use noise-cancelling headphones to reduce auditory distractions. Some individuals with ADHD report that wordless noise can help them concentrate on verbal tasks, this can include "white noise," fan sounds, classical music, New Age music, or nature sounds. This is consistent with research findings that people with ADHD do best when they have the optimal level of stimulation—not too much or too little.
- Ask others not to interrupt, post a sign on a door, or consider nonverbal cues (e.g., headphones on).

If the client has control over the work environment, consider the following:

- If quiet is important to concentrate, brainstorm about how to obtain a quiet work environment.
- If avoiding distractions at home is important to concentrate, consider going to a work space where there are minimal distractions, such as a library. Some individuals with ADHD can work well at coffee houses because the distractions of home are not available, while others are too distracted by the hubbub in this environment.
- Ask family members or roommates not to disturb while working. Close the door. Put up a sign if necessary.

MANAGE INTERNAL DISTRACTIBILITY

Psychotherapist: Sounds like you're really bothered by the piles of mail around the house. Are you feeling ready to make a plan to work on it? . . . Okay, so here's one important thing to keep in mind. Most people with ADHD want to solve problems immediately. However, this sounds like one of those problems that is best worked on a little at a time. Some things in life are just too complicated to do all at once. Developing your skills to work on projects over time helps you to achieve long-term goals. We can use this mail task as practice for that. How does that sound? . . . What time of day can you concentrate best? . . . What time during the day does your medicine feel like it's the most effective? . . . Given that, what time of day do you think would be best to work on this project? . . . How many minutes sound like a very doable amount of time to work on it? . . . When you start it, keep a pad handy and if you're distracted thinking of other things to do, make a note of that idea, then go back to the task for the full 10 minutes, okay?

When working on boring tasks, such as sorting out piles of unopened mail, individuals with ADHD are readily distracted by their own thoughts. The psychotherapist in the previous example assesses motivation and provides some psychoeducation about the importance of developing the skill of working on projects over time. Then the psychotherapist and the client make a very concrete plan to work on the task, including setting a specific date and time to work on it. Additional tips to reduce distractibility include (National Resource Center on AD/HD, 2003; Solanto, 2011):

- When distracted by thoughts of other tasks, write them down, then refocus on the task at hand (Safren et al., 2010).
- Do one task at a time, and do not start new ones until the current one is done.
- Set an alarm for every 30 minutes. At that time, clients can reassess whether they are still on track with the work they had been planning to do (Safren, Perlman, et al., 2005)—and refocus if they became distracted with something else.

"Distractibility delay" is a technique to help the client focus on one topic for an extended period of time (Sprich et al., 2012). When using this technique, a client chooses a doable amount of time to concentrate on one task, perhaps 15 minutes. When distractions enter the mind, they make a note of them on a piece of paper and then set them aside. At the end of the 15 minutes, clients review the distractions and decide whether they need to go on the task list or whether they can be ignored. Overall, the goal is to help the client develop greater awareness of distractibility and increase skills toward redirecting attention toward the task at hand (Sprich et al., 2012).

ADJUST THE LEVEL OF STIMULATION FOR IMPROVED CONCENTRATION

Clara: At school, I have to work in a "bullpen" with the other teachers. I play ambient music on my headphones to drown out the sounds around me so I can focus.

Psychotherapist: It sounds like you've figured out a great solution to help you concentrate at work.

Maintaining an optimal level of stimulation improves the performance of individuals with ADHD. Individuals with ADHD have a narrower range of stimulation in which they operate well. If they have too much stimulation, they get overwhelmed and then procrastinate or avoid. If they have too little stimulation, they get easily bored, and their attention wanders to their own thoughts and external distractions; then they lose concentration and do not finish the task. When they have an optimal level of stimulation, they are able to perform to a higher level and they can ignore distractions better (Forster, Robertson, Jennings, Asherson, & Lavie, 2014).

Noise can be an effective tool to adjust the amount of stimulation and improve cognitive performance (Söderlund, Sikström, & Smart, 2007). If the client is overstimulated with external distractions, carefully chosen noise can reduce stimulation to a more optimal level by masking distractions, such as coworkers talking. Clara does this in the previous example. If the client is understimulated, noise can increase stimulation, resulting in better concentration. Clients report that nonverbal noise (classical music, ambient music, nature sounds, light jazz, etc.) helps concentration on verbal tasks, while verbal noise (podcasts, comedy videos, soundtracks from TV shows) helps concentration on nonverbal tasks.

EMOTIONAL DYSREGULATION

Clara: My mother and I often argue. In retrospect, most of these arguments are so trivial. She is just like me; I think she has ADHD as well, but she doesn't want to admit it. We are very close, but these arguments are upsetting.

Psychotherapist: Like many people with ADHD, it sounds like you're struggling with getting angry quickly and your mother may well be having the same problem. Your biggest challenge here is to build in a brief moment to think about your reaction. It sounds like one of you gets irritated, then you both end up being reactive and having an argument. Is that true? . . . So the challenge here is not to escalate the situation. Remember, it takes two people to have an argument. If you can refrain from escalating, that may eliminate a lot of arguments, even if your mother doesn't make any changes herself. Do you think it's worth a try?

As mentioned in previous chapters, about half of adults with ADHD have problems with emotional dysregulation, specifically being emotionally labile, overly irritable, easily overwhelmed by problems, and prone to temper outbursts. Clara and her mother are both reactive, yet they regret these arguments, and they realize that these arguments do not contribute to their long-term goal of having a good mother–daughter relationship. While there is some evidence that stimulant medication and atomoxatine may help with emotional dysregulation, psychotherapy has an important role as well (Shaw, Stringaris, Nigg, & Leibenluft, 2014).

We can help our clients identify their emotions and learn ways of coping other than immediately reacting. We can help them explore whether their behaviors are appropriate in the moment and whether these behaviors help them move toward their long-term goals. In the previous example, Clara's long-term goal is to have a better and more peaceful relationship with her mother, and she realizes that being reactive to minor irritations is not conducive to that goal. So the psychotherapist collaborates with her to help her think of alternative behaviors in advance, since her reactivity does not allow her to do that in the moment. Mindfulness training can also encourage greater awareness of what is happening in the moment in a less reactive way (Shaw et al., 2014).

Since exercise is frequently helpful for emotional modulation in anxiety and depression, it may help with emotional dysregulation in ADHD. Clients have reported significant improvement in emotional dysregulation after starting an exercise program.

Family-based interventions may also help with emotional dysregulation (Shaw et al., 2014). When the family is getting along better and communicates in a more positive manner, there is much less to be irritated or angry about.

CALENDAR SKILLS

Psychotherapist: So, Troy, do you have a calendar to keep track of your appointments?

Troy: No, my wife does that for me. She keeps track of the kids' schedules too.

P: What about you; have you ever kept a calendar for yourself?

T: I've tried to, but it's never seemed to work out.

P: Why?

T: Well, I tried a Franklin planner, but it was bulky and I didn't want to carry it around with me. So I kept leaving it at home and of course that wasn't working out. Then I tried to keep everything on the wall calendar at home, but I would forget to check it and add things to it. I missed my dental appointment, and we had to pay a $50 fee. I've also missed the kids' games because I lost track of them. My wife got fed up and she decided that she'd keep track of everything for me.

P: This is a common phenomenon among adults who have ADHD. Often they get all fired up about a new calendar system, and, while it is new, for the first few days or weeks, they feel motivated. Then it becomes boring and they lose all motivation.

T: That's definitely it. At first, I got all fired up, but then I lost track of it and my schedule got all disorganized again.

P: So how does your wife keep track of everything?

T: She has it all in her phone, and she reminds me if I have things that I need to do. She has everything in there, my appointments, hers and the kids' schedules too.

P: How do you feel about this system?

T: Well, it mostly works, but I feel like another one of her kids that she has to keep track of.

P: Are there any problems with this system?

T: Well, occasionally, I forget to tell her about something that I'm doing, and she gets irritated with me all over again.

P: Okay. I really think that you can make progress in this area if we work together on it. Is that something you would like to work on?

T: Yes, I think it's about time.

P: Do you and your wife have the same kind of phone?

T: Yes, but I never use the calendar functions on it.

P: Okay. Sometimes I talk with people about whether they'd prefer to use a paper or electronic calendar, but I'm guessing that it would be best to just go with the system that your wife has already started. What do you think?

T: Yes.

P: Okay. So here's what I'd suggest to get started. Can you have a talk with your wife this week about your family calendar and tell her that you're going to be working on keeping better track of your own appointments yourself? Then sit down with her and figure out how to sync your phone to the family calendar that your wife has going. Also, these electronic calendars can often be set up to have subcalendars for personal events, family events, and so on. Can you check to see if she has set these up and work out how to fit your appointments into whatever plan she has going?

T: Sure. She'll be happy that I'm making an effort on this.

P. Great. Also, I'd suggest that you try to figure out how to access your calendar from any other devices that you often use, okay? The more readily available your calendar is, the more likely you'll be to use it. What other devices do you often use?

T: Just a laptop.

P: So in our next session, let's talk about how to use the calendar more effectively, once you've got everything set up, okay?

T: Sounds good.

Next session:

P: So, how did things go with your wife and the calendar?

T: (pulls phone out) Good. We talked about the calendar. She doesn't use the sub-calendar function; she just keeps everything in one calendar. We decided that it would be best for me to just add to that calendar so we can both see what everyone in the family is up to at any given time.

P: Okay, that sounds good.

T: I also figured out how to access the calendar from my laptop.

P: Great! You've done an excellent job with all the legwork you need to do to get started. Keep in mind that using this calendar will need to become a new habit, and, like all new habits, it takes time and lots of practice to get going. But once you've developed it as a habit, it will become easier to maintain and a lot of things in your life will be more pleasant and less chaotic for both you and your family. So, here's my first question: Are your therapy appointments in your calendar?

T: No. I know that they are at the same time every week, so I just keep track of them that way.

P: Okay, so the first thing about using your calendar effectively is to put all appointments in it, even if you think you'll remember them. Remember that time you came late because you had to meet with one of your son's teachers and you didn't realize there was a conflict until that morning? Putting everything in the calendar will help reduce that kind of problem.

T: Okay. I hear you.

P. So why don't you put our appointments in there right now? Put in your regular time at 8am on Tuesday, and then be sure that you've set it up as a weekly recurring appointment.

T: (Enters therapy appointments into phone.) Okay, done.

P: Is there anything else that you don't have in there, anything you've been doing regularly?

T: Yes, I have my baseball game on Tuesday evenings.

P: Okay, so let's go ahead and enter that into your calendar now.

T: (Enters game into phone.) Okay.

P: Great! Now all you need to add are your one-time appointments. This brings us to the second point about using your calendar effectively. Right at the moment that you're making any appointment, or scheduling any get-together with friends or family, check your calendar right then and enter it in. This is a really essential new habit to develop, and I'd like to ask you to work really hard on doing this over the next week.

T: Sure.

P: That helps prevent schedule conflicts like you've run into in the past. Also, you can be sure that you have enough time to get to whatever you've scheduled in. Now didn't you mention that you were taking your family to the Grand Canyon next month?

T: Yes.

P: So let's coordinate our calendars about that. Can you look and see what week that is?

T: It's the week of July 2nd.

P. Okay. So I'll delete our appointment that week, and why don't you delete our appointment that week in your calendar right now as well? (Both remove that appointment.) Also, I'm going to be out the week of August 5th. Can you delete our appointment that week? (Both delete that appointment.)

T: Done.

P: Great! So now we've got our schedules coordinated for the next two months. So here's the final thing to keep in mind about the calendar—check it regularly. It's best to check it first thing in the morning, so you have everything in mind that you're doing throughout the day. Keep checking it throughout the day as you need to. Then take a look at it toward the end of the day or in the evening to get in mind what you have coming up the next day. Also, it's good to take a look at the whole upcoming week every few days or so, so you have an idea about what's coming up. It's easiest to do that on the laptop, because the screen is bigger.

T: Okay, I'll try to do that.

P: Sounds good. Let me know how things go next week, and we can problem-solve as needed. So, remember to enter everything into your calendar and to check it regularly, okay?

T: Okay.

P: If you're not perfect, that's okay. This is a process and it may not all happen overnight. If you run into any trouble, let me know what went wrong next week and we'll problem-solve about it, okay?

T: Okay.

The psychotherapist could have gone further with calendar issues in the first session but chose not to. Helping the client learn to set doable goals is an important self-management skill for ADHD, and the goals set seemed doable to the client. Once the client had the electronic calendar synced to his phone, further work was done in the next session. Sporadic checks on calendar use will continue until Troy is regularly and effectively using his calendar. Troy is encouraged to practice calendar skills immediately, during the psychotherapy session. If the client comes in with a planner stuffed full of fliers, sticky notes, and other bits of information with appointments on them, you can work collaboratively to consolidate the calendar during the session (Sprich et al., 2012).

Troy's experiences with calendars are common, although not universal, among adults with ADHD. Often they have made countless aborted attempts to use a calendar. When the calendar is a new project, it is novel and interesting, but then it quickly becomes a boring chore and the individual does not stick with it long enough for it to become an automatic, effortless habit (Sprich et al., 2012). As in Troy's case, often spouses or other family members compensate for the individual's skill deficit. In most cases, you will want to have a discussion with the client about preferences for a paper calendar versus electronic, but in the previous example, it was best to go with the system that Troy's wife had already started. Some general principles for effective calendar use are (Solanto, 2011):

- Have only one calendar. It does not matter if it is paper or electronic, just that the client will stick with that one. Choose the one that the client thinks would be easiest.
- The calendar must be portable and with the client at all times.
- No appointments are agreed to without checking the calendar first.
- All appointments must be entered into the calendar at the time that they are made.
- The calendar should be checked at least every morning and evening.
- The calendar can be used to schedule tasks as well as appointments.

Encouragement and praise are especially important for adults with ADHD, because they have had so many experiences of failure and lack self-confidence about their ability to organize their lives. So be positive about progress, even when the progress is partial. It is likely that partial progress in the past has led to all-or-none thinking and then giving up, rather than effective problem-solving.

TASK LIST SKILLS

Psychotherapist: How are you doing with keeping track of tasks that you need to do?

Clara: Okay, I guess. At work they call me the Post-it Queen.

P: Because?

C: Because I've got post-it notes all over my computer and sticking out all over from my calendar. (Pulls calendar out of bag; there are indeed many post-its hanging out of it.)

P: How does that seem to be working?

C: Honestly, not so well. I keep losing track of stuff I need to do, even though I have a post-it for it, and I miss deadlines.

P: So you need a system that keeps track of deadlines?

C: Right. And sometimes I get overwhelmed by the post-its and just ignore all of them.

P: So there's no way to choose what to do first, and you get overwhelmed by the volume of tasks.

C: And then sometimes I do things that aren't that important and lose track of the high-priority tasks.

P: Okay, so you need help with prioritizing things too.

C: Yes, the whole thing is just a mess, honestly. I have no idea how to fix it.

P: Okay, let's try to make some progress with this. First, like we did with your calendar, we need to figure out whether you want to keep a paper or electronic to-do list. What are your thoughts about that?

C: Well, I prefer paper, but that doesn't seem to be working out so well.

P: True. I'm hearing from you that you've got lots of things to keep track of, and the post-it system isn't working. Because of the sheer quantity of to-do items, I'm thinking that it might be worth trying an electronic system.

C: Okay, I'll give it a try.

P: So here's what I'd suggest for the next week. Choose one electronic to-do system. Most of them can be accessed on your phone and on a computer, and I'd strongly recommend that you chose one of those. I use one with the ridiculous name of Toodledo. Do you want me to write that down for you?

C: Sure.

P: You don't need to use that one. If you want to do some research and find a different one, that's fine. Just be sure it can prioritize items, list deadlines, make multiple separate to-do lists, and be accessed on your phone and your computer. So once you've chosen one, access it on your computer. Then take all the post-its and enter them all into one big list. If there are any deadlines for any of the items, enter those in too.

C: Okay.

P: Then install the app and be sure you can access the list on your phone. That way if you are out and about, you can add things to your list right away when you are thinking of them.

C: Got it.

P: Does that sound doable?

C: Yes, I think I can do that. If I have any trouble, I'll ask my sister; she's a whiz with computers.

P: Sounds good. If you want extra credit, go through the list and prioritize the items. Only things that need to be done within the next couple of days should be in the highest priority category. You might also want to put make more than one list, such as work and home, but don't make it too complicated, okay?

C: Okay, will do.

P: The main thing is choosing a system and getting everything in there. We can work together next time on prioritizing.

Next session:

P: How did things go with the to-do list?

C: I entered in everything from all the post-its that were floating around. Everyone at work was shocked that the post-its were all gone! Once I got them all on the list, it was much easier to prioritize them. I also realized that a bunch of the post-its were about stuff that I wanted to get done over the summer, so I put those on a separate list and it helped a lot to get them off the main list.

P: Wow—I'm really impressed with the progress that you made on this!

C: Thanks. I did this all yesterday, so I don't know how it will go yet.

P: Well, you've got a great start. So the main point is to be sure to enter things in when they come up, along with their priorities and due dates, so you don't lose track of them. It's also helpful to have the list, because if you have a spare 10 minutes, you can scan the list for something that can be done in a brief amount of time and get it over with.

C: Sure, that makes sense.

P: So let me know how things are going with this next week. We can problem-solve like we did with the calendar.

As with calendars, choose between either an electronic or paper task list. Clara needed a flexible system that could accommodate many tasks with varying deadlines, so an electronic list was preferable for her. Troy only needs to track a few personal tasks at a time, so a small paper list that he keeps with him works fine. There are multiple apps available for keeping track of tasks, otherwise known as to-do lists. Be flexible, because different work settings will need different methods of tracking tasks. For example, a supervisor with ADHD may need to buy project management software so the team can work together to track tasks and deadlines. Others may find spreadsheets helpful for tracking certain kinds of tasks. Many experts recommend that the client purchase a small notebook to use to keep track of to-do items and write to-do lists in. This is a good system for many clients, but it can become unwieldy if the client has a long list, as Clara does. Once a system is chosen, the client needs to develop new habits to enter in tasks and check the list regularly.

Prioritizing the task list is essential. Otherwise, all the tasks will seem essential, then the list will seem long and overwhelming, and your client will procrastinate again. Electronic task lists are easy to reprioritize, which can be helpful if a lot of tasks need to be tracked. If needed, help the client develop a priority system.

It is important that clients look at their task lists every day (Sprich et al., 2012). There is a tendency to get all excited about making a task list but then never check it again in the future, so it is not much use (Sprich et al., 2012). Note that this may have started with Clara, since she put together the task list in one burst of effort—a typical way of operating for individuals with ADHD. So the psychotherapist will need to carefully monitor her use of the task list and help her problem-solve so that it can be used most effectively.

Because many people with ADHD have problems with working memory, using lists effectively is especially important. Other types of lists and notes that can be helpful:

- Take extensive notes during class or meetings to keep track of information, due dates, and so on.
- When trying to work out plans, priorities, or timetables, write them down.
- Make a list when doing any shopping.
- Keep a notepad in a pocket or purse to write down information that is easily forgotten (Murphy, 2005).

EMAIL, TEXT MESSAGES, AND PHONE CALLS

Psychotherapist: What does your email look like?

Clara: I have two accounts, one for work and one for home. Both of them have over 1,000 emails in them.

P: Do you ever lose track of important emails?

C: All the time. My family gets mad at me because sometimes I don't get back to them about things they ask me on email, then they have to call me to get the answer. I missed out on signing up for the flexible medical spending plan at work because the email just moved to the second page and I forgot about it. My husband explained how much money we were losing and I felt terrible.

Many adults with ADHD struggle with keeping track of and responding to email, text messages, and phone calls. An individual may have difficulties in none of these areas, one, or more. So check in with your client:

- How are you doing with keeping track of phone messages? Do you return calls in a timely fashion? Are you deleting the old messages? Are you keeping track of information from the phone messages?
- Do you have any problems with responding to text messages in a timely fashion? Are you losing track of text messages?
- How are you doing with email? How many messages are in your inbox? How do you keep track of important emails? Are you keeping track of important information, events, and things to do from the emails?

You may find that the client is not integrating calendar and to-do list usage with these incoming messages. Problem-solve these issues. Consider the following goals:

- Delete all phone messages in a timely manner, at least once a week.
- Transfer information from email, phone messages, and text messages to the calendar and to-do list daily.
- Return calls and text messages within one day, whenever possible.
- Keep only emails that require a response or attention or have not yet been read today in the inbox. Any email the client might want later should be saved in the archive. Tell clients not to bother with elaborate email filing systems—use search functions to find old email instead—and to unsubscribe from as many email lists as possible.
- Start a second email address for important email from friends and family. This is helpful if the client is overwhelmed with unimportant email that should nonetheless be saved. Let all the receipts, less important listservs, and so on go to the first email address.
- Do not check email, phone calls, and texts all day; it is too distracting. Turn off notifications of new messages. Close out email tabs on the computer browser because they are too distracting. Check for messages only during intentional breaks from other work and be ready to respond to them then.

PAPERWORK

Psychotherapist: How is your personal paperwork organized?

Clara: On my desk there are piles of paperwork. I try to sort it out every once in a while, but then I get overwhelmed and stop again.

P: How does this feel?

C: I hate it. Every time I look at these piles, I feel guilty and bad about myself. I wonder: why can't I get this under control like everyone else? The mess makes me feel anxious and out of control every time I see it. And I can't find important documents when I need them without spending all kinds of time digging through the piles.

P: That sounds stressful. Sounds like you could do with some help with this.

C: I hired an organizer once. She set up color-coded files for me, but I never use them.

P: I understand why you are struggling with this. Paperwork and filing does not come easily to people with ADHD. The best system for anyone with ADHD is a simple system that is easy to maintain. It is also important to have a routine for dealing with paperwork. I recommend that we think about one day per week that you can set aside a little time to do your paperwork. What day would work best for you?

C: I could do this on Sunday before I do grading.

P: That sounds good. So let's work on setting up a routine for the next week. It's not so important how much you accomplish at first; it's more important that you work on it regularly. That way, it will all get done eventually. Does that make sense?

C: Sure.

Typically, individuals with ADHD wrestle with paperwork. As with other projects, they get excited at first about solving the problem with a new organizational system but then lose enthusiasm after a few days or weeks, leaving paperwork only partially organized. Here are some key suggestions to pass along:

- Keep the filing system as simple as possible and do not spend more time on organizing than is saved by being organized (Tuckman, 2007). A simple, easily implemented system is better than an optimal system.
- Keep and file only the most important items and throw everything else away (Safren, Perlman, et al., 2005) so that clutter does not build up.
- Designate a central location for incoming bills, paperwork, receipts, and so on—maybe a basket, tray, or even a corner of a desk (Safren, Perlman, et al., 2005).
- Set up recurring automatic online bill payments; this will help reduce financial disorganization (Murphy, 2005).
- Choose one time per week to regularly work on paperwork.

The following is a list of types of paperwork and some suggested solutions:

- Permanent
  - Examples: Education records (diploma, transcripts), employment records, family health records, mortgage contract, real estate deed and title, birth certificates, marriage licenses, divorce decrees, passports, military service and discharge records, investment statements, social security card, adoption papers, advance directives, death certificates for immediate relatives, citizenship papers, powers of attorney, stock and bond certificates, wills

    - Storage solution: Keep in alphabetized file folders at home. Ideally, some of this should be kept in a fireproof box at home or in a safety deposit box.
- Should be kept over one year, until replaced or updated
    - Examples: Appliance warranties and service contracts, other contracts (e.g., loans, employment, leases), health and other insurance benefit and policy information, pet records (e.g., microchip number, vaccinations), receipts for items under warranty, vehicle title and purchase contract
    - Storage solution: Alphabetized file folders at home
- Save for taxes
    - Examples: Property tax records, charitable deduction receipts, W-2s
    - Storage solution: As they come in, put these items into a folder labeled Income Taxes [current year]. Put tax returns in this folder when completed. Start a new folder each year.
- Short-term
    - Examples: Bank statements, credit card statements, bills, receipts
    - Storage solution: Save these items in an accordion folder prelabeled with the months. Shred as much of this as possible. If the client owns a business, have the client talk to an accountant about tracking paperwork for the business.

If a client is really struggling with piles of paperwork, you could have him or her bring in a pile to the session to work on together. Consider initially sorting the paperwork into three piles: File, Action Needed, and Trash (Solanto, 2011), then help the client determine how to move forward from there. Inform the client that office supply stores generally offer secure shredding services if there are too many documents to shred at home.

MANAGING MULTISTEP PROJECTS

Psychotherapist: Do you have any larger projects you've been meaning to do?

Clara: I've been meaning to clean out my walk-in closet for months, but it's a wreck. I just keep the door closed. My husband doesn't even like to look in there.

P: What happens when you try to sort it out?

C: I just have to do the whole thing all at once or I'll never finish it. It takes hours. Then the clothes I'm going to donate to charity sit around the house in bags for weeks until my husband gets tired of looking at them and donates them himself. He gets mad at me for not finishing the job, but I keep procrastinating.

P: This pattern of procrastinating on large projects is typical of ADHD. Also, doing almost the entire project in one big burst of effort is typical as well. A lot of people with ADHD will procrastinate indefinitely on projects that can't be done in one big burst. Then they have difficulties winding up the last details of the project, like you did with donating the clothes.

C: That's totally me.

P: Okay, let's think about this closet project and see if we can work out a plan. Can we use it to practice working on a project in pieces, rather than in one big burst?

C: Yes, I really need to learn to do that.

P: Let's start with making a list of all the tasks that go into cleaning out the closet. Let's also try to figure out how to do it without making a mess that irritates your husband. (Hands pad to Clara.)

C: Okay, I need to sort out the shoes, the scarves, the jewelry, the clothes, other stuff I have in there . . . I have to take the donations in.

P: How about next weekend you sort out only one or two categories, put what you are going to donate in bags, then put the bags in your car trunk so they aren't in your husband's way? Drop off the bags at charity when you are out driving around. I know you have a lot to do with school at this time of year, so let's not take on the whole thing at once—that would be too time-consuming. But you can still do part and feel that you're making progress. How does that sound?

C: Good. I'll sort out only the clothes next week and leave the rest for later.

P: Okay, let's check in on how this goes next week. Remember the general principle—if you haven't worn it in a year, get rid of it, no matter how expensive it was.

C: I was thinking of taking the expensive things to a resale shop.

P: So what would be a good way to manage this?

C: I'll start a box for things to go to resale, and once I'm done with the whole project, I'll take that in.

P: Sounds like a great idea.

I always tell clients that "planning out the project is always the first step in getting it done." So break down a larger task into smaller steps, as Clara and the psychotherapist do in the example. If there is a due date, work up a timetable for the project with these steps allocated to weeks or days leading up to the due date. Be sure each step feels doable within the client's attention span; if it is not, break it down further. Remember: "If you're having trouble getting started, then the first step is too big" (Solanto, 2011, p. 111). Other tips to help the client with long-term projects include (National Resource Center on AD/HD, 2003; Tucker, 2007):

- Use positive self-talk to reward self for completing each step.
- Set up regular meetings with others—boss, spouse, coworkers, faculty advisors—to enhance accountability for keeping on schedule

KEY POINTS

- Carefully assess which problem is most pertinent for your client with ADHD today. Your client will be most motivated to work on this.
- Or start with basic skills such as getting regular meals and sleep or effective use of calendars and task lists.
- Educate the client about effective habit formation.
- Take a collaborative and encouraging stance.

12

Comorbid Conditions, Emotional Distress, and Dysfunctional Cognitions

Even though at least 70% of adults with ADHD have at least one comorbid disorder (Knouse & Safren, 2011), most clinical trials exclude patients who have both ADHD and comorbid mental health disorders (Sobanski, Paslakis, Schredl, Daffner, & Alm, 2013). Thus treatment recommendations for this highly comorbid population are based primarily on clinical experience rather than outcome data. Since depression, anxiety, and substance abuse are the most common comorbidities (Ramsay, 2010b), those are the focus of this chapter.

Why are people with ADHD more likely to have anxiety and depression? Perhaps there is shared genetic vulnerability. Perhaps certain environmental risk factors increase both the risk of ADHD and of anxiety or depression. Plus, the stresses of living with ADHD make people feel anxious and depressed. Most likely, it is a combination of these reasons (Turgay et al., 2012).

ADDRESS NEGATIVE COGNITIONS ABOUT SELF

"ADHD is not caused by maladaptive cognitions" (Ramsay, 2010a, p. 40). However, adults with ADHD have more negative automatic thoughts, even when they are not depressed (Mitchell, Benson, Knouse, Kimbrel, & Anastopoulos, 2013). These negative cognitions probably stem from their own reactions to their difficulties and from the feedback that parents or teachers have given in the past (Mitchell, Benson, et al., 2013). The experience of living with ADHD has a negative impact on self-esteem, hope for the future, and beliefs about one's abilities, leading to dysfunctional negative cognitions (Ramsay, 2010a). These negative beliefs are often maintained by procrastination, avoidance, and executive functioning deficits (Ramsay, 2010a). These cognitions may be especially problematic for adults who were not diagnosed with ADHD during childhood and who have long attributed their difficulties to personal failings. Examples of these negative cognitions include (Knouse & Safren, 2011; Ramsay & Rostain, 2005; Ramsay & Rostain, 2008b; Ramsay, 2010a; Safren, Perlman, Sprich, & Otto, 2005, Solanto, 2011):

- "I never do anything right."
- "I can't handle normal responsibilities."
- "I let myself down."
- "I am too inept to handle the basic demands of life."
- "Everything in my life is a mess and will never get better."
- "My life will always be chaotic and in turmoil."
- "I'm careless and am going to do this wrong."
- "This is going to take forever."
- "I'm lazy."
- "I'm stupid."
- "I'm a failure."
- "I'm inadequate."
- "I'm an imposter, a fraud."
- "I'm a bad, flawed person."
- "I'm unmotivated."
- "My life is out of control."
- "I haven't fulfilled my potential."
- "I'm an underachiever."
- "Everyone else can do it. Why can't I?"

These negative cognitions lead to increased self-criticism, emotional distress and avoidance (Ramsay & Rostain, 2008b). The belief that they need to do things in the same manner that others do leads to continued frustration and ineffective coping (Ramsay & Rostain, 2008b).

Pessimism and an expectation of repeated and continued failures is a prominent theme in the aforementioned beliefs. Research has shown that psychoeducation focusing on biological explanations decreases blame but tends to increase pessimism (Kvaale et al., 2013). Reiterating that ADHD can be effectively treated and emphasizing the client's own ability to work on successful implementation of skills will help decrease pessimism.

Negative self-esteem is another common theme in the stated beliefs. Related themes in these beliefs include self-mistrust, incompetence, and instability (Ramsay & Rostain, 2008a). A literature review found consistent evidence across multiple studies that decreased self-esteem is common in adults with ADHD (Cook, Knight, Hume, & Qureshi, 2014). Increased self-efficacy and life functioning due to skills acquisition should have a positive effect on self-esteem.

Examine these cognitions as you would with any other client. As usual, orient the client to the idea of maladaptive automatic thoughts and the importance of paying attention to, monitoring, and examining them. You might want to share a list of thinking errors (many are readily available online or in other books about cognitive therapy that you may possess, or you can use the ones in Safren,

Perlman, et al., 2005, p. 95, or in Ramsay & Rostain, 2015, p. 74). Many psychotherapists like to use a thought record as a tool for structuring this examination of cognitions (many versions of this available online, in other books, or in Safren, Perlman, et al., 2005, p. 101). On the other hand, you may have a strong hunch that your client would find written homework to be tedious or boring, which would contribute to it not being done, and additional feelings of failure. In that case, discuss the issues thoroughly during the session instead, and ask the client to practice substituting more helpful cognitions between sessions.

ADDRESS MALADAPTIVE POSITIVE COGNITIONS

Psychotherapist: How is your graduate level class going?

Clara: Great.

P: I seem to remember that you said that you have a final paper in this class? How is that going?

C: I haven't started it yet, but I have plenty of time to get it done.

P: When exactly is that paper due?

C: It's due in about a month.

P: Can you remind me what is involved in this final paper?

C: I'm writing it about high-functioning autistic children in the science classroom. I'm really excited about this, because I don't know that much about autistic children yet. I'm looking forward to learning more about it.

P: It sounds like you need to do a lot of library research and reading before you can start writing this paper. Have you started that at all?

C: No, but I have still have lots of time.

P: Let's think about that. I know you often talk to me about how much time you have to spend on grading and preparing for class. How much time in a week do you devote to this class that you are taking?

C: I usually fit in about three or four hours on Sunday afternoon to work on the class.

P: So let's think about what's involved in writing this paper. How long do you think it would take to do the literature search and find the articles and books that you need?

C: I would say I could do it in one or two hours. Plus, I might need to go to the library to pick up the books.

P: How long do you think it would take you to read those articles and books?

C: I am not sure, but the instructor said that we need to have at least eight references.

P: I have read a lot of those kinds of articles. I know they are not always easy to get through. I would say it would take at least half an hour per article, if not more. What do you think?

C: That's probably about right.

P: Okay, we've already gotten at least six hours of work just to prepare to write the paper. How long do you think it would take to write the paper?

C: I can write really fast under pressure. This is supposed to be a 10-page paper. I think I could write it in about eight hours.

P: In the past you've always done everything at the last minute, which has worked out for you okay. However, you've told me many times that you've often thought you could do better work if you allowed yourself more time. How about trying that this time?

C: Okay, I think that would be a good idea.

P: So you're telling me that you got at least 14 hours of work to do this paper. You told me before that you don't want to ask for an extension at the last minute again. We've talked in the past about how you often have a tendency to underestimate how long projects will take. So I'm guessing that it's more realistic to multiply your time estimate by 2. So, let's say that this paper is likely to take 30 hours of work. Does that sound reasonable given your past experience?

C: That sounds like a lot, but you're probably right.

P: So if it takes 30 hours to do this paper, and you have four weeks left, you'll need to spend somewhere around 7 to 8 hours per week on it from now on, until it is due, in order to get it done.

C: Wow. It sounds like I don't have a lot of time to do it after all.

P: Okay, here's a pad and a pen. Let's work on a timetable of you what you will do each week in order to get this paper done on time.

Knouse and Mitchell (2015) wisely point out that maladaptive positive cognitions often maintain dysfunctional behavior in adults with ADHD. The maladaptive positive cognitions maintain self-esteem and self-image, as well as reduce aversive emotions in the short term. Thus the avoidant behavior is maintained, and improved compensatory skills are not developed. Clara verbalizes two maladaptive positive cognitions: "I have still have lots of time" and "I can write really fast under pressure." As the example illustrates, she does not actually have "lots of time" left. Her past experience shows that she often needs to ask for extensions at the last minute. Plus, she knows that if she did not write the paper in such a rush, it would be a much better paper. Yet these maladaptive positive cognitions maintain the avoidance that contributes to dysfunctional results. The psychotherapist helps Clara re-examine these maladaptive positive cognitions, and they begin to work on compensatory skills—planning a timetable of tasks. I strongly recommend that you read Knouse and Mitchell's (2015) article, which contains much clinical wisdom and helpful advice.

SUSCEPTIBILITY TO STRESS

Adults with ADHD feel more stress and have more stressors (Hirvikoski, Lindholm, Nordenström, Nordström, & Lajic, 2009). This stress is associated with increased depression and anxiety (Hirvikoski et al., 2009). Why?

- More life stressors occur due to impulsiveness or lack of foresight and planning.
- They have ineffective coping skills due to executive functioning deficits.
- Emotional dysregulation leads to increased perception of stress.
- They have a heightened psychological reaction to stress (Lackschewitz, Hüther, & Kröner-Herwig, 2008).

Provide emotional support and problem-solving to help with stress management. Developing improved coping skills and executive functioning skills will reduce life stressors and enhance emotional well-being.

DEPRESSION

Contemplating the impairments of ADHD can lead to feeling sad and demoralized. When the depression is mild, I recommend treating the ADHD with medication and treating both the ADHD and depression with psychotherapy (McGough, 2014). Antidepressant medications are less effective for mild depression anyway (Arif, Leventhal, Khan, & Brown, 2002; Kirsch et al., 2008). In most cases, as clients improve, they feel encouraged and more positive about their life circumstances, and the mild depression lifts without a need for antidepressants (Kooij et al., 2010).

Major depression complicates the clinical picture and can make it difficult to determine whether ADHD is actually present, since many cognitive symptoms are similar (chapter 3). Depression is especially common in women with ADHD (Ramsay & Rostain, 2008b). A careful clinical interview comparing longitudinal symptoms of depression and ADHD in both educational and work contexts can usually clarify the diagnostic picture. When the client has major depression, consider carefully whether the depression or the ADHD is more impairing (McGough, 2014). If the major depression is significantly impairing, treating it with both antidepressants and psychotherapy can be a wise place to start. Psychotherapy about ADHD can begin immediately as well. Once the depression begins to lift, the client will have more energy and motivation to address ADHD.

ANXIETY, WORRY, RUMINATION, AND PERFECTIONISM

Adults with ADHD may be especially prone to worry, rumination, and negative automatic thoughts (Abramovitch & Schweiger, 2009; Mitchell, Benson, et al., 2013). Clients are distressed about the disorganization and unpredictability in their lives, which leads to anxiety. Because the anxiety is—at least in part—reality based, I recommend initially treating the ADHD with medication and treating both the ADHD and anxiety with psychotherapy (McGough, 2014). Generally, antianxiety medications are not needed, and effective psychotherapy of the ADHD will result in dramatically reduced anxiety. Standard cognitive behavioral techniques can be used to address worry and negative automatic thoughts. Worry is generally future oriented and focuses on anticipating threats (Nolen-Hoeksema, Wisco, & Lyubomirsky, 2008). Once life becomes more manageable and predictable, anxiety improves (Kooij et al., 2010). When clients are reluctant to give up worrying, explore whether the associated distress has helped them get motivated and stop procrastinating (Ramsay & Rostain, 2008b). A minority of clients may need medication for anxiety.

Rumination is typically triggered by emotional distress or a distressing event (Smith & Alloy, 2008). Ruminative thoughts focus on the past and themes of self-worth, meaning, and loss (Nolen-Hoeksema et al., 2008). When ruminating, the individual repetitively and passively focuses on the causes, consequences, and symptoms of the distress (Nolen-Hoeksema et al., 2008). So rumination has a prominent circular quality, with the same upsetting thoughts being repeated over and over in the same way. Rumination has a strong connection to both anxiety and depression (Smith & Alloy, 2008) and is passive, rather than focusing on active problem-solving (Nolen-Hoeksema et al., 2008).

Individuals with ADHD seem to be particularly prone to rumination, possibly because of cognitive differences, such as their tendency to hyperfocus and to be distracted by their own thoughts when working on tasks. To treat rumination, first provide psychoeducation and examine the effects of rumination on the client:

- Educate the client to distinguish between rumination and reflection/contemplation.
- Explore whether there is an underlying unexamined belief that rumination is helpful.
- Explore the relationships between rumination, depression, and anxiety.
- Recognize that rumination exacerbates and prolongs distress and can trigger depressive episodes.
- Normalize the client's struggle by providing education that rumination is common among people with depression and/or anxiety.
- Recognize that time and energy is spent on ruminating instead of coping and problem-solving.

Next encourage the client to work on identifying rumination when it is occurring and assist with self-talk to interrupt the rumination process ("I've gone through these thoughts hundreds of times exactly the same way; I don't need to do this again"). Encourage the client to refocus cognitively on neutral or positive activities that are engrossing, distracting, and/or uplifting (Nolen-Hoeksema et al., 2008). These can be anything that works for the client—perhaps a hobby, physical activity, reading, watching TV, or talking with a friend or relative. Later, it may be helpful to examine the maladaptive content of ruminations in psychotherapy (Nolen-Hoeksema, et al., 2008).

Perfectionism is often present and has been found in one study to be—by far—the most common cognitive distortion among adults with ADHD (Strohmeier, Rosenfeld, DiTomasso, & Ramsay, 2016). Perfectionism may have a functional purpose of encouraging the client to check and recheck work—which can be adaptive, because individuals with ADHD are error-prone. However, perfectionism can cause them to waste time and feel miserable about their mistakes. Perfectionism may also contribute to procrastination, because the individual is waiting for "the right time" to get started on a task (Strohmeier et al., 2016). Here are some common perfectionistic cognitions among individuals with ADHD:

- "I should be able to work at top efficiency for the entire day."
- "This project needs to be done without any errors in order for it to be acceptable."
- "No one else makes any errors. Why do I make them all the time?"

Often clients with ADHD have an unrealistically positive view of how efficient and accurate others' work is. They think of coworkers as not making errors at all and then expect that they must reach this level of perfection to perform adequately. I often suggest that a reasonable goal is not perfection but instead improving one's accuracy and work skills to an average level.

SUBSTANCE ABUSE

Substance abuse is common in individuals with ADHD. Substances can be used for the following reasons:

- Self-medication relieves ADHD symptoms such as restlessness, inattention, impulsivity, and sleep problems (Kooij et al., 2010).
- Substance use is considered novel and exciting (Kooij et al., 2010).
- Getting drunk or high helps the client avoid emotional distress.

Ask about the benefits of substance use (Ramsay & Rostain, 2008b). Once substance abuse starts, it generally becomes a self-sustaining and separate problem needing targeted interventions. Adults with ADHD often take twice as long to achieve remission from substance abuse (Wilens, 2011).

Expert opinions differ about whether it is appropriate to prescribe stimulants for a client with ADHD who abuses substances (Mariani & Levin, 2007). Experts recommend that drug or alcohol abuse should be targeted first as the primary disorder, but treating ADHD in conjunction with the substance use disorder is also a possibility when there is good treatment compliance (Kooij et al., 2010). In some cases, it is wise to encourage the client to begin substance abuse treatment or self-help groups, and show a commitment to working on abstinence, prior to prescribing any medications. More severe addictions may require residential treatment (Wilens, 2004).

Substance abuse clients can abuse stimulants. The doses of stimulants prescribed for ADHD do not activate opioid receptors in the brain, but higher doses do, and are more addicting (Biederman, 2016). Some individuals will crush stimulant tablets and snort them for a high. If the client has a history of abusing or selling stimulant medication, treat with atomoxetine (Mariani & Levin, 2007) and/or psychotherapy. Other medications are off-label and are not significantly effective for treating ADHD (Coghill, 2013; Faraone & Glatt, 2010; Volkow & Swanson, 2013).

Each client's situation must be examined on an individualized basis for likelihood of continued adherence to mental health and substance abuse treatment before medication is prescribed. If a client has not abused stimulant medication, shows dedication to abstinence, and demonstrates good compliance with substance abuse treatment, stimulant medication may be appropriate. Medicine can improve concentration during substance abuse treatment and facilitate learning new coping skills. Extended-release stimulants or atomoxetine are strongly recommended, rather than short-acting stimulants (Mariani & Levin, 2007). For additional input on monitoring and treating the client with both ADHD and substance abuse, see Upadhyaya (2007).

Diversion, which means giving or selling prescribed medication to someone else, sometimes happens with stimulant medication (Upadhyaya, 2007). Among college students, some of this diverted ADHD medication is used by individuals without ADHD to focus when studying, but more of it may be "snorted" as a recreational drug (Barrett, Darredeau, Bordy, & Pihl, 2005). McGough (2014) recommends counseling the client not to sell or share medication, keeping careful medication records, and noting any patterns of lost prescriptions or seeking additional prescriptions.

KEY POINTS

- Check out the Recommended Reading and Resources section of this book for further reading about effective psychotherapy for ADHD.
- Negative cognitions about self are nearly universal among adults with ADHD due to negative feedback and life experiences.
- Maladaptive positive cognitions can be present as well and reinforce procrastination and poor executive functioning skills.

- Adults with ADHD feel more stressed and have more stressors. Adaptive functioning skills help considerably.
- Mild depression and anxiety can often be treated with psychotherapy alone when ADHD is being effectively treated with psychotherapy and medications.
- Substance abuse clients must be carefully evaluated on an individual basis to determine whether stimulant medications will be used as prescribed.

13

Medications

Clara: When the kids turn in their lab write-ups in, I tend to procrastinate on grading. I get distracted and putter around the house, binge-watching TV, or taking my dog for a walk instead of sitting down and focusing on the work. Then I get angry and frustrated with myself and ask myself why I can't just get it done like everyone else.

Psychotherapist: You can't get it done like everyone else because your brain tends to function in a different way. This is where medication can really help. The medication is likely to help your concentration a lot during challenging tasks like grading. Also, it helps reduce both your own distracting thoughts and your susceptibility to external distractions.

An understanding of the benefits of medication treatment for ADHD is helpful for clients and facilitates collaboration with psychiatrists and other prescribers.

NEUROTRANSMITTERS AND ADHD

The *dopamine deficit theory* of ADHD hypothesizes that there is a deficit or dysregulation of dopamine in the brains of individuals with ADHD, which causes their affective, cognitive, and behavioral difficulties (Bush, 2010; Swanson et al., 2007). Dopamine is a *neurochemical*, in other words, a chemical that nerve cells use to communicate with each other. Stimulant medication increases dopamine release in the synapses between neurons (Aguiar, Eubig, & Schantz, 2010), thus increasing the amount of active dopamine in the brain.

How other neurotransmitters are involved in ADHD is not yet clear (Bush, 2010), but norepinephrine does appear to be involved (Solanto, 2002). Interestingly, the other medication that has been FDA approved for treating ADHD is Strattera (atomoxetine), which is a norepinephrine reuptake inhibitor.

STIMULANT MEDICATIONS

Psychotherapy is helpful for organizational skills but leaves the client with continued cognitive difficulties. Stimulant medications significantly help with these cognitive problems and stimulants are currently considered the most scientifically validated treatment of ADHD (Ramsay, 2010b; see chapter 9). All current practice guidelines for treatment of ADHD recommend a trial of stimulant medication (Gibbins & Weiss, 2007). Stimulant medications are significantly more effective than non-stimulants in treating ADHD symptoms (Faraone & Glatt, 2010; Moriyama, Polanczyk, Terzi, Faria, & Rohde, 2013; Ramsay, 2010b). Many psychiatrists prefer extended-release stimulants because:

- There is a reduced potential for abuse (Hammerness, 2013).
- Once-daily medication is easier for clients to remember (Hammerness, 2013), resulting in improved medication adherence (Spencer et al., 2011).

Symptoms improve within an hour of taking the medication, and the beneficial effects last for 6 to 10 hours (Volkow & Swanson, 2013). The effective dose of each medication varies by individual. The most commonly used brand names (generic names in parentheses) for long-acting stimulant medications are:

- Adderall XR (dextroamphetamine/amphetamine)
- Vyvanse (lisdexamfetamine, long-acting formulation)
- Focalin XR (dexmethylphenidate hydrochloride, extended release)
- Concerta (methylphenidate, extended release, same medicine as in Ritalin)

If a short-acting stimulant is prescribed for ADHD, it needs to be taken multiple times during the day in order to be effective all day. So short-acting stimulants are less often prescribed, although they appear to be equally effective (Faraone & Glatt, 2010). Sometimes psychiatrists will prescribe a small dose of a shorter-acting stimulant for the client to take in the afternoon as needed, when the client feels that the morning dose of a long-acting stimulant is wearing off. The following are the brand names for short-acting stimulant medications (generic names in parentheses):

- Ritalin (methylphenidate)
- Dexadrine (dextroamphetamine)
- Adderall (dextroamphetamine/amphetamine)

Over time, there is a possibility that some clients might develop a tolerance to stimulant medication. In other words, the same dose of stimulant medication will be less effective for treating ADHD symptoms than before. Planned drug holidays may be helpful in preventing tolerance (Kolar et al., 2008). However, long-term studies of adults who continue to take stimulant medication have found that the medication continues to be effective and well-tolerated (Fredriksen, Halmøy, Faraone, & Haavik, 2013).

Be aware that currently more than half of stimulant medication prescriptions are written by nonpsychiatrist physicians (Olfson, Blanco, Wang, & Greenhill, 2013). Primary care physicians are rarely extensively trained in assessment and diagnosis of ADHD. At times, stimulants may be prescribed by a primary care physician through young adulthood when the individual has not been evaluated by a mental health professional to determine whether ADHD symptoms remain or have abated.

CONTRAINDICATIONS AND SIDE EFFECTS

Stimulants are well tolerated by clients and have been prescribed safely for decades. Adults who do not have preexisting substance abuse problems and who are given stimulants to treat their ADHD are *not* at increased risk for developing substance use disorders or addiction to stimulants (Barkley, Fischer, Smallish, & Fletcher, 2003; McGough, 2014).

Side effects and adverse effects for stimulant medications can include nervousness, agitation, increased heart rate, elevated blood pressure, insomnia, decreased appetite, dry mouth, headache, nausea, abdominal pain, gastrointestinal upset, dizziness, depression, irritability, and weight loss (Hammerness, 2013; McGough, 2014; Merkel & Kuchibhatla, 2009; Volkow & Swanson, 2013). In very rare cases, psychosis can be an adverse effect of stimulants (Merkel & Kuchibhatla, 2009). Some individuals experience increased irritability or rebound hyperactivity when medications wear off in the late afternoon (McGough, 2014). Some clients experience a "crash" as the medication wears off, but usually the client and the psychiatrist are able to adjust the medications to minimize this phenomenon. Despite this long list of possible side effects, few clients complain about the side effects of stimulants, and most side effects that do occur are manageable through modifying the dose or making minor lifestyle changes.

Large studies have not found increased cardiac mortality among individuals taking stimulant medication, but some concern about cardiac risk remains (McCarthy et al., 2009; McGough, 2014). Psychiatrists assess cardiac risk factors (McGough, 2014) and will order further testing, if needed, before prescribing any medication.

Appetite suppression can occur after taking stimulants, which requires careful attention to the timing of meals and medications. If this is an issue, be sure that the client eats a good breakfast before taking stimulant medication, carefully considers whether to eat lunch—even if not hungry—and eats a good supper when the medication wears off.

Insomnia is a possible side effect, but dosage adjustments can generally alleviate this problem. If your client is having insomnia in response to medication, recommend a discussion with the psychiatrist. However, most adults with ADHD actually find that nighttime sleep is improved when they are taking stimulant medication during the day (Sobanski et al., 2013).

Stimulants can affect anxiety in two ways, and it is not possible to predict how a given client with anxiety is going to react. A few clients feel jittery, which contributes to anxiety. Because they have heard of this side effect, anxious clients may be hesitant to take stimulants. Educate them that many individuals actually have less anxiety on stimulants. Improving distractibility and concentration usually helps people feel less distractible and get things done, thus reducing worry and improving anxiety.

Most psychiatrists minimize the risk of side effects by starting with a very low dose of stimulant and then increasing slowly as tolerated. In conclusion, "in the vast majority of cases, the harm done by not treating ADHD far outweighs the risk of treatment . . . these medicines are generally quite safe" (Merkel, 2010, p. 929).

Some people cannot take stimulants because of medical reasons (Hammerness, 2013; Volkow & Swanson, 2013):

- Prior allergic reactions to similar medications
- Certain medical conditions, including hyperthyroidism, glaucoma, and seizures
- History of psychosis
- History of tics
- History of cardiovascular disease in the client or his or her immediate family
- Any signs of abnormal heart rate or blood pressure (these must be evaluated medically first)
- Client is taking a medication that should not be prescribed with a stimulant (includes MAO inhibitors)
- Epilepsy (stimulants can lower the seizure threshold; Nutt et al., 2007)

Whether to take stimulants when pregnant remains an area of uncertainty. There is some evidence that stimulants cross the placenta in animal studies, and they are probably in breast milk as well (McGough, 2014). Currently, there is some evidence of safety during pregnancy but not enough to rule out risk yet. Discontinuation of stimulants during pregnancy for mild to moderate ADHD is recommended because of insufficient information on safety during pregnancy (Nonacs, 2014). If the client has severe ADHD symptoms, which may interfere with daily functioning and affect the pregnancy, the client and her psychiatrist will need to weigh the pros and cons carefully (McGough, 2014; Nonacs, 2014).

ATOMOXETINE (STRATTERA)

Only one nonstimulant medication, atomoxetine (brand name Strattera), has been approved by the FDA for adults with ADHD. While stimulants are immediately effective, atomoxetine takes three to four weeks for maximal improvement (McGough, 2014). Effectiveness data indicates that atomoxetine is definitely helpful for ADHD symptoms, but not as much as stimulant medication (Ramsay,

2010b), and is safe and well tolerated (Surman et al., 2010). One advantage to atomoxetine is that cognitive improvements are constant throughout waking hours, whereas stimulant medication varies in its effectiveness depending on when the dose was taken and whether it is wearing off.

There is some evidence that atomoxetine may help with affective dysregulation, if present (Reimherr et al., 2005). Also, atomoxetine can be helpful when stimulants are not tolerated, when there are comorbid tic or anxiety disorders, or when irritability is a side effect of stimulants (McGough, 2014). Atomoxetine can treat comorbid ADHD and depression (Ding et al., 2014). It is also helpful because there is not the stimulant "crash" that many clients described in the late afternoon (McGough, 2014). Side effects include headache, nausea, dry mouth, drowsiness, and erectile dysfunction but typically subside quickly (McGough, 2014; Ramsay, 2010b).

OTHER NONSTIMULANT MEDICATIONS FOR ADHD

Other nonstimulant medications have been used with ADHD "off-label," but research indicates that these medications are less effective than stimulant medications for treating ADHD (Faraone & Glatt, 2010) and have less evidence supporting their use (Volkow & Swanson, 2013). It is recommended that these medications not be used unless the client does not tolerate stimulants or atomoxetine (McGough, 2014). These medications appear to affect dopamine and/or norepinephrine in the brain to cause some symptom improvement (Coghill, 2013). The following is a list of the nonstimulant medications (Coghill, 2013; Faraone & Glatt, 2010). The generic names are in parentheses.

- Clonidine and guanfacine: These are the generic names for two antihypertensive medications that are FDA approved for treating ADHD in children but not adults
- Provigil (modafinil)
- Wellbutrin (buproprion, also marketed under the trade name Zyban for smoking cessation), an antidepressant
- Tofranil (imipramine) and Norpramin (desipramine): both are tricyclic antidepressants

Some psychiatrists may use a stimulant plus one of these medications if the client does not show sufficient improvement with the stimulant alone (Coghill, 2013).

NONSTIMULANT MEDICATIONS FOR COMORBID CONDITIONS

As was discussed in chapter 3, most adults with ADHD will have comorbid conditions. Sometimes these conditions will be severe enough to consider psychotropic medication. Anxiety and depression will make preexisting problems with attention and concentration worse. However, depression and anxiety often lift when the ADHD is treated sufficiently through psychotherapy and stimulant medication (McGough, 2014). See chapter 12 for further discussion of treatment of ADHD and comorbid depression or anxiety. For further information about when medication is essential, recommended, and optional, see Willer (2014).

MEDICATION ACCEPTANCE AND ADHERENCE

Individuals with ADHD may be reluctant to take medication. In these cases, inquire about the client's concerns about medication. Sometimes these concerns can be addressed through further psychoeducation. Here are some common concerns and suggested responses:

- Concern: "I may become addicted to it." Response: "We've talked about substances, and you don't have a history of any abuse of substances, right? Research has found that there is not a risk of addiction for people who don't have any history of substance abuse."
- Concern: "I might have side effects." Response: "Most people aren't bothered by side effects, but some are. Usually people tell me that any side effects are mild compared to the benefits. Remember, if you stop taking it, the side effects go away. So it's really a cost-benefit analysis. If you decide that you don't like it, you could always try another medication or just stop taking it. It's completely up to you."
- Concern: "I don't want to be dependent on a medication." Response: "You don't have to take stimulant medication all the time if you don't want to. I would just like you to consider it because I know how difficult it is for you to concentrate at times. You have to spend so much energy to get things done. It's not your fault that your brain is organized in this way. I just feel that you deserve some help. I encourage you to try it, or even just have a consultation with a psychiatrist, so you can make the most informed choice. If you don't like it, you don't have to continue to take it."
- Concern: "I don't want to take a medication for the rest of my life. This would be for the rest of my life, wouldn't it?" Response: "Yes, it is true that adult ADHD does not go away. But with the right treatment, most of the symptoms can be managed effectively. Medication is very helpful in this regard. Do you have to take it for a lifetime? It's really up to you. If you find it helpful, you can continue to take it. If your life circumstances are such that you don't feel you need it anymore, you don't need to take it."

Medication adherence can be a problem for adults with ADHD, since their lives tend to be disorganized. Also, some clients prefer to take their medication only when absolutely necessary and skip it on days when they have fewer work or academic responsibilities. Since ADHD medication is taken in the morning, I usually suggest that they pair taking the medication with something that they always do in the morning—perhaps breakfast or brushing their teeth. I suggest that they take the medication *before* they do the other regular morning activity. They might even need to put a little note on the cereal box or by their toothbrush. If they take extra "booster" medication in the afternoon, this medication should be kept in a purse, bag, or backpack that is always with the client. The client will usually notice loss of focus, and that will help with remembering to take the extra medication when needed. For further suggestions on managing medication adherence, see Willer (2014).

WHEN DO PEOPLE WITH ADHD DO WELL WITHOUT MEDICATION?

Some people with ADHD function pretty well without medication. This is an understudied area of research, so little is known, other than what can be gleaned from clinical experience. Adults with ADHD can do well if they have others in their lives to help organize and attend to difficult and boring tasks, such as a spouse, a housekeeper, and/or an executive assistant. If the adult with ADHD has found a career that is interesting, this can be sufficiently motivating to do well. Increased insight and life experience help a person with ADHD work toward long-term goals, despite the inherent difficulty of doing so. Those with milder ADHD symptoms are most likely to be able to cope effectively without medications (Ramsay, 2010b). Nonetheless, these individuals are likely to still struggle with organizational challenges in their personal lives.

KEY POINTS

- Stimulant medication remains the most well-validated and -researched treatment for adult ADHD.
- For clients who cannot tolerate stimulants well, or have medical reasons not to take them, Strattera (atomoxetine) is an FDA-approved alternative.
- If the client cannot take these medications, there are other medicines that may help improve symptoms, although to a significantly lesser extent.

14

Review of Other Treatments for ADHD

Many treatments have been suggested for ADHD over the years. I focus on the most common ones here. Although some of the treatments in this chapter could be labeled "complementary and alternative medicine," I agree with Carroll (2015), who argues that this label is not helpful. Either a treatment is scientifically proven to be effective or it is not, or perhaps more study is needed. Generally, less research has been done regarding these potential treatments in adults than in children.

OMEGA-3 FATTY ACIDS HELP CHILDREN WITH ADHD

In children, daily supplementation of omega-3 fatty acids results in modest symptom improvement after three to four months (Hawkey & Nigg, 2014; McGough, 2014). Conclusion: "There is evidence from well-conducted studies for a small effect" with children who have ADHD (Stevenson et al., 2014, p. 416).

While there is strong evidence that omega-3 supplementation improves ADHD symptoms in children, the degree of improvement is much smaller than with stimulant medications (Bloch & Qawasmi, 2011; Sonuga-Barke et al., 2013). Therefore, omega-3 fatty acid supplementation should be considered *an adjunctive treatment rather than a primary treatment* (Bloch & Qawasmi, 2011; Ramsay, 2010b). However, in cases where medication is refused or contraindicated, omega-3 fatty acid supplementation is encouraged as one part of treatment (Bloch & Qawasmi, 2011).

It remains unproven whether omega-3 fatty acid supplementation is an effective adjunctive treatment for adults with ADHD. However, it is known that our current American diet does not typically supply enough omega-3 fatty acids (Nigg, 2012). If you wish to discuss these findings with your client, educate the client that sufficient omega-3 intake is necessary for general neurological health and cognitive functioning (Dyall & Michael-Titus, 2008; Mazza, Pomponi, Janiri, Bria, & Mazza, 2007). Be sure to caution the client that supplementation is *not* an effective stand-alone treatment for ADHD (Sonuga-Barke, 2015), but it may help with mild symptom improvement over time, especially if depression is present (Ramsay, 2010b). Appendix 3 provides a handout that you can give to your clients about omega-3 fatty acid supplementation.

OTHER DIETS OR SUPPLEMENTS: NOT PROVEN EFFECTIVE

No additional dietary interventions have been proven to be helpful for treating ADHD. Numerous dietary changes have been proposed to improve ADHD symptoms. The following is a brief list of these and the related scientific evidence:

- *Artificial food color elimination*: Controversy has raged for years about whether artificial food colors affect ADHD symptoms. Recent research suggests that a subgroup of children with ADHD shows significant symptom improvement when eating a diet free of artificial food colors (Nigg et al., 2012; Sonuga-Barke et al., 2013; Stevens, Kuczek, Burgess, Hurt, & Arnold, 2010). Conclusion: This is "a potentially valuable treatment" for children with ADHD, but the degree of effectiveness and for whom it is effective are unknown (Stevenson et al., 2014, p. 416). Further research is needed before any recommendations can be definitively made (Stevenson et al., 2014). Also, any improvement that might occur is likely to be small (Ramsay, 2010b). Due to lack of evidence of effectiveness, elimination of artificial food colorings from diets of adults with ADHD cannot be recommended at this time (Ramsay, 2010b).
- *Vitamin and mineral supplementation*: There is some promising preliminary evidence that vitamin and mineral supplementation could be helpful for adults with ADHD (Rucklidge, Frampton, Gorman, & Boggis, 2014), but this research has not progressed to the point where any specific recommendations can be made for treatment.
- *Caffeine*: This does not contribute to ADHD symptoms in children, and, in fact, since it is a stimulant, caffeine may even help ADHD symptoms (Nigg, 2012).
- *Sugar*: Although commonly believed to worsen childhood ADHD, sugar was *not* found to increase ADHD symptoms (Nigg, 2012).
- *Pesticides in food*: Pesticides have been suggested as a possible contributing factor to development of ADHD in childhood that is worthy of further research (Nigg, 2012). However, any connection between current pesticide intake and adult ADHD is unclear.
- *Feingold diet*: Some have proposed that childhood hyperactivity is caused by increased sensitivity to certain foods, including synthetic food colors, synthetic flavors, preservatives, and certain nuts and fruits (McGough, 2014). There is no current evidence that this diet is effective (McGough, 2014).

- *Elimination diet:* Some have proposed that hyperactivity is a reaction to certain foods, including dairy, eggs, nuts, whole wheat products, and citrus. There is no current evidence that this diet is effective (Sonuga-Barke et al., 2013)—plus, it is restrictive and likely to cause nutritional deficiencies (McGough, 2014).
- *Amino acid supplementation:* Any benefits have been found to be short-lived (Ramsay, 2010b).
- *Herbal treatments, including ginseng, ginko biloba and St John's wort:* These have not been shown to be effective (Ramsay, 2010b).

None of these dietary changes or supplements have yet been proven to improve ADHD in children, and they are understudied in adults. However, encouragement of healthy eating and reducing processed foods is recommended for adults with ADHD, who tend to be disorganized and inattentive to good health habits.

COGNITIVE REHABILITATION: CURRENTLY NOT PROVEN EFFECTIVE

Cognitive rehabilitation utilizes computerized training programs to help an individual learn to compensate for cognitive deficits. Cognitive rehabilitation training is very time-consuming. The client attends 30- to 40-minute daily training sessions five days a week for five weeks (Ramsay, 2010b). The cognitive rehabilitation practitioner needs specialized training to administer the protocol and use the software.

There is significant evidence that cognitive rehabilitation can be helpful for adults who have sustained traumatic brain injuries and have related cognitive dysfunction (Cappa et al., 2005; Cicerone et al., 2005; Cicerone et al., 2011). However, rehabilitating an injured brain and training an intact brain with ADHD are different tasks. With ADHD, cognitive training has focused on these four deficits: visual working memory, verbal working memory, response inhibition, and attention (Sonuga-Barke, Brandeis, Holtmann, & Cortese, 2014).

Although some studies have found positive effects of cognitive rehabilitation training on ADHD symptoms in children, a meta-analysis found that these may be due to lack of blind ratings (Sonuga-Barke et al., 2013). It has not been proven yet to be an effective treatment for the cognitive deficits of ADHD in children or adults (Cortese et al., 2015; McGough, 2014; Melby-Lervóg & Hulme, 2013; Rapport, Orban, Kofler, & Friedman, 2013; Sonuga-Barke et al., 2014). More research in this area is needed.

NEUROFEEDBACK: EFFECTIVENESS REMAINS CONTROVERSIAL

Neurofeedback is a specialized form of biofeedback. The neurofeedback professional gathers EEG data from readings of electrical activity at multiple points in a specialized cap fitted to the client's head. First, the client's typical EEG patterns are measured, and these readings are interpreted through specialized computer programs and compared to a population standard. The treatment involves the client playing various computer "games," which the client is winning when the brain waves are modifying in the desired direction (S. Effarah, personal communication, 2015; Ramsay, 2010b). Neurofeedback is time consuming, often taking 30 to 40 sessions or more to achieve benefits (Arns, Heinrich, & Strehl, 2014; McGough, 2014; Ramsay, 2010b). Practitioners of neurofeedback need considerable specialized training and software, as well as expensive equipment.

The goal of neurofeedback treatment is to modify the brain-wave patterns to look more like the patterns of an individual without ADHD by increasing some brain waves while decreasing others. Neurofeedback treatment for ADHD has been highly controversial over the years (Ramsay, 2010b). In the past, neurofeedback practitioners have stated the effectiveness of their treatment before sufficient well-designed studies had been published in support (Ramsay, 2010b).

Nonetheless, recent research studies of neurofeedback have shown symptom improvement in children with improved research design, (Arns et al., 2014; Mayer, Wyckoff, & Strehl, 2013; Ramsay, 2010b). A literature review found six studies that indicated similar benefits to children from neurofeedback and stimulant medication (Arns et al., 2014). One meta-analysis determined that neurofeedback was an effective treatment for ADHD in children (Hodgson, Hutchinson, & Denson, 2012), but another found that neurofeedback was ineffective when there was a placebo control and concluded that positive effects of neurofeedback may be due to lack of blind ratings (Sonuga-Barke et al., 2013). Some placebo control studies found similar improvements in sham neurofeedback and actual neurofeedback groups, although these studies have been criticized for their methodology (Arns et al., 2014).

Thus the debate about the effectiveness of neurofeedback rages on. To address methodological issues, experts in ADHD and neurofeedback are currently collaborating in a large double-blind study, funded by the National Institute of Mental Health, evaluating neurofeedback treatment of children with ADHD; the study is ongoing at the time of writing (Arns et al., 2014; Kerson, 2013). Only pilot study results have been published to date, and they do not support neurofeedback over sham neurofeedback (Arnold et al., 2013), but additional study design refinements are likely, so no firm conclusions can be drawn at this time.

In conclusion, many research questions remain, and adults who receive neurofeedback for ADHD are clearly understudied in the research literature. Prominent researchers consider neurofeedback to be a still unproven treatment for ADHD and do not recommend it (McGough, 2014), or they consider the findings inconclusive at present (Ramsay, 2010b).

MINDFULNESS TRAINING: PROMISING BUT FURTHER RESEARCH NEEDED

Mindfulness training generally has two components: meditation practice and encouraging the client to be more aware of the present moment. There are three main types of meditation practice: cultivating focused attention, cultivating awareness of all internal and external sensations, and cultivating compassion toward self and others—otherwise known as loving-kindness meditation (Ricard, Lutz, & Davidson, 2014). In recent decades, mindfulness training and meditation have been utilized by many innovative cognitive-behavioral approaches. Considerable research documents the benefits of mindfulness training, and many of these benefits could be particularly helpful for ADHD:

- Enhanced ability to regulate and monitor one's own attention, reducing mind wandering
- Enhanced emotional self-regulation, decreased reactivity to stress, and increased emotional equanimity
- Improved ability to self-observe
- Improved self-compassion and decreased self-esteem problems through loving-kindness meditation practice
- Improved persistence
- Improved biological processes conducive to health and resilience to stress
- Decreased depression and rumination
- Activation of the prefrontal cortex (an underactive area in adults who have ADHD)

These emotional and cognitive changes have been documented to occur in adults who have practiced regular meditation (Baer, 2003; Chiesa & Serretti, 2010; Farb, Anderson, & Segal, 2012; Hölzel, et al., 2011; Ricard et al., 2014; Zylowska, Smalley, & Schwartz, 2009). Regular meditation results in changes in brain volume, activity, and connectivity in certain areas, including the default network and frontal areas, which are affected in ADHD (Hölzel et al., 2011; Mitchell, Zylowska, & Kollins, 2015; Ricard et al., 2014). Mindfulness training programs also usually have particularly good retention rates (Baer, 2003). So it is reasonable to speculate that adults with ADHD would see similar benefits.

A program of mindful awareness practice for adults with ADHD is detailed in Zylowska et al. (2009). This program adapts mindfulness and meditation practices to the attention challenges of clients with ADHD by using brief guided meditations—at first 5 minutes and building up to 15 minutes. Walking meditation is offered as an alternative, because many clients with ADHD are restless (Mitchell et al., 2015).

Two pilot studies of this program (Mitchell, McIntyre, et al., 2013; Zylowska et al., 2008), a study of mindfulness-based cognitive therapy (Schoenberg et al., 2014), studies of dialectical behavior therapy treatment (Fleming, McMahon, Moran, Peterson, & Dreessen, 2015; Hirvikoski et al., 2011), and a program of Tai Chi training—which involves mindful movement training (Converse, Ahlers, Travers, & Davidson, 2014)—were all found to show improvements in attention and other measures of ADHD cognition. A recent study showed mindfulness training improvements were comparable to improvements from cognitive-behavioral therapy (Edel, Hölter, Wassink & Juckel, 2014). Future research is likely to examine whether adding mindfulness to cognitive-behavioral therapy protocols results in improved treatment outcomes (Mitchell, McIntyre, et al., 2015).

Basic mindfulness and meditation practices can be easily implemented in the psychotherapy office, but experts recommend that these techniques not be taught by anyone who has not personally practiced meditation and mindfulness. The client must practice regularly and consistently in order to see benefits. Clearly, not all ADHD clients are ready for this intervention, but those who are may see improvements in self-understanding and self-management.

Further research is needed, but this approach appears promising. The only known risk to this treatment is that it could be ineffective. Psychotherapists with adequate knowledge and training could consider using these practices for any client who is interested. Referral to a meditation group may be helpful in encouraging compliance or if the psychotherapist is not experienced with mindfulness practices. Alternatively, Zylowaska's (2012) book, which can be used in a self-guided manner, is described Recommended Reading and Resources section of this book.

COACHING: PROMISING BUT FURTHER RESEARCH NEEDED

Since many psychotherapists have not been trained to recognize or treat adult ADHD, the nascent field of coaching has stepped in to fill this treatment gap. The primary focus of coaching is intensive work on behavior change and skills development, whereas psychotherapists may focus on cognitions and emotions as well as behavior and skills (Knouse, Cooper-Vince, Sprich, & Safren, 2008). Coaches are not trained to address psychiatric comorbidities. Coaches see their role as (Tuttle, Ahmann, & Wright, 2016):

- Egalitarian, nonclinical, and with a personal development focus
- Focused on skills development and implementation
- Available by phone, text, or email between sessions (increased availability provides additional support, accountability, and engagement)
- Able to meet in person, remotely, and in nontraditional settings

Note that coaches are not reimbursed by health insurance, although some flexible spending accounts have been reported to reimburse for coaching services (E. Ahmann, personal communication, 2016). There are not licensure requirements for coaches, and the titles of "coach" or "ADHD coach" are not regulated by state or federal governments, so anyone can legally use these titles.

Coaches may work with clients on their own or in collaboration with psychotherapists. If you would like to collaborate with a coach, the following credentials are commonly found and respected (L. J. Tuttle, personal communication, 2016):

- Certification from the International Coaching Federation (initials after the coach's name would be ACC, PCC, or MCC [Associate, Professional, or Master Certified Coach, respectively])

- Certification from the Center for Credentialing and Education (BCC [Board Certified Coach])
- Certification from the Professional Association of ADHD Coaches (CACP, PCAC, MCAC [Certified ADHD Coach Practitioner, Professional Certified ADHD Coach, or Master Certified ADHD Coach, respectively])

Other coaching credentials are available, and over a dozen separate programs train ADHD coaches, several specifically specialize in ADHD. If you would like to collaborate with a coach, inquire about that individual's training credentials and years of experience working with clients who have ADHD (L. J. Tuttle, personal communication, 2016). Some websites for finding coaches are:

- ADHD Coaches Organization's "Find Your Coach" listing
- Children and Adults with ADHD (CHADD) online professional resource directory
- International Coach Foundation's Coach Referral Service

Research to date reports positive results from coaching adults, mostly university students (Field, Parker, Sawilowsky, & Rolands, 2013; Kubik, 2009; Parker, Hoffman, Sawilowsky, & Rolands, 2011; Tuttle et al., 2016). A recent review identified areas of improvement due to coaching, including well-being, academic performance, and social functioning (Tuttle et al. 2016). Since coaching provides increased accountability and scaffolding, these improvements are expected. These are promising findings, but more randomized trials are necessary before firm conclusions about the effectiveness of coaching can be drawn (Tuttle et al., 2016). Also, whether coaching provides lasting benefits, once the coaching is over, remains unclear.

INEFFECTIVE AND UNPROVEN TREATMENTS

Other potential treatments have been recommended over the years. None of the following have been shown to be effective treatments for ADHD: acupuncture, chiropractic adjustment, interactive metronome training (done by occupational therapists), repetitive transcranial magnetic stimulation, sensory integration training (done by occupational therapists), vision therapy (done by optometrists), massage, mirror feedback, or vestibular and cerebellar exercises (McGough, 2014; Ramsay, 2010b). Some have tried homeopathy, but there is no evidence that homeopathy is ever effective in treating anything at all (McGough, 2014).

KEY POINTS

- *Omega-3 fatty acids* have been well-documented as essential to healthy brain functioning. Plus, there is some evidence that omega-3s may be helpful for individuals with ADHD, especially those who also have depression. Appendix 3 provides a handout for the adult client who is interested in omega-3 supplementation. This should not be considered an effective stand-alone treatment for ADHD.

- *Mindfulness techniques:* While there is limited support for mindfulness interventions at this time, considerable research has documented cognitive and emotional changes in general client populations that would benefit the ADHD client. If you have personal experience with meditating and mindfulness practices, consider incorporating these with ADHD clients who are receptive to this approach, but first read Zylowaska et al. (2009) to learn how to use these methods with ADHD clients.
- *Coaching:* Collaborating with a coach specializing in ADHD could be helpful for clients who need additional structure between sessions and who have the financial resources to afford this assistance. Further research is necessary to document clinical effectiveness and lasting benefits.
- No other dietary changes, supplements, or proposed treatments have sufficient evidence to be recommended for adults with ADHD at the present time.

AFTERWORD: SOME FINAL THOUGHTS

Troy: For a long time, I thought that adults couldn't have ADHD. I knew on some level that something was different about me, but I didn't think that was it. I'm glad Aimee looked all this up online and helped me find you.

Clara: I got therapy for anxiety a couple times before, but it never helped that much. I didn't feel like I made a lot of progress on my issues until I figured out that I had ADHD and sought treatment for it.

UNDERDIAGNOSIS AND LACK OF TREATMENT HAS HIGH SOCIETAL COSTS

Multiple studies have described the costs to society of untreated adult ADHD. These societal costs include (Asherson et al., 2012; Bernfort, Nordfeld, & Persson, 2008; Birnbaum et al., 2005):

- *Expenses of treating comorbid disorders* that tend to arise when ADHD remains untreated.
- *Increased medical care costs* for adults with ADHD because they are accident-prone and engage in risky behavior.
- *More traffic accidents*: Since many adults with ADHD are poor drivers, they contribute to increased traffic accidents, often resulting in bodily injury.
- *Criminal justice costs*: Individuals with ADHD are overrepresented among those who commit crimes and are imprisoned. Of course, this is a small fraction of those people who are diagnosed with ADHD. There are considerable societal costs associated with the criminal justice system, not to mention the suffering of crime victims.

- *Lost economic productivity* because of absenteeism and inefficient work habits.
- *Reduced economic productivity due to undereducation*: Many adults with ADHD are significantly less educated than their peers. They earn less income. All this contributes to reduced productivity in the economy.
- *Reduced household income,* when the household includes an adult with ADHD.

STEREOTYPES PERSIST, ENCOURAGED BY TOO MUCH RESEARCH ON WHITE BOYS

Researchers continue to study too many hyperactive white middle-class preadolescent boys and too few people from any other group who have ADHD (Ramsay & Rostain, 2008a). This contributes to societal stereotypes; many people think of a typical person with ADHD as being a white hyperactive boy.

Women, first- or second-generation immigrants, and ethnic, racial, and cultural minorities are especially likely have undiagnosed ADHD (Rostain, Ramsay. & Waite, 2015; Rothe, 2005; Stevens, Harman, & Kelleher, 2005). There is concern that black children with ADHD are seen as "bad" and punished, whereas white children are seen as having a mental illness and treated (Asherson et al., 2012). ADHD is also generally underdiagnosed in any population with barriers to treatment—such as financial barriers, language barriers, low educational level, or poor access to healthcare (Able, Johnston, Adler, & Swindle, 2007; Rothe, 2005). Diagnosis and treatment of these individuals at a younger age might have helped alleviate their dysfunction considerably (Biederman et al., 2006).

In reality, ADHD crosses all gender and demographic lines. These stereotypes and knowledge gaps help contribute to underdiagnosis of ADHD and lack of treatment. This results in untold suffering and dysfunction among untreated individuals with ADHD.

POOR INFORMATION DISSEMINATION AND STIGMA LEAD TO LACK OF TREATMENT

Effective communication between psychotherapy researchers and psychotherapists who practice in the community has long been a significant problem in mental health (Weisz, Ng, & Bearman, 2014). This problem is especially acute regarding adult ADHD. Many psychotherapists are entirely unaware of the extensive scientific evidence supporting the adult ADHD diagnosis and do not know how to recognize and treat these clients. Only 1 out of 10 adults with ADHD received any treatment for their ADHD in the past year (Kessler et al., 2011). Psychotherapy that does not address ADHD is unlikely to be effective and may even lead to worse self-esteem (Ratey, Greenberg, Bemporad, & Lindem, 1992). Lack of information for the general public remains a problem as well. The media often presents ADHD as a controversial diagnosis, which it is not.

Most mental health professionals do not recognize ADHD in their clients and thus do not treat it (Biederman et al., 2006; Kessler et al., 2005). Among adults with ADHD in treatment for comorbid conditions, three-fourths did not have their ADHD addressed at all (Kessler et al., 2011). Yet it is likely that 1 out of every 5 to 10 psychotherapy clients has ADHD (Asherson, 2013).

Other mental health professionals explicitly reject known ADHD clients. They are stigmatized as "lazy and unmotivated." Professionals have told me that they will not work with ADHD clients because they consider them to be too much trouble because "they run late and they don't follow-up."

ADVANTAGES TO ADHD? UNCLEAR

Troy: My boss says that my ADHD is BS. But he also says that he likes to have me around, because I tend to have "out-of-the-box" ideas. He has no idea that I think these two things are one and the same.

There is a movement among people with autism to embrace their diagnosis and reject the assumption that they are necessarily dysfunctional because of their neurological differences. They refer to people who do not have autism as "neurotypical" and embrace "neurodiversity" as normal and beneficial. Many are applying these ideas to ADHD as well (Armstrong, 2015; Smalley, 2008).

The possible advantages to having an ADHD brain are generally ignored by researchers, with a very few exceptions (e.g., Ramsay, Giwerc, McGrath, & Niemiec, 2016). There is preliminary evidence that a neurodiverse group including two children without ADHD and one with ADHD can be much more successful at problem-solving (Kuester & Zentall, 2011; Zentall, Kuester, & Craig, 2011). Many individuals with ADHD are artists and have other creative pursuits. They feel that their ADHD is related to their creativity. Many individuals with ADHD are self-employed. They say that their ADHD is related to their passion and drive to succeed. ADHD is clearly related to novelty-seeking, which may be an adaptive trait in certain circumstances (Tierney, 2012). It is time to examine these claims (Smalley, 2008). Strengths associated with ADHD may have contributed to the genes for ADHD persisting over time (Bush, 2010).

COMPASSION FOR PEOPLE WITH ADHD

Clara: I feel a lot better about myself now. I understand more about how my own brain works and how it is different from the brains that other people have. This helps me let go of blaming myself and find solutions that work for me. My husband is easier on me now, because I've shared what I've learned with him and he knows that I am trying.

Troy: I always felt like the biggest screw-up ever. Now I know that people like me often have a lot of trouble adjusting when they are young adults, just like I did. So I can cut myself a little slack. After all, I have a job that I like and a loving family, so I figure I'm doing pretty well. I'm working on not being so impulsive and blurting things out, and I've made progress with that. Aimee is happy that I'm working with her and her calendar system. We are getting along much better now.

Since beginning to write this book, I have been working with more clients who have adult ADHD. Adults with ADHD bring their suffering into the psychotherapist's office. Accurately diagnosing ADHD is the first step. Enhancing the client's self-understanding through psychoeducation alleviates much suffering. Effective treatment through medication and skills training improves functioning.

People who have ADHD live in a world that was devised for people who do not have it. Those who do not have ADHD continue to stigmatize those who do. Their criticisms are demoralizing and lead to depression and anxiety, rather than effective coping. A greater understanding of neurodiversity might help everyone become more encouraging and supportive of the efforts of people with ADHD, rather than being so critical of their errors. Anyone who works or lives with a person who has ADHD realizes that, due to fluctuating attention, minor errors are inevitable. It is not helpful to overemphasize these errors.

Some people might argue that Clara does not have ADHD because, over the years, she has learned some ways to compensate. She graduated from college, she makes it to school on time, her students learn a lot from her, and she is happily married. Yet she still experiences frequent daily struggles and emotional pain from her symptoms of ADHD. I would argue that she is just as deserving of our compassion and professional help for her struggles and pain as any other client.

The disorganization, inattention, and impulsiveness of ADHD often bring out negative judgments. Troy has had many interpersonal and work problems over the years, and he struggles with smoking too much marijuana. But he's dedicated to being a good father to his children, a good husband to his wife, and providing for his family. He takes his psychotherapy seriously because he knows that any improvements he can make will help his whole family.

Clara, Troy, and our other clients with ADHD can make dramatic improvements in emotional and adaptive functioning. These improvements will radiate out, positively affecting their relationships with their families, coworkers, students, and others around them. Because they are so used to being judged, our compassion, encouragement, and understanding are especially healing to adults with ADHD.

APPENDIX 1

Psychological Assessment of ADHD

This appendix overviews commonly used psychological tests to assess adult ADHD and provides a recommended assessment protocol. Psychotherapists who are not psychologists may benefit from reading this appendix to learn more about psychological assessment of ADHD.

WHO CAN OBTAIN AND USE PSYCHOLOGICAL TESTING INSTRUMENTS

Some questionnaires can be purchased by anyone but should be used with supervision and consultation by anyone who does not have graduate training in psychological testing. The Barkley questionnaires discussed later in this chapter are in this category.

Other questionnaires are only available to professionals who have graduate training in psychological testing. Generally, these individuals have a doctoral degree in psychology or possibly a master's degree. The companies who publish these questionnaires will not sell them to you if you do not have the necessary qualifications. Commonly used instruments that are limited to use by psychologists include the Behavior Rating Inventory of Executive Function (BRIEF) and the Conners' Adult ADHD Rating Scales (CAARS).

HOW QUESTIONNAIRES CAN HELP WITH ADHD DIAGNOSIS AND TREATMENT

The questionnaires described later in this chapter were, for the most part, devised to be sensitive to ADHD symptoms specifically. The scales of these questionnaires address important issues regarding ADHD, such as self-concept, time management, sluggish cognitive tempo symptoms, and more. These questionnaires are highly sensitive to ADHD symptoms and should detect symptoms if they are present.

Several studies have found much a stronger statistical relationship between an executive functioning (EF) questionnaire (the Barkley Deficits in Executive Functioning Scale, described later in this chapter) and frequent ADHD functional outcomes (such as occupational dysfunction and deviant or antisocial behavior) than traditional neuropsychological EF tests (Barkley & Murphy, 2010). Other researchers agree that self-reported behavior scales are helpful in assessing EF deficits (Biederman et al., 2007). Barkley (2014a) asserts that neuropsychological tests of EF are not complex enough to measure life challenges, which is why most people with ADHD score in the normal range. In other words, he asserts that neuropsychological assessments of EFs are not sufficiently *ecologically valid*. For that reason, he assesses EFs with questionnaires (Barkley & Murphy, 2010). This is a convincing argument.

Questionnaires, such as the ones discussed in this chapter, can be particularly helpful in the following circumstances:

- The psychologist wants use the most sensitive indicators of ADHD symptoms.
- The psychologist wants to understand these particular areas of dysfunction: negative self-concept, emotional dysregulation, hyperactivity, sluggish cognitive tempo, and daily EF problems.

RETROSPECTIVE ASSESSMENT OF CHILDHOOD ADHD SYMPTOMS

If your client did not have a diagnosis of ADHD during childhood, you will want to assess whether childhood ADHD symptoms were present. Two questionnaires are commonly used to obtain retrospective self-reports of childhood symptoms from clients: The Barkley Adult ADHD Rating Scale-IV (BAARS-Childhood), Self-Report: Childhood Symptoms and the Wender Utah Rating Scale (WURS).

The WURS is in the public domain. It has a long version and a commonly used short version. Although it has been used in many studies, the WURS can be challenging to interpret:

- The scale includes questions assessing mood problems, irritability, hot temper, and moodiness (Wender, 1995), which not all adults with ADHD had as children (McGough & Barkley, 2004).
- The scale includes questions assessing significant behavioral problems, low self-esteem, and emotional distress, which not all clients with ADHD had (McGough & Barkley, 2004).
- It may give false positives for dysfunctional personality traits, depression, or childhood anxiety (Hill, Pella, Singh, Jones, & Gouvier, 2009; Mancini, Van Amerigen, Oakman, & Figueiredo, 1999; McCann, Scheele, Ward, & Roy-Byrne, 2000; Wierzbicki, 2005).

If your client reports no history of emotional problems as a child, good relationships with parents, and probable inattentive type ADHD, this questionnaire will not help you determine whether the client had childhood ADHD. These are exactly the individuals whose ADHD is usually missed during childhood. So despite good psychometric properties (Taylor, Deb, & Unwin, 2011), this scale is often not useful in many practice settings. However, it may be more helpful when working with clients who come from high-risk backgrounds.

For these reasons, I recommend use of the BAARS-Childhood. The BAARS-Childhood and the WURS are the only two instruments available to retrospectively assess childhood ADHD, and only the BAARS-Childhood may have the sensitivity to detect past ADHD in most clients. It can be purchased from Guilford Press and then copied and used indefinitely after purchase (list price as of writing is \$160, but discounts are often available). It is two pages long and retrospectively assesses childhood inattention and hyperactivity/impulsivity. The BAARS-Childhood also has an other-report version if a parent or childhood caretaker is available to assist with the evaluation.

CURRENT INATTENTIVENESS, HYPERACTIVITY, AND IMPULSIVITY

Two instruments are commonly used to assess current adulthood inattentiveness, hyperactivity, and impulsivity: the CAARS and the BAARS, Self-Report: Current Symptoms (BAARS-Current). Both have self-report and other-report versions.

The CAARS is highly recommended. The CAARS is actually a family of questionnaires; there are long, short, and screening versions of the questionnaires for the client and for the informant, resulting in six versions of the questionnaire. The CAARS-Self-Report: Long Version is two pages long and has 66 questions; the Short Version is one page long and has 26 questions. It can only be purchased by individuals with graduate training in psychological assessment. A complete kit with all the different versions included can be purchased from Multi-Health Systems for \$379 at the time of writing, but a more affordable option is to purchase the technical manual (\$81) and 25 self-report short or long forms (\$55).

The CAARS is one of the most commonly used instruments for assessing adult ADHD in research and clinical practice (Wasserstein, 2005) and has the best and most thoroughly assessed psychometric properties (Knouse & Safren, 2010; Taylor et al., 2011). In addition to DSM symptoms of ADHD, the CAARS also has a factor-derived scale that assesses Impulsiveness/Emotional Lability and has a scale to assess Problems with Self-Concept. Of note, there is an Inconsistency index validity scale. Be aware that adults who have anxiety, depression, or substance abuse *without ADHD* can score high on the CAARS (Van Voorhees, Hardy, & Kollins, 2011) because of the cognitive symptoms of those disorders.

The BAARS-Current is recommended. The same book from Guilford Press discussed in the previous section includes the BAARS Self-Report: Current Symptoms, which is two pages long and has 27 questions. In addition to DSM symptoms, the BAARS Current Symptoms assesses sluggish cognitive tempo, which can be helpful with certain clients. Note that the current self-report version has considerable overlap with the Adult ADHD Self-Report Scale Symptom Checklist (ASRS). However, unlike the ASRS, norms are available for all four of the symptom clusters assessed (inattention, hyperactive, impulsive, and sluggish cognitive temp), as well as Total ADHD symptoms, so it provides a more fine-grained assessment of symptom severity.

Since the BAARS-Current and CAARS measure somewhat different constructs, they can be administered together if desired. When data is somewhat inconsistent between the two instruments, rely on the data from the CAARS, since it has well-documented excellent psychometric properties, or compare items to determine what types of questions are leading to the discrepancy. Also, the CAARS has norms for the informant versions, and the BAARS-Current does not. Note that neither of these instruments measure EF symptoms. So either questionnaire should always be paired with at least one measure of EF when assessing adult ADHD.

One scale that I did not fully review here is the Brown Attention Deficit Disorder Scales. It has 40 items and five subscales, which combine some DSM symptoms with some EF symptoms: organization/work, attention, energy/effort, mood, and memory (Taylor et al., 2011). Some use it in conjunction with the CAARS (e.g., Wasserstein, 2005), or it can be used as a stand-alone measure that provides coverage of many adult ADHD symptoms.

Be aware that if the client is currently taking stimulant medication, current ADHD symptoms may be somewhat elevated but may drop below the level of clinical significance.

QUESTIONNAIRES FOR EF ASSESSMENT

When assessing EF, two questionnaires are commonly used: Behavior Rating Inventory of Executive Function Adult Version (BRIEF-A) and the Barkley Deficits in Executive Functioning Scale (BDEFS for Adults). Both have self-report and other-report versions.

The BRIEF-A is highly recommended to assess EF deficits in adult ADHD (Adler, Barkley, & Wilens, 2006). This instrument was developed to assess EF in any clinical population, not just ADHD. The BRIEF-A asks about EF in the past month. It is two pages long and has 75 questions. It can only be purchased by individuals with graduate training in psychological assessment. An introductory kit with both versions and a manual included can be purchased from Psychological Assessment Resources, Inc. for $226 at the time of writing. It has excellent psychometric properties (Roth, Lance, Isquith, Fischer, & Giancola, 2013). Adults with ADHD have significantly worse scores on the Meta-Cognition Factors and associated subscales, as well as the Self-Monitor and Inhibit subscales of the BRIEF-A as compared to controls (Roth et al., 2013). A significant strength of the BRIEF-A is its three validity scales measuring inconsistency in responses, over-endorsement of infrequent items, and a mindset of negativity (Roth, Isquith, & Gioia, 2005).

The BRIEF-A is more sensitive to actual behavioral EF difficulties than neuropsychological tests of EF (Biederman et al., 2011). A suggested cut-off for significant executive dysfunction is a T-score of 65 or more on 2 or more scales of the BRIEF-A (Biederman, Fried, et al., 2011). Improvement on the BRIEF-A was closely associated with improvement in DSM ADHD symptoms when stimulant medication was administered (Biederman, Fried, et al., 2011).

The BDEFS is highly recommended. This instrument was developed especially to assess EF in ADHD populations. The BDEFS asks about EF over the past six months. It is five pages long and has 89 questions. There is a self version and an other version, plus short versions of each. It can be purchased from Guilford Press and then copied and used indefinitely after purchase (list price as of writing is $160, but discounts are often available). The self and other reports were found to be highly correlated in a research study (Barkley & Murphy, 2010). The relationships between life dysfunction and EF have ecological validity (Barkley & Murphy, 2010). Other evidence of reliability and validity of this instrument is presented in the manual (Barkley, 2011b).

I recommend administration of both instruments, if possible. Each provides unique information. The BDEFS provides valuable information about the client's difficulties managing time, which is not addressed on the BRIEF-A. The BRIEF-A provides valuable information about working memory, proneness to errors, and unfinished tasks (Task Monitor subscale), disorganized and lost items (Organization of Materials), and distress over set-shifting (Shift)—this information is not available from the BDEFS. At times, the results from these two questionnaires will be inconsistent; this is likely due to item differences, so you may wish to examine specific responses. There are no norms available for the informant version of the BDEFS, so use the BRIEF-A if you are gathering information from informants.

ASSESSING ATYPICAL REWARD SENSITIVITY

Despite a growing understanding of the importance of atypical reward sensitivity in ADHD, no normed and standardized instruments exist to assess this. However, the Quick Delay Questionnaire (Clare, Helps, & Sonuga-Barke, 2010) has been developed for research, and in two preliminary studies it has shown good psychometric properties (Clare et al., 2010; Mitchell et al., 2016). The questionnaire has 10 items and has Delay Aversion and Delay Discounting subscores. However, neither norms nor cut-offs are currently available for this instrument (E. Sonuga-Barke, personal communication, 2015). If you wish to use it, the answers can be used in a qualitative manner to further understand reward sensitivity in a particular client. The questionnaire is available for your use in Appendix 2.

WHEN TO ADMINISTER INFORMANT REPORTS

Administer informant reports in two situations. First, administer informant reports when you suspect that a client has reasons to exaggerate symptoms, perhaps to obtain stimulants. Populations at risk include college students and individuals in high-pressure white-collar careers. Second, administer informant reports when you wonder if a client is minimizing symptoms—these individuals are often young adults with limited insight (Sibley et al., 2012b). Note that the CAARS and the BRIEF-A have norms for the informant versions, while the BAARS and the BDEFS do not.

A RECOMMENDED ADHD PSYCHOLOGICAL TESTING PROTOCOL

The clinical interview should include a thorough assessment of depression, anxiety, and substance abuse, since these conditions are so often comorbid with ADHD. Also, the client should be screened for other conditions that may be comorbid (chapter 3).

To thoroughly assess ADHD, give the client the following questionnaires:

- *Sleep problems*: Use the Pittsburgh Sleep Quality Index, as discussed in chapter 5.
- *Childhood ADHD*: Use the BAARS, Self-Report: Childhood Symptoms. If the client comes from a high-risk background, the WURS could be informative.
- *Current DSM ADHD symptoms*: Use the CAARS: Self-Report, either short or long version. An alternative or additional instrument would be the BAARS, Self-Report: Current Symptoms.
- *Executive functioning*: Consider administering both the BDEFS and the BRIEF-A. Either is helpful alone but does not provide as much data on problematic areas of functioning. If you need to use just one instrument, use the BRIEF-A.
- *Functioning problem areas:* Administer the Weiss Functional Impairment Rating Scale.
- *Atypical reward sensitivity*: Administer the Quick Delay Questionnaire if desired. Follow up with interview questions.
- *Informant reports*: Administer the CAARS and BRIEF-A informant versions if needed.
- Utilize other instruments to assess psychopathology as indicated by professional judgment.

APPENDIX 2

The Quick Delay Questionnaire

Name: ________________________________ Age: __________

Birth Date: _____/_____/_____ Today's Date: ____/_____/___ Gender: M F

INSTRUCTIONS:

Please circle a number below which best describes your behaviour over the past 6 months, from

1: 'Not at all like me' to 5: 'Very much like me'.

Please try to rate all items.

I will not give up, even if I have to wait a long time for something important.	1	2	3	4	5
I am usually calm when I have to wait in queues.	1	2	3	4	5
I will often choose a task which helps me in the long term even if I don't get anything from it right away.	1	2	3	4	5
I feel calm when waiting for things.	1	2	3	4	5
I often give up on things I cannot have straightaway.	1	2	3	4	5
I hate waiting for things.	1	2	3	4	5
I try to avoid tasks that will only give me something in the long-term and not straight away.	1	2	3	4	5
I feel annoyed when I have to wait for someone else to be ready before I can do something.	1	2	3	4	5
Having to wait for things makes me feel stressed and tense.	1	2	3	4	5
The future is not important. I only consider instant outcomes of my actions.	1	2	3	4	5

Note: Reprinted from Clare, S., S. Helps, & E. J. Sonuga-Barke (2010). The quick delay questionnaire: A measure of delay aversion and discounting in adults. *ADHD Attention Deficit and Hyperactivity Disorders, 2*(1), 43–48, with permission of Springer and the authors.

Scoring for Quick Delay Questionnaire
Delay Aversion Scale: Add items 2 (reverse code), 4 (reverse code), 6, 8, 9
Delay Discounting Scale: Add items 1 (reverse code), 3 (reverse code), 5, 7, 10

APPENDIX 3

Omega-3 Fatty Acids Client Handout

GENERAL INFORMATION

- Our current American diet usually does not supply enough omega-3 fatty acids.
- Sufficient omega-3 intake is necessary for general neurological health and cognitive functioning.

OMEGA-3S AND ADHD

- Research shows that omega-3 supplementation helps cognitive functioning and behavior.
- The effect is small, but reliably there.
- To see benefits, you must use them for three to four months and consistently thereafter.
- There are no known risks to omega-3 supplementation.
- Make a plan for consistent and daily addition of omega-3 fatty acids.

Try one the following options for safe and effective doses of omega-3 fatty acid supplementation for adults:

- 2–4 tablespoons of ground flaxseed taken with lots of water (or perhaps sprinkled over breakfast cereal), OR
- 1–2 tablespoons of flaxseed oil

Plant-based sources are better for the environment.
If you prefer fish-based options, try one of the following:

- 3,000–4,000 mg standardized fish oils per day in capsule form, OR
- 2–3 servings of fatty fish (salmon, mackerel, halibut, sardines, herrings, anchovies, tuna, oyster, lobster) per week

Remember: Supplementation is not an effective stand-alone treatment for your ADHD. But it may help over time, especially if you have some problems with depression.

Sources: McGough (2014); Mazza, Pomponi, Janiri, Bria, and Mazza (2007); Ramsay (2010b).

RECOMMENDED READING AND RESOURCES

Chapter 1

Faraone, S. V., P. Asherson, T. Banaschewski, J. Biederman, J. K. Buitelaar, J. A. Ramos-Quiroga, . . . Barbara Franke. (2015). Primer: Attention-deficit/hyperactivity disorder. *Nature Reviews: Disease Primers, 1*, Article 15020.

Faraone and colleagues provide a succinct description of all important issues in ADHD, including genetics, developmental issues, and brain functioning. There is a helpful timeline of the history of ADHD and an interesting figure illustrating brain regions that have a role in ADHD. This article is quite heavy in scientific jargon but is an excellent review of most major issues in understanding ADHD.

Chapter 2

Barkley, R. A., Murphy, K. R., & Fischer, M. (2008). *ADHD in adults: What the science says*. New York: Guilford Press.

See especially Chapter 7: Identifying New Symptoms of ADHD in Adulthood.

Chapter 5

Wasserstein, J. (2005). Diagnostic issues for adolescents and adults with ADHD. *Journal of Clinical Psychology/In Session, 61*(5), 535–547.

Wasserstein provides an excellent overview of the general process of assessing adult ADHD.

Chapter 6

Walters, A. S., Silvestri, R., Zucconi, M., Chandrashekariah, R., & Konofal, E. (2008). Review of the possible relationship and hypothetical links between attention deficit hyperactivity disorder (ADHD) and the simple sleep related movement disorders, parasomnias, hypersomnias, and circadian rhythm disorders. *Journal of Clinical Sleep Medicine, 4*(6), 591–600.

The authors provide a thorough discussion of the current understanding of the relationship between ADHD and sleep disorders.

Chapter 7

Akutagava-Martins, G. C., Salatino-Oliveira, A., Kieling, C. C., Rohde, L. A. & Hutz, M.H. (2013). Genetics of attention-deficit/hyperactivity disorder: Current findings and future directions. *Expert Review of Neurotherapeutics, 13*(4), 435–445.

The authors summarize important findings about genetics and ADHD to date.

Chapter 8

Nigg, J. (2013). Attention-deficit/hyperactivity disorder and adverse health outcomes. *Clinical Psychology Review, 33*(2), 215–228.

Nigg, a foremost expert on ADHD, reviews the literature on adverse health outcomes in ADHD in this timely article.

Pera, G., & Robin, A. L. (Eds.). (2016). *Adult ADHD-focused couple therapy.* New York: Routledge.

The editors compile helpful chapters on various difficulties faced by couples with one ADHD partner, and various treatment approaches are presented.

Pera, G. (2008). *Is it you, me or adult A.D.D.: Stopping the roller coaster when someone you love has attention deficit disorder.* San Francisco, CA: 1201 Alarm Press.

Based on informal surveys and considerable experience with online and in-person support groups, journalist Pera shares insights and common observations to help partners understand the difficulties they are having with their ADHD spouse.

Chapter 9

Quinn, P. O. (2011). *100 questions & answers about attention-deficit hyperactivity disorder (ADHD) in women and girls.* Sudbury, MA: Jones & Bartlett Learning.

This is an especially helpful book for women with ADHD. The author carefully grounds her information in the scientific literature. Highly recommended.

Ramsay, J. R., & Rostain, A. L. (2014). *The adult ADHD tool kit: Using CBT to facilitate coping inside and out.* New York: Routledge.

The authors provide detailed advice on coping skills for adults with ADHD. While this book is designed to stand alone, it could also be used effectively in conjunction with psychotherapy. Highly recommended.

Safren, S. A., Perlman, C. A., Sprich, S., & Otto, M. W. (2005). *Mastering your adult ADHD: A cognitive-behavioral treatment program client workbook.* New York: Oxford University Press.

This client workbook is accompanied by a therapist guide that is cited under "Chapter 12." Client can work through this at their own pace or in conjunction with therapy sessions. This book is highly recommended and based on the best psychotherapy practices for adult ADHD.

www.chadd.org

CHADD (Children and Adults with ADD) is a national organization in the United States that provides education, support, and training regarding ADHD. Some local chapters sponsor support groups for adults who have ADHD. Many chapters sponsor support groups for parents of children with ADHD. Many of your clients with ADHD will fall into both groups. Many interesting articles are available on the website that may enhance clients' self-understanding, and CHADD publishes an interesting monthly magazine about ADHD.

Chapter 10

Nigg, J. (2006). *What causes ADHD? Understanding what goes wrong and why.* New York: Guilford Press.

This book provides an in-depth explanation of cognitive issues in ADHD.

Castellanos F. X., & Proal, E. (2012). Large-scale brain systems in ADHD: Beyond the prefrontal-striatal model. *Trends in Cognitive Sciences, 16*(1), 17–26.

The authors describe the major neural networks of the brain and how each one may be involved in ADHD.

Chapter 11

Ramsay, J. R., & Rostain, A. L. (2016). Adult attention-deficit/hyperactivity disorder as an implementation problem: Clinical significance, underlying mechanisms, and psychosocial treatment. *Practice Innovations, 1*(1), 36–52.

The authors review the cognitive and biological bases of implementation problems in ADHD and provide multiple helpful suggestions for overcoming these difficulties.

Chapter 12

Sprich, S. E., Knouse, L. E., Cooper-Vince, C., Burbridge, J., & Safren, S. A. (2012). Description and demonstration of CBT for ADHD in adults. *Cognitive Behavioral Practice, 17*(1), 9–15.

This highly recommended article provides a concise summary of the main points of the authors' CBT treatment for ADHD. In addition, a copy of this article hosted on NIH.gov includes eight short videos illustrating the techniques described in the article.

www.apsard.org

Website for American Professional Society of ADHD and Related Disorders (APSARD), an organization that has an annual conference on ADHD research as well as informative videos on the most recent research. Free continuing education credits are available.

www.adhdinadults.com

This website provides free continuing education credits for viewing videos about adult ADHD by leading experts. At the time of writing, it appears that these credits are only valid for physicians, but the educational videos are free to be viewed by any professional.

Knouse, L. E., & Mitchell, J. T. (2015). Incautiously optimistic: Positively valenced cognitive avoidance in adult ADHD. *Cognitive and Behavioral Practice, 12*, 192–202.

This article provides additional insight into dysfunctional positive cognitions and ADHD.

Ramsay, J. R., & Rostain, A. L. (2014). *Cognitive-behavioral therapy for adult ADHD: An integrative psychosocial and medical approach* (2nd ed.). New York: Routledge.

The authors are important researchers in the field of ADHD. Here, they share their clinical insights about CBT, pharmacotherapy, and complicating factors. Four longer case examples illustrate effective treatment principles.

Safren, S. A., Sprich, S., Perlman, C. A., & Otto, M. W. (2005). *Mastering your adult ADHD: A cognitive-behavioral treatment program therapist guide*. New York: Oxford University Press.

This therapist guide accompanies a client workbook. It is short and very readable. It provides many concrete and helpful suggestions for therapists to implement with their clients. The authors have done important research on psychotherapy for adult ADHD.

Solanto, M. V. (2011). *Cognitive-behavioral therapy for adult ADHD: Targeting executive dysfunction*. New York: Guilford Press.

Solanto presents a group psychotherapy format for adult ADHD in this treatment manual. However, many of the interventions recommended would be equally valuable for individual therapy. She provides many helpful clinical examples. The author has done important research on psychotherapy for adult ADHD.

Tuckman, A. (2007). *Integrative treatment for adult ADHD: A practical, easy-to-use guide for clinicians*. Oakland, CA: New Harbinger.

Tuckman is a clinician who specializes in treatment of ADHD. He provides many helpful clinical suggestions for managing symptoms of ADHD. He goes into detail about medications, working with the partner or spouse, and occupational counseling.

Upadhyaya, H. P. (2007). Managing attention-deficit/hyperactivity disorder in the presence of substance use disorder. *Journal of Clinical Psychiatry*, *68*(Suppl. 11), 23–30.

The author provides useful advice on managing clients with both ADHD and substance abuse beyond what is covered in the current chapter. Highly recommended.

Waite, R., & Ramsay, J. R. (2010). A Hispanic woman with ADHD—A case example. *Journal of Attention Disorders*, *13*(4), 424–432.

This article presents a helpful case study of a young, lesbian Latina woman, illustrating some cultural issues in treatment.

CHAPTER 14

Ramsay, J. R. (2010b). *Nonmedication treatments for adult ADHD: Evaluating impact on daily functioning and well-being*. Washington DC: APA Books.

Chapters 6 and 7 of this book review the status of treatments discussed in this chapter in more detail.

Zylowaska, L. (2012). *The mindfulness prescription for adult ADHD*. Boston: Trumpeter.

Dr. Zylowska wrote this book as a self-guided introduction to mindfulness and meditation practices for the adult with ADHD. The guided meditation exercises in this book are freely available on this website: http://www.shambhala.com/MindfulnessPrescription

Zylowaska, L., Smalley, S. L., & Schwartz, J. M. (2009). Mindful awareness and ADHD. In F. Didonna (Ed.), *Clinical handbook of mindfulness*. New York: Springer Science+Business Media, 319–338.

This chapter details the rationale and structure of group mindfulness and meditation training for adults with ADHD.

REFERENCES

Abikoff, H. B., Jensen, P. S., Arnold, L. E., Hoza, B., Hechtman, L., Pollack, S., . . . Vitiello, B. (2002). Observed classroom behavior of children with ADHD: Relationship to gender and comorbidity. *Journal of Abnormal Child Psychology, 30*(4), 349–359.

Able, S. L., Johnston, J. A., Adler, L. A., & Swindle, R. W. (2007). Functional and psychosocial impairment in adults with undiagnosed ADHD. *Psychological Medicine, 37*(1), 97–107.

Abramovitch, A., Goldzweig, G., & Schweiger, A. (2013). Correlates of physical activity with intrusive thoughts, worry and impulsivity in adults with attention deficit/hyperactivity disorder: A cross-sectional pilot study. *The Israel Journal of Psychiatry and Related Sciences, 50*(1), 47–54.

Abramovitch, A., & Schweiger, A. (2009). Unwanted intrusive and worrisome thoughts in adults with attention deficit/hyperactivity disorder. *Psychiatry Research, 168*, 230–233.

Adamou, M., Arif, M., Asherson, P., Aw, T. C., Bolea, B., Coghill, D., . . . Pitts, M. (2013). Occupational issues of adults with ADHD. *BMC Psychiatry, 13*(1), Article 59.

Adler, L. A., Barkley, R. A., Wilens, T. A., & Ginsberg, D. L. (2006). Differential diagnosis of attention-deficit/hyperactivity disorder and comorbid conditions. *Primary Psychiatry, 13*(5) Suppl 3, 1–13.

Adler, L. A., Clemow, D. B., Williams, D. W., & Durell, T. M. (2014). Atomoxetine effects on executive function as measured by the BRIEF-A in young adults with ADHD: A randomized, double-blind, placebo-controlled study. *PloS One, 9*(8), e104175.

Adler, L. A., & Cohen, J. (2004). Diagnosis and evaluation of adults with attention-deficit/hyperactivity disorder. *Psychiatric Clinics of North America, 27*(2), 187–201.

Adler, L. A., Spencer, T. J., Levine, L. R., Ramsey, J. L., Tamura, R., Kelsey, D., . . . Biederman, J. (2008). Functional outcomes in the treatment of adults with ADHD. *Journal of Attention Disorders, 11*(6), 720–727.

Aguiar, A., Eubig, P. A., & Schantz, S. L. (2010). Attention deficit/hyperactivity disorder: A focused overview for children's environmental health researchers. *Environmental Health Perspectives, 118*(12), 1646–1653.

Akutagava-Martins, G. C., Salatino-Oliveira, A., Kieling, C. C., Rohde, L. A., & Hutz, M. H. (2013). Genetics of attention-deficit/hyperactivity disorder: Current findings and future directions. *Expert Review of Neurotherapeutics, 13*(4), 435–445.

Alpert, J. E., Maddocks, A., Nierenberg, A. A., O'Sullivan, R., Pava, J. A., Worthington, J. J., . . . Fava, M. (1996). Attention deficit hyperactivity disorder in childhood among adults with major depression. *Psychiatry Research*, *62*(3), 213–219.

American Psychiatric Association. (2013). *Diagnostic and statistical manual of mental disorders* (5th ed.). Washington, DC: American Psychiatric Publishing.

American Psychiatric Publishing. (2013a). Attention deficit/hyperactivity disorder. Retrieved from http://www.dsm5.org/documents/adhd%20fact%20sheet.pdf

American Psychiatric Publishing. (2013b). Highlights of changes from DSM-IV-TR to DSM-5. Retrieved from http://www.dsm5.org/Documents/changes%20from%20dsm-iv-tr%20to%20dsm-5.pdf

Amons, P. J. T., Kooij, J. J. S., Haffmans, P. M. J., Hoffman, T. O., & Hoencamp, E. (2006). Seasonality of mood disorders in adults with lifetime attention-deficit/hyperactivity disorder (ADHD). *Journal of Affective Disorders*, *91*(2), 251–255.

Antshel, K. M., Faraone, S. V., Maglione, K., Doyle, A., Fried, R., Seidman, L., & Biederman, J. (2009). Is adult attention deficit hyperactivity disorder a valid diagnosis in the presence of high IQ? *Psychological Medicine, 39*(8), 1325–1335.

Antshel, K. M., Faraone, S. V., Maglione, K., Doyle, A. E., Fried, R., Seidman, L. J., & Biederman, J. (2010). Executive functioning in high-IQ adults with ADHD. *Psychological Medicine*, *40*(11), 1909–1918.

Archer, D. (2014, May 14). ADHD: The entrepreneur's superpower. *Forbes*. Retrieved from http://www.forbes.com/sites/dalearcher/2014/05/14/adhd-the-entrepreneurs-superpower/

Archer, T., & Kostrzewa, R. M. (2012). Physical exercise alleviates ADHD symptoms: Regional deficits and development trajectory. *Neurotoxicity Research*, *21*(2), 195–209.

Arif, K., Leventhal, R. M., Khan, S. R., & Brown, W. A. (2002). Severity of depression and response to antidepressants and placebo: An analysis of the Food and Drug Administration database. *Journal of Clinical Psychopharmacology, 22*(1), 40–45.

Armstrong, T. (2015). The myth of the normal brain: Embracing neurodiversity. *AMA Journal of Ethics*, *17*(4), 348–352.

Arnold, L. E., Hodgkins, P., Caci, H., Kahle, J., & Young, S. (2015). Effect of treatment modality on long-term outcomes in attention-deficit/hyperactivity disorder: A systematic review. *PloS One*, *10*(2), e0116407

Arnold, L. E., Lofthouse, N., Hersch, S., Pan, X., Hurt, E., Bates, B., . . . Grantier, C. (2013). EEG neurofeedback for ADHD: Double-blind sham-controlled randomized pilot feasibility trial. *Journal of Attention Disorders*, *17*(5), 410–419.

Arns, M., Heinrich, H., & Strehl, U. (2014). Evaluation of neurofeedback in ADHD: The long and winding road. *Biological Psychology*, *95*, 108–115.

Arns, M., van der Heijden, K. B., Arnold, L. E., & Kenemans, J. L. (2013). Geographic variation in the prevalence of attention-deficit/hyperactivity disorder: The sunny perspective. *Biological Psychiatry*, *74*(8), 585–590.

Asherson, P. (2005). Clinical assessment and treatment of attention deficit hyperactivity disorder in adults. *Expert Review of Neurotherapeutics*, *5*(4), 525–539.

Asherson, P. (2013). ADHD in adults: A clinical concern. In C. B. H. Surman (Ed.), *ADHD in adults: A practical guide to evaluation and management* (pp. 1–13). New York: Humana Press.

Asherson, P., Akehurst, R., Kooij, J. S., Huss, M., Beusterien, K., Sasané, R., . . . Hodgkins, P. (2012). Under-diagnosis of adult ADHD: Cultural influences and societal burden. *Journal of Attention Disorders*, *16*(5 suppl.), 20S–38S.

Attention Deficit Disorder Association. (2006). *Guiding principles for the diagnosis and treatment of attention deficit/hyperactivity disorder*. Pottstown, PA: Author.

Bacchini, D., Affuso, G., & Trotta, T. (2008). Temperament, ADHD and peer relations among schoolchildren: The mediating role of school bullying. *Aggressive Behavior, 34*, 447–459.

Baer, R. A. (2003). Mindfulness training as a clinical intervention: A conceptual and empirical review. *Clinical Psychology: Science and Practice, 10*(2), 125–143.

Baird, A. L., Coogan, A. N., Siddiqui, A., Donev, R. M., & Thome, J. (2012). Adult attention-deficit hyperactivity disorder is associated with alterations in circadian rhythms at the behavioural, endocrine and molecular levels. *Molecular Psychiatry, 17*(10), 988–995.

Banerjee, T. D., Middleton, F., & Faraone, S. V. (2007). Environmental risk factors for attention-deficit hyperactivity disorder. *Acta Paediatrica, 96*(9), 1269–1274.

Barbaresi, W. J., Colligan, R. C., Weaver, A. L., Voigt, R. G., Killian, J. M., & Katusic, S. K. (2013). Mortality, ADHD, and psychosocial adversity in adults with childhood ADHD: A prospective study. *Pediatrics, 131*(4), 637–644.

Barkley, R. A. (2002). Major life activity and health outcomes associated with attention-deficit/hyperactivity disorder. *The Journal of Clinical Psychiatry, 63*, 10–15.

Barkley, R. A. (2006a). ADHD in adults: Developmental course and outcome of children with ADHD, and ADHD in clinic-referred adults. In R. A. Barkley (Ed.), *Attention-deficit hyperactivity disorder: A handbook for diagnosis and treatment* (3rd ed., pp. 248–296). New York: Guilford Press.

Barkley, R. A. (2006b). A theory of ADHD. In R. A. Barkley (Ed.), *Attention-deficit hyperactivity disorder: A handbook for diagnosis and treatment* (3rd ed., pp. 297–334). New York: Guilford Press.

Barkley, R. A. (2010a). *Taking charge of adult ADHD*. New York: Guilford Press.

Barkley, R. A. (2010b). Why emotional impulsiveness should be a central feature of ADHD. *The ADHD Report, 18*(4), 1–5.

Barkley, R. A. (2011a). *Adult ADHD Rating Scale-IV (BAARS-IV)*. New York: Guilford Press.

Barkley, R. A. (2011b). *Barkley Deficits in Executive Functioning Scale (BDEFS)*. New York: Guilford Press.

Barkley, R. A. (2012). Distinguishing sluggish cognitive tempo from attention-deficit/hyperactivity disorder in adults. *Journal of Abnormal Psychology, 121*(4), 978–990.

Barkley, R. A. (2014a). *Attention-deficit hyperactivity disorder: A handbook for diagnosis and treatment* (4th ed.). New York: Guilford Press.

Barkley, R. A. (2014b). Sleep problems and ADHD—An overview. *The ADHD Report, 22*(3), 6–11.

Barkley, R. A. (2014c). Sluggish cognitive tempo (concentration deficit disorder?): Current status, future directions, and a plea to change the name. *Journal of Abnormal Child Psychology, 42*(1), 117–125.

Barkley, R. A., & Benton, C. M. (2010). Why money matters are so challenging for you . . . and what you can do about it. Retrieved from http://www.chadd.org/Membership/Attention-Magazine/View-Articles/Money-Matters.aspx

Barkley, R. A., & Brown, T. E. (2008). Unrecognized attention-deficit/hyperactivity disorder in adults presenting with other psychiatric disorders. *CNS Spectrums, 13*(11), 977–984.

Barkley, R. A., Cook, E. H., Dulcan, M., Campbell, S., Prior, M., Atkins, M., . . . Lewandowski, L. (2002). Consensus statement on ADHD. *European Child & Adolescent Psychiatry, 11*(2), 96–98.

Barkley, R. A., & Cox, D. (2007). A review of driving risks and impairments associated with attention-deficit/hyperactivity disorder and the effects of stimulant medication on driving performance. *Journal of Safety Research, 38*(1), 113–128.

Barkley, R. A., & Fischer, M. (2010). The unique contribution of emotional impulsiveness to impairment in major life activities in hyperactive children as adults. *Journal of the American Academy of Child & Adolescent Psychiatry, 49*(5), 503–513.

Barkley, R. A., Fischer, M., Smallish, L., & Fletcher, K. (2003). Does the treatment of attention-deficit/hyperactivity disorder with stimulants contribute to drug use/abuse? A 13-year prospective study. *Pediatrics, 111*(1), 97–109.

Barkley, R. A., Fischer, M., Smallish, L., & Fletcher, K. (2004). Young adult follow-up of hyperactive children: Antisocial activities and drug use. *Journal of Child Psychology and Psychiatry, 45*(2), 195–211.

Barkley, R. A., Fischer, M., Smallish, L., & Fletcher, K. (2006). Young adult outcome of hyperactive children: Adaptive functioning in major life activities. *Journal of the American Academy of Child & Adolescent Psychiatry, 45*(2), 192–202.

Barkley, R. A., & Murphy, K. R. (2010). Impairment in occupational functioning and adult ADHD: The predictive utility of executive function (EF) ratings versus EF tests. *Archives of Clinical Neuropsychology, 25*(3), 157–173.

Barkley, R. A., Murphy, K. R., & Bush, T. (2001). Time perception and reproduction in young adults with attention deficit hyperactivity disorder. *Neuropsychology, 15*(3), 351–360.

Barkley, R. A., Murphy, K. R., & Fischer, M. (2008). *ADHD in adults: What the science says.* New York: Guilford Press.

Barrett, S. P., Darredeau, C., Bordy, L. E., & Pihl, R. O. (2005). Characteristics of methylphenidate misuse in a university student sample. *Canadian Journal of Psychiatry, 50*(8), 457–461.

Beaty, R. E., Benedek, M., Wilkins, R. W., Jauk, E., Fink, A., Silvia, P. J., . . . Neubauer, A. C. (2014). Creativity and the default network: A functional connectivity analysis of the creative brain at rest. *Neuropsychologia, 64*, 92–98.

Beck, J. S., & Broder, F. R. (2016, January 19). The new "homework" in cognitive behavior therapy. Retrieved from https://www.beckinstitute.org/category/uncategorized/

Becker, S. P. (2013). Topical review: Sluggish cognitive tempo: Research findings and relevance for pediatric psychology. *Journal of Pediatric Psychology, 38*(10), 1051–1057.

Becker, S. P., Langberg, J. M., Luebbe, A. M., Dvorsky, M. R., & Flannery, A. J. (2014). Sluggish cognitive tempo is associated with academic functioning and internalizing symptoms in college students with and without attention-deficit/hyperactivity disorder. *Journal of Clinical Psychology, 70*(4), 388–403.

Becker, S. P., Luebbe, A. M., & Langberg, J. M. (2014). Attention-deficit/hyperactivity disorder dimensions and sluggish cognitive tempo symptoms in relation to college students' sleep functioning. *Child Psychiatry & Human Development, 45*(6), 675–685.

Becker, S. P., Marshall, S. A., & McBurnett, K. (2014). Sluggish cognitive tempo in abnormal child psychology: An historical overview and introduction to the special section. *Journal of Abnormal Child Psychology, 42*(1), 1–6.

Beebe, D. W., & Gozal, D. (2002). Obstructive sleep apnea and the prefrontal cortex: Towards a comprehensive model linking nocturnal upper airway obstruction to daytime cognitive and behavioral deficits. *Journal of Sleep Research, 11*(1), 1–16.

Berck, J. (2015, September 28). Is it old age or A.D.H.D.? *The New York Times*. Retrieved from http://well.blogs.nytimes.com/2015/09/28/is-it-alzheimers-or-a-d-h-d/?_r=0

Berman, M. G., Peltier, S., Nee, D. E., Kross, E., Deldin, P. J., & Jonides, J. (2010). Depression, rumination and the default network. *Social Cognitive and Affective Neuroscience*, 6(5), 548–555.

Bernardi, S., Faraone, S. V., Cortese, S., Kerridge, B. T., Pallanti, S., Wang, S., & Blanco, C. (2012). The lifetime impact of attention deficit hyperactivity disorder: Results from the National Epidemiologic Survey on Alcohol and Related Conditions (NESARC). *Psychological Medicine*, *42*(4), 875–887.

Bernfort, L., Nordfeldt, S., & Persson, J. (2008). ADHD from a socio-economic perspective. *Acta Paediatrica*, *97*(2), 239–245.

Biederman, J. (2011). The course and persistence of ADHD throughout the life-cycle. In J. Buitelaar, C. C. Kan, & P. J. Asherson (Eds.), *ADHD in adults: Characterization, diagnosis, and treatment* (pp. 1–8). Cambridge, UK: Cambridge University Press.

Biederman, J. (2016, January). Neurobiological evidence for a separation between working memory and ADHD. Paper presented at the American Professional Society of ADHD and Related Disorders, Washington, DC.

Biederman, J., & Faraone, S. V. (2004). The Massachusetts General Hospital studies of gender influences on attention-deficit/hyperactivity disorder in youth and relatives. *Psychiatric Clinics of North America*, *27*(2), 225–232.

Biederman, J., Faraone, S. V., Mick, E., Spencer, T., Wilens, T., Kiely, K., . . . Warburton, R. (1995). High risk for attention deficit hyperactivity disorder among children of parents with childhood onset of the disorder: A pilot study. *The American Journal of Psychiatry*, *152*(3), 431–435.

Biederman, J., Faraone, S. V., & Monuteaux, M. C. (2002). Differential effect of environmental adversity by gender: Rutter's index of adversity in a group of boys and girls with and without ADHD. *The American Journal of Psychiatry*, *159*(9), 1556–1562.

Biederman, J., Faraone, S. V., Monuteaux, M. C., Bober, M., & Cadogen, E. (2004). Gender effects on attention-deficit/hyperactivity disorder in adults, revisited. *Biological Psychiatry*, *55*(7), 692–700.

Biederman, J., Faraone, S., Spencer, T., Mick, E., Monuteaux, M., & Aleardi, M. (2006). Functional impairments in adults with self-reports of diagnosed ADHD. *The Journal of Clinical Psychiatry*, *67*, 524–540.

Biederman, J., Fried, R., Petty, C. R., Henin, A., Wozniak, J., Corkum, L., . . . Faraone, S. V. (2012). Examining the association between stimulant treatment and cognitive outcomes across the life cycle of adults with attention-deficit/hyperactivity disorder: A controlled cross-sectional study. *The Journal of Nervous and Mental Disease*, *200*(1), 69–75.

Biederman, J., Fried, R., Petty, C., Mahoney, L., & Faraone, S. V. (2012). An examination of the impact of attention-deficit hyperactivity disorder on IQ: A large controlled family-based analysis. *Canadian Journal of Psychiatry*, *57*(10), 608–616.

Biederman, J., Fried, R., Petty, C. R., Wozniak, J., Doyle, A. E., Henin, A., . . . Faraone, S. V. (2011). Cognitive development in adults with attention-deficit/hyperactivity disorder: A controlled study in medication-naive adults across the adult life cycle. *The Journal of Clinical Psychiatry*, *72*(1), 11–16.

Biederman, J., Kwon, A., Aleardi, M., Chouinard, V. A., Marino, T., Cole, H., . . . Faraone, S. V. (2005). Absence of gender effects on attention deficit hyperactivity disorder: Findings in nonreferred subjects. *The American Journal of Psychiatry, 162*, 1083–1089.

Biederman, J., Mick, E., Faraone, S. V., Braaten, E., Doyle, A., Spencer, T., . . . Johnson, M. A. (2002). Influence of gender on attention deficit hyperactivity disorder in children referred to a psychiatric clinic. *The American Journal of Psychiatry, 159*(1), 36–42.

Biederman, J., Mick, E., Fried, R., Wilner, N., Spencer, T. J., & Faraone, S. V. (2011). Are stimulants effective in the treatment of executive function deficits? Results from a randomized double blind study of OROS-methylphenidate in adults with ADHD. *European Neuropsychopharmacology, 21*(7), 508–515.

Biederman, J., Petty, C. R., Evans, M., Small, J., & Faraone, S. V. (2010). How persistent is ADHD? A controlled 10-year follow-up study of boys with ADHD. *Psychiatry Research, 177*(3), 299–304.

Biederman, J., Petty, C. R., Fried, R., Fontanella, J., Doyle, A. E., Seidman, L. J., & Faraone, S. V. (2007). Can self-reported behavioral scales assess executive function deficits? A controlled study of adults with ADHD. *The Journal of Nervous and Mental Disease, 195*(3), 240–246.

Birnbaum, H. G., Kessler, R. C., Lowe, S. W., Secnik, K., Greenberg, P. E., Leong, S. A., & Swensen, A. R. (2005). Costs of attention deficit–hyperactivity disorder (ADHD) in the US: Excess costs of persons with ADHD and their family members in 2000. *Current Medical Research and Opinion, 21*(2), 195–205.

Bleck, J. R., DeBate, R. D., & Olivardia, R. (2015). The comorbidity of ADHD and eating disorders in a nationally representative sample. *The Journal of Behavioral Health Services & Research, 42*(4), 437–451.

Bloch, M. H., & Qawasmi, A. (2011). Omega-3 fatty acid supplementation for the treatment of children with attention-deficit/hyperactivity disorder symptomatology: Systematic review and meta-analysis. *Journal of the American Academy of Child & Adolescent Psychiatry, 50*(10), 991–1000.

Boonstra, A. M., Kooij, J. J., Oosterlaan, J., Sergeant, J. A., Buitelaar, J. K., & Van Someren, E. J. (2007). Hyperactive night and day? Actigraphy studies in adult ADHD: A baseline comparison and the effect of methylphenidate. *Sleep, 30*(4), 433–442.

Boonstra, A. M., Oosterlaan, J., Sergeant, J. A., & Buitelaar, J. K. (2005). Executive functioning in adult ADHD: A meta-analytic review. *Psychological Medicine, 35*(8), 1097–1108.

Bouchard, M. F., Bellinger, D. C., Wright, R. O., & Weisskopf, M. G. (2010). Attention-deficit/hyperactivity disorder and urinary metabolites of organophosphate pesticides. *Pediatrics, 125*(6), e1270–e1277.

Bramham, J., Young, S., Bickerdike, A., Spain, D., McCartan, D., & Xenitidis, K. (2009). Evaluation of group cognitive behavioral therapy for adults with ADHD. *Journal of Attention Disorders, 12*(5), 434–441.

Bridgett, D. J., & Walker, M. E. (2006). Intellectual functioning in adults with ADHD: A meta-analytic examination of full scale IQ differences between adults with and without ADHD. *Psychological Assessment, 18*(1), 1–14.

Brod, M., Pohlman, B., Lasser, R., & Hodgkins, P. (2012). Comparison of the burden of illness for adults with ADHD across seven countries: A qualitative study. *Health and Quality of Life Outcomes, 10*(1), 1–17.

Brod, M., Schmitt, E., Goodwin, M., Hodgkins, P., & Niebler, G. (2012). ADHD burden of illness in older adults: A life course perspective. *Quality of Life Research, 21*(5), 795–799.

Brook, J. S., Brook, D. W., Zhang, C., Seltzer, N., & Finch, S. J. (2013). Adolescent ADHD and adult physical and mental health, work performance, and financial stress. *Pediatrics, 131*(1), 5–13.

Brown, T. E. (2005). *Attention deficit disorder: The unfocused mind in children and adults.* New Haven, CT: Yale University Press.

Brown, T. E. (2006). Executive functions and attention deficit hyperactivity disorder: Implications of two conflicting views. *International Journal of Disability, Development and Education, 53*(1), 35–46.

Brown, T. E. (2008). ADD/ADHD and impaired executive function in clinical practice. *Current Psychiatry Reports, 10*(5), 407–411.

Brown, T. E. (2013). *A new understanding of ADHD in children and adults: Executive function impairments.* New York: Routledge.

Brown, T. E., Brams, M., Gao, J., Gasior, M., & Childress, A. (2010). Open-label administration of lisdexamfetamine dimesylate improves executive function impairments and symptoms of attention-deficit/hyperactivity disorder in adults. *Postgraduate Medicine, 122*(5), 7–17.

Brown, T. E., & Landgraf, J. M. (2010). Improvements in executive function correlate with enhanced performance and functioning and health-related quality of life: Evidence from 2 large, double-blind, randomized, placebo-controlled trials in ADHD. *Postgraduate Medicine, 122*(5), 42–51.

Brown, T. E., Reichel, P. C., & Quinlan, D. M. (2009). Executive function impairments in high IQ adults with ADHD. *Journal of Attention Disorders, 13*(2), 161–167.

Buckner, R. L., Andrews-Hanna, J. R., & Schachter, D. L. (2008). The brain's default network: Anatomy, function, and relevance to disease. *Annals of the New York Academy of Sciences, 1124*(1), 1–38.

Buitelaar, J. K. (2011). Afterward: ADHD in adults: Toward a new definition in DSM-V. In J. Buitelaar, C. C. Kan, & P. J. Asherson (Eds.), *ADHD in adults: Characterization, diagnosis, and treatment* (pp. 297–304). Cambridge, UK: Cambridge University Press.

Bush, G. (2010). Attention-deficit/hyperactivity disorder and attention networks. *Neuropsychopharmacology Reviews, 35*(1), 278–300.

Canadian ADHD Resource Alliance. (2011). Canadian ADHD practice guidelines (3rd ed.). Toronto: Author. Retrieved from http://www.caddra.ca/cms4/

Canu, W. H., Newman, M. L., Morrow, T. L., & Pope, D. L. (2007). Social appraisal of adult ADHD: Stigma and influences of the beholder's big five personality traits. *Journal of Attention Disorders, 11*(6), 700–710.

Cappa, S. F., Benke, T., Clarke, S., Rossi, B., Stemmer, B., & Heugten, C. M. (2005). EFNS guidelines on cognitive rehabilitation: Report of an EFNS task force. *European Journal of Neurology, 12*(9), 665–680.

Carroll, A. E. (2015, August 10). Labels like "alternative medicine" don't matter. The science does. *The New York Times.* Retrieved from http://www.nytimes.com/2015/08/11/upshot/labels-like-alternative-medicine-dont-matter-the-science-does.html?_r=0

Carson, S. H., Peterson, J. B., & Higgins, D. M. (2003). Decreased latent inhibition is associated with increased creative achievement in high-functioning individuals. *Journal of Personality and Social Psychology, 85*(3), 499–506.

Castellanos, F. X. (2015). Is adult-onset ADHD a distinct entity? *The American Journal of Psychiatry, 172*(10), 929–931.

Castellanos, F. X., & Proal, E. (2012). Large-scale brain systems in ADHD: Beyond the prefrontal–striatal model. *Trends in Cognitive Sciences, 16*(1), 17–26.

Castellanos, F. X., Sharp, W. S., Gottesman, R. F., Greenstein, D. K., Giedd, J. N., & Rapoport, J. L. (2003). Anatomic brain abnormalities in monozygotic twins discordant for attention deficit hyperactivity disorder. *The American Journal of Psychiatry, 160*(9), 1693–1696.

Castellanos, F. X., & Tannock, R. (2002). Neuroscience of attention deficit/hyperactivity disorder: The search for endophenotypes. *Nature Reviews: Neuroscience, 3*, 617–628.

Chang, W. P., Davies, P. L., & Gavin, W. J. (2009). Error monitoring in college students with attention-deficit/hyperactivity disorder. *Journal of Psychophysiology, 23*(3), 113–125.

Chang, Y. K., Labban, J. D., Gapin, J. I., & Etnier, J. L. (2012). The effects of acute exercise on cognitive performance: A meta-analysis. *Brain Research, 1453*, 87–101.

Chen, Q., Sjölander, A., Runeson, B., D'Onofrio, B. M., Lichtenstein, P., & Larsson, H. (2014). Drug treatment for attention-deficit/hyperactivity disorder and suicidal behaviour: Register based study. *BMJ, 348*, g3769.

Cherkasova, M., Sulla, E. M., Dalena, K. L., Pondé, M. P., & Hechtman, L. (2013). Developmental course of attention deficit hyperactivity disorder and its predictors. *Journal of the Canadian Academy of Child and Adolescent Psychiatry, 22*(1), 47–54.

Cheung, C. H., Rijsdijk, F., McLoughlin, G., Brandeis, D., Banaschewski, T., Asherson, P., & Kuntsi, J. (2016). Cognitive and neurophysiological markers of ADHD persistence and remission. *The British Journal of Psychiatry, 208*(6), 548–555.

Chiesa, A., & Serretti, A. (2010). A systematic review of neurobiological and clinical features of mindfulness meditations. *Psychological Medicine, 40*(8), 1239–1252.

Chronis-Tuscano, A., Seymour, K. E., Stein, M. A., Jones, H. A., Jiles, C. D., Rooney, M. E., . . . Robb, A. S. (2008). Efficacy of osmotic-release oral system (OROS) methylphenidate for mothers with attention-deficit/hyperactivity disorder (ADHD): Preliminary report of effects on ADHD symptoms and parenting. *The Journal of Clinical Psychiatry, 69*(12), 1938–1947.

Chronis-Tuscano, A., & Stein, M. A. (2012). Pharmacotherapy for parents with attention-deficit hyperactivity disorder (ADHD). *CNS Drugs, 26*(9), 725–732.

Cicerone, K. D., Dahlberg, C., Malec, J. F., Langenbahn, D. M., Felicetti, T., Kneipp, S., . . . Laatsch, L. (2005). Evidence-based cognitive rehabilitation: Updated review of the literature from 1998 through 2002. *Archives of Physical Medicine and Rehabilitation, 86*(8), 1681–1692.

Cicerone, K. D., Langenbahn, D. M., Braden, C., Malec, J. F., Kalmar, K., Fraas, M., . . . Azulay, J. (2011). Evidence-based cognitive rehabilitation: Updated review of the literature from 2003 through 2008. *Archives of Physical Medicine and Rehabilitation, 92*(4), 519–530.

Clare, S., Helps, S., & Sonuga-Barke, E. J. (2010). The quick delay questionnaire: A measure of delay aversion and discounting in adults. *ADHD Attention Deficit and Hyperactivity Disorders, 2*(1), 43–48.

Coghill, D. (2013). Non-stimulant drug treatments for adults with ADHD. In C. B. H. Surman (Ed.), *ADHD in adults: A practical guide to evaluation and management* (pp. 89–117). New York: Humana Press.

Coghill, D., & Banaschewski, T. (2009). The genetics of attention-deficit/hyperactivity disorder: *Expert Review of Neurotherapeutics, 9*(10), 1547–1565.

Combs, M. A., Canu, W. H., Broman Fulks, J. J., & Nieman, D. C. (2014). Impact of sluggish cognitive tempo and attention-deficit/hyperactivity disorder symptoms on adults' quality of life. *Applied Research in Quality of Life, 9*(4), 981–995.

Combs, M. A., Canu, W. H., Broman Fulks, J. J., Rocheleau, C. A., & Nieman, D. C. (2015). Perceived stress and ADHD symptoms in adults. *Journal of Attention Disorders, 19*(5), 425–434.

Converse, A. K., Ahlers, E. O., Travers, B. G., & Davidson, R. J. (2014). Tai chi training reduces self-report of inattention in healthy young adults. *Frontiers in Human Neuroscience, 8*(13), 1–7.

Cook, J., Knight, E., Hume, I., & Qureshi, A. (2014). The self-esteem of adults diagnosed with attention-deficit/hyperactivity disorder (ADHD): A systematic review of the literature. *ADHD Attention Deficit and Hyperactivity Disorders, 6*(4), 249–268.

Corbett, B., & Stanczak, D. E. (1999). Neuropsychological performance of adults evidencing attention-deficit hyperactivity disorder. *Archives of Clinical Neuropsychology, 14*(4), 373–387.

Cortese, S., Faraone, S. V., Konofal, E., & Lecendreux, M. (2009). Sleep in children with attention-deficit/hyperactivity disorder: Meta-analysis of subjective and objective studies. *Journal of the American Academy of Child & Adolescent Psychiatry, 48*(9), 894–908.

Cortese, S., Ferrin, M., Brandeis, D., Buitelaar, J., Daley, D., Dittmann, R. W., . . . Zuddas, A. (2015). Cognitive training for attention-deficit/hyperactivity disorder: Meta-analysis of clinical and neuropsychological outcomes from randomized controlled trials. *Journal of the American Academy of Child & Adolescent Psychiatry, 54*(3), 164–174.

Cortese, S., Konofal, E., Lecendreux, M., Arnulf, I., Mouren, M. C., Darra, F., & Dalla Bernardina, B. (2005). Restless legs syndrome and attention-deficit/hyperactivity disorder: A review of the literature. *Sleep, 28*(8), 1007–1013.

Cramond, B. (1994). Attention-deficit hyperactivity disorder and creativity—What is the connection? *The Journal of Creative Behavior, 28*(3), 193–210.

Csikszentmihalyi, M. (1990). *Flow: The psychology of optimal experience.* New York: Harper Perennial.

Dalsgaard, S. (2016, January). Morbidity, mortality and functional impact of ADHD: Findings from Danish National Registers. Paper presented at the annual meeting of the American Professional Society of ADHD and Related Disorders, Washington, DC.

Dalsgaard, S., Østergaard, S. D., Leckman, J. F., Mortensen, P. B., & Pedersen, M. G. (2015). Mortality in children, adolescents, and adults with attention deficit hyperactivity disorder: A nationwide cohort study. *The Lancet, 385*(9983), 2190–2196.

Davidson, M. A. (2008). ADHD in adults: A review of the literature. *Journal of Attention Disorders, 11*(6), 628–641.

Davis, J. M., Takahashi, T., Shinoda, H., & Gregg, N. (2012). Cross-cultural comparison of ADHD symptoms among Japanese and US university students. *International Journal of Psychology, 47*(3), 203–210.

Deacon, B. J., & Baird, G. L. (2009). The chemical imbalance explanation of depression: Reducing blame at what cost? *Journal of Social and Clinical Psychology, 28*(4), 415–435.

Deault, L. C. (2010). A systematic review of parenting in relation to the development of comorbidities and functional impairments in children with attention-deficit/hyperactivity disorder (ADHD). *Child Psychiatry & Human Development, 41*(2), 168–192.

Dias, T. G. C., Kieling, C., Graeff-Martins, A. S., Moriyama, T. S., Rohde, L. A., & Polanczyk, G. V. (2013). Developments and challenges in the diagnosis and treatment of ADHD. *Revista Brasileira de Psiquiatria, 35*, S40–S50.

Ding, Y.-S., Naganawa, M., Gallezot, J.-D., Nabulsi, N., Lin, S.-F., Ropchan, J. . . . Laruelle, M. (2014). Clinical doses of atomoxetine significantly occupy both norepinephrine and serotonin transports: Implications on treatment of depression and ADHD. *NeuroImage, 86*, 164–171.

Division of Sleep Medicine, Harvard Medical School. (2014). Narcolepsy self-evaluation. Retrieved from http://healthysleep.med.harvard.edu/narcolepsy/diagnosing-narcolepsy/narcolepsy-self-evaluation

D'Onofrio, B. M., Rickert, M. E., Frans, E., Kuja-Halkola, R., Almqvist, C., Sjölander, A., . . . Lichtenstein, P. (2014). Paternal age at childbearing and offspring psychiatric and academic morbidity. *JAMA Psychiatry, 71*(4), 432–438.

Durell, T. M., Adler, L. A., Williams, D. W., Deldar, A., McGough, J. J., Glaser, P. E., . . . Fox, B. K. (2013). Atomoxetine treatment of attention-deficit/hyperactivity disorder in young adults with assessment of functional outcomes: A randomized, double-blind, placebo-controlled clinical trial. *Journal of Clinical Psychopharmacology, 33*(1), 45–54.

Durmer, J. S., & Dinges, D. F. (2005, March). Neurocognitive consequences of sleep deprivation. *Seminars in Neurology, 25*(1), 117–129.

Dyall, S. C., & Michael-Titus, A. T. (2008). Neurological benefits of omega-3 fatty acids. *Neuromolecular Medicine, 10*(4), 219–235.

Eakin, L., Minde, K., Hechtman, L., Ochs, E., Krane, E., Bouffard, R., . . . Looper, K. (2004). The marital and family functioning of adults with ADHD and their spouses. *Journal of Attention Disorders, 8*(1), 1–10.

Edel, M. A., Enzi, B., Witthaus, H., Tegenthoff, M., Peters, S., Juckel, G., & Lissek, S. (2013). Differential reward processing in subtypes of adult attention deficit hyperactivity disorder. *Journal of Psychiatric Research, 47*(3), 350–356.

Edel, M. A., Hölter, T., Wassink, K., & Juckel, G. (2014). A comparison of mindfulness-based group training and skills group training in adults with ADHD: An open study. *Journal of Attention Disorders*. Advance online publication.

Eisenbarth, H., Alpers, G. W., Conzelmann, A., Jacob, C. P., Weyers, P., & Pauli, P. (2008). Psychopathic traits in adult ADHD patients. *Personality and Individual Differences, 45*(6), 468–472.

Ek, A., & Isaksson, G. (2013). How adults with ADHD get engaged in and perform everyday activities. *Scandinavian Journal of Occupational Therapy, 20*(4), 282–291.

Ellis, B., & Nigg, J. (2009). Parenting practices and attention-deficit/hyperactivity disorder: New findings suggest partial specificity of effects. *Journal of the American Academy of Child & Adolescent Psychiatry, 48*(2), 146–154.

Engelhardt, P. E., Ferreira, F., & Nigg, J. T. (2011). Language production strategies and disfluencies in multi-clause network descriptions: A study of adult attention-deficit/hyperactivity disorder. *Neuropsychology, 25*(4), 442–453.

Engleman, H. M., & Douglas, N. J. (2004). Sleep·4: Sleepiness, cognitive function, and quality of life in obstructive sleep apnoea/hypopnoea syndrome. *Thorax, 59*(7), 618–622.

Epperson, C. N., Pittman, B., Czarkowski, K. A., Bradley, J., Quinlan, D. M., & Brown, T. E. (2011). Impact of atomoxetine on subjective attention and memory difficulties in perimenopausal and postmenopausal women. *Menopause, 18*(5), 542–548.

Epperson, C. N., Shanmugan, S., Kim, D. R., Mathews, S., Czarkowski, K. A., Bradley, J., . . . Brown, T. E. (2015). New onset executive function difficulties at menopause: A possible role for lisdexamfetamine. *Psychopharmacology, 232*(16), 3091–3100.

Faraone, S. (2016, January). Findings from the MGH on Late-onset ADHD. Paper presented at the annual meeting of the American Professional Society of ADHD and Related Disorders, Washington, DC.

Faraone, S. V., Asherson, P., Banaschewski, T., Biederman, J., Buitelaar, J. K., Ramos-Quiroga, J. A., . . . Franke, B. (2015). Primer: Attention-deficit/hyperactivity disorder. *Nature Reviews: Disease Primers, 1*, 1–23.

Faraone, S. V., & Biederman, J. (2005). What is the prevalence of adult ADHD? Results of a population screen of 966 adults. *Journal of Attention Disorders*, 9(2), 384–391.

Faraone, S., Biederman, J., & Mick E. (2006).The age-dependent decline of attention-deficit/hyperactivity disorder: A meta-analysis of follow-up studies. *Psychological Medicine*, *36*(2), 159–165.

Faraone, S. V., Biederman, J., Spencer, T., Mick, E., Murray, K., Petty, C., . . . Monuteaux, M. C. (2006). Diagnosing adult attention deficit hyperactivity disorder: Are late onset and subthreshold diagnoses valid? *The American Journal of Psychiatry, 163*(10), 1720–1729.

Faraone, S. V., Biederman, J., Spencer, T., Wilens, T., Seidman, L. J., Mick, E., & Doyle, A. E. (2000). Attention-deficit/hyperactivity disorder in adults: An overview. *Biological Psychiatry*, *48*(1), 9–20.

Faraone, S. V., Biederman, J., & Wozniak, J. (2012). Examining the comorbidity between attention deficit hyperactivity disorder and bipolar I disorder: A meta-analysis of family genetic studies. *The American Journal of Psychiatry, 169*, 1256–1266.

Faraone, S. V., & Glatt, S. J. (2010). A comparison of the efficacy of medication for adult attention-deficit/hyperactivity disorder using meta-analysis of effect sizes. *The Journal of Clinical Psychiatry, 71*(6), 754–763.

Farb, N. A., Anderson, A. K., & Segal, Z. V. (2012). The mindful brain and emotion regulation in mood disorders. *Canadian Journal of Psychiatry. 57*(2), 70–77.

Farrell, N. R., Lee, A. A., & Deacon, B. J. (2015). Biological or psychological? Effects of eating disorder psychoeducation on self-blame and recovery expectations among symptomatic individuals. *Behaviour Research and Therapy*, *74*, 32–37.

Fedele, D. A., Hartung, C. M., Canu, W. H., & Wilkowski, B. M. (2010). Potential symptoms of ADHD for emerging adults. *Journal of Psychopathology and Behavioral Assessment*, *32*(3), 385–396.

Ferini-Strambi, L., Baietto, C., Di Gioia, M. R., Castaldi, P., Castronovo, C., Zucconi, M., & Cappa, S. F. (2003). Cognitive dysfunction in patients with obstructive sleep apnea (OSA): Partial reversibility after continuous positive airway pressure (CPAP). *Brain Research Bulletin*, *61*(1), 87–92.

Field, S., Parker, D. R., Sawilowsky, S., & Rolands, L. (2013). Assessing the impact of ADHD coaching services on university students' learning skills, self-regulation, and well-being. *Journal of Postsecondary Education and Disability*, *26*(1), 67–81.

Fischer, M., Barkley, R. A., Smallish, L., & Fletcher, K. (2002). Young adult follow-up of hyperactive children: Self-reported psychiatric disorders, comorbidity, and the role of childhood conduct problems and teen CD. *Journal of Abnormal Child Psychology*, *30*(5), 463–475.

Fischer, M., Barkley, R. A., Smallish, L., & Fletcher, K. (2007). Hyperactive children as young adults: Driving abilities, safe driving behavior, and adverse driving outcomes. *Accident Analysis & Prevention*, *39*(1), 94–105.

Fischer, B. L., Gunter-Hunt, G., Steinhafel, C. H., & Howell, T. (2012). The identification and assessment of late-life ADHD in memory clinics. *Journal of Attention Disorders, 16*(4), 333–338.

Flannery, A. J., Becker, S. P., & Luebbe, A. M. (2016). Does emotion dysregulation mediate the association between sluggish cognitive tempo and college students' social impairment? *Journal of Attention Disorders, 20*(9), 802–812.

Fleming, A. P., McMahon, R. J., Moran, L. R., Peterson, A. P., & Dreessen, A. (2015). Pilot randomized controlled trial of dialectical behavior therapy group skills training for ADHD among college students. *Journal of Attention Disorders, 19*(3), 260–271.

Fliers, E., Rommelse, N., Vermeulen, S. H., Altink, M., Buschgens, C. J., Faraone, S. V., . . . Buitelaar, J. K. (2007). Motor coordination problems in children and adolescents with ADHD rated by parents and teachers: Effects of age and gender. *Journal of Neural Transmission, 115*(2), 211–220.

Fones, C. S., Pollack, M. H., Susswein, L., & Otto, M. (2000). History of childhood attention deficit hyperactivity disorder (ADHD) features among adults with panic disorder. *Journal of Affective Disorders, 58*(2), 99–106.

Forster, S., Robertson, D. J., Jennings, A., Asherson, P., & Lavie, N. (2014). Plugging the attention deficit: Perceptual load counters increased distraction in ADHD. *Neuropsychology, 28*(1), 91–97.

Franke, B., Faraone, S. V., Asherson, P., Buitelaar, J., Bau, C. H., Ramos-Quiroga, J. A., . . . International Multicentre persistent ADHD CollaboraTion (IMpACT). (2012). The genetics of attention deficit/hyperactivity disorder in adults: A review. *Molecular Psychiatry, 17*(10), 960–987.

Frazier, T. W., Demaree, H. A., & Youngstrom, E. A. (2004). Meta-analysis of intellectual and neuropsychological test performance in attention-deficit/hyperactivity disorder. *Neuropsychology, 18*(3), 543–555.

Fredriksen, M., Halmøy, A., Faraone, S. V., & Haavik, J. (2013). Long-term efficacy and safety of treatment with stimulants and atomoxetine in adult ADHD: A review of controlled and naturalistic studies. *European Neuropsychopharmacology, 23*(6), 508–527.

Fried, R. (2016, January). Clinical correlates of working memory deficits in youth with and without ADHD. Paper presented at the annual meeting of the American Professional Society of ADHD and Related Disorders, Washington, DC.

Frost, R. O., Steketee, G., & Tolin, D. F. (2011). Comorbidity in hoarding disorder. *Depression and Anxiety, 28*(10), 876–884.

Fugate, C. M., Zentall, S. S., & Gentry, M. (2013). Creativity and working memory in gifted students with and without characteristics of attention deficit hyperactive disorder: Lifting the mask. *Gifted Child Quarterly, 57*(4), 234–246.

Fulda, S., & Schulz, H. (2001). Cognitive dysfunction in sleep disorders. *Sleep Medicine Reviews, 5*(6), 423–445.

Gapin, J. I., Labban, J. D., & Etnier, J. L. (2011). The effects of physical activity on attention deficit hyperactivity disorder symptoms: The evidence. *Preventive Medicine, 52*, S70–S74.

Gaub, M., & Carlson, C. L. (1997). Gender differences in ADHD: A meta-analysis and critical review. *Journal of the American Academy of Child & Adolescent Psychiatry, 36*(8), 1036–1045.

Gershon, J. (2002). A meta-analytic review of gender differences in ADHD. *Journal of Attention Disorders, 5*(3), 143–154.

Gibbins, C., & Weiss, M. (2007). Clinical recommendations in current practice guidelines for diagnosis and treatment of ADHD in adults. *Current Psychiatry Reports, 9*(5), 420–426.

Gimpel, G. A., Collett, B. R., Veeder, M. A., Gifford, J. A., Sneddon, P., Bushman, B., . . . Odell, J. D. (2005). Effects of stimulant medication on cognitive performance of children with ADHD. *Clinical Pediatrics, 44*(5), 405–411.

Gizer, I. R., Ficks, C., & Waldman, I. D. (2009). Candidate gene studies of ADHD: A meta-analytic review. *Human Genetics, 126*(1), 51–90.

Gonzalez, R. A., Kallis, C., & Coid, J. W. (2013). Adult attention deficit hyperactivity disorder and violence in the population of England: Does comorbidity matter? *PloS One, 8*(9), e75575.

Goodman, D. W., Mitchell, S., Rhodewalt, L., & Surman, C. B. (2016). Clinical presentation, diagnosis and treatment of attention-deficit hyperactivity disorder (ADHD) in older adults: A review of the evidence and its implications for clinical care. *Drugs & Aging, 33*(1), 27–36.

Gudjonsson, G. H., Sigurdsson, J. F., Sigfusdottir, I. D., & Young, S. (2012). A national epidemiological study of offending and its relationship with ADHD symptoms and associated risk factors. *Journal of Attention Disorders, 18*(1), 3–13.

Guo, W., Yao, D., Jiang, J., Su, Q., Zhang, Z., Zhang, J., . . . Xiao, C. (2014). Abnormal default-mode network homogeneity in first-episode, drug-naive schizophrenia at rest. *Progress in Neuro-Psychopharmacology and Biological Psychiatry, 49*, 16–20.

Haavik, J., Halmøy, A., Lundervold, A. J., & Fasmer, O. B. (2010). Clinical assessment and diagnosis of adults with attention-deficit/hyperactivity disorder. *Expert Review of Neurotherapeutics, 10*(10), 1569–1580.

Hallowell, E. M., & Ratey, J. J. (2001). *Driven to distraction: Recognizing and coping with attention deficit disorder from childhood through adulthood.* New York: Anchor Books.

Halperin, J. M., & Schulz, K. P. (2006). Revisiting the role of the prefrontal cortex in the pathophysiology of attention-deficit/hyperactivity disorder. *Psychological Bulletin, 132*(4), 560–581.

Halperin, J. M., Trampush, J. W., Miller, C. J., Marks, D. J., & Newcorn, J. H. (2008). Neuropsychological outcome in adolescents/young adults with childhood ADHD: Profiles of persisters, remitters and controls. *Journal of Child Psychology and Psychiatry, 49*(9), 958–966.

Hamilton, J. P., Furman, D. J., Chang, C., Thomason, M. E., Dennis, E., & Gotlib, I. H. (2011). Default-mode and task-positive network activity in major depressive disorder: Implications for adaptive and maladaptive rumination. *Biological Psychiatry, 70*(4), 327–333.

Hammerness, P. (2013). Stimulant pharmacotherapy for adults with ADHD. In C. B. H. Surman (Ed.), *ADHD in adults: A practical guide to evaluation and management* (pp. 71–87). New York: Humana Press.

Harpin, V. A. (2005). The effect of ADHD on the life of an individual, their family, and community from preschool to adult life. *Archives of Disease in Childhood, 90*(Suppl. 1), i2–i7.

Harrison, A. G., Edwards, M. J., & Parker, K. C. (2007). Identifying students faking ADHD: Preliminary findings and strategies for detection. *Archives of Clinical Neuropsychology, 22*(5), 577–588.

Hart, H., Radua, J., Nakao, T., Mataix-Cols, D., & Rubia, K. (2013). Meta-analysis of functional magnetic resonance imaging studies of inhibition and attention in attention-deficit/hyperactivity disorder: Exploring task-specific, stimulant medication, and age effects. *JAMA Psychiatry*, *70*(2), 185–198.

Harvey, A. G., Lee, J., Williams, J., Hollon, S. D., Walker, M. P., Thompson, M. A., & Smith, R. (2014). Improving outcome of psychosocial treatments by enhancing memory and learning. *Perspectives on Psychological Science*, *9*(2), 161–179.

Hawkey, E., & Nigg, J. T. (2014). Omega-3 fatty acid and ADHD: Blood level analysis and meta-analytic extension of supplementation trials. *Clinical Psychology Review*, *34*(6), 496–505.

Healey, D. M., & Rucklidge, J. J. (2008). The relationship between ADHD and creativity. *The ADHD Report*, 16(3), 1–5.

Hill, B. D., Pella, R. D., Singh, A. N., Jones, G. N., & Gouvier, W. D. (2009). The Wender Utah Rating Scale: Adult ADHD diagnostic tool or personality index? *Journal of Attention Disorders*, *13*(1), 87–94.

Hillman, C. H., Erickson, K. I., & Kramer, A. F. (2008). Be smart, exercise your heart: Exercise effects on brain and cognition. *Nature Reviews Neuroscience*, *9*(1), 58–65.

Hillman, C. H., Pontifex, M. B., Castelli, D. M., Khan, N. A., Raine, L. B., Scudder, M. R., . . . Kamijo, K. (2014). Effects of the FITKids randomized controlled trial on executive control and brain function. *Pediatrics*, *134*(4), e1063–e1071.

Hinshaw, S. P., & Blachman, D. R. (2005). Attention-deficit/hyperactivity disorder in girls. In D. J. Bell, S. L. Foster, & E. J. Mash (Eds.), *Handbook of behavioral and emotional problems in girls* (pp. 117–147). New York: Kluwer Academic/Plenum.

Hinshaw, S. P., Owens, E. B., Zalecki, C., Huggins, S. P., Montenegro-Nevado, A. J., Schrodek, E., & Swanson, E. N. (2012). Prospective follow-up of girls with attention-deficit/hyperactivity disorder into early adulthood: Continuing impairment includes elevated risk for suicide attempts and self-injury. *Journal of Consulting and Clinical Psychology*, *80*(6), 1041–1051.

Hirvikoski, T., Lindholm, T., Nordenström, A., Nordström, A. L., & Lajic, S. (2009). High self-perceived stress and many stressors, but normal diurnal cortisol rhythm, in adults with ADHD (attention-deficit/hyperactivity disorder). *Hormones and Behavior*, *55*(3), 418–424.

Hirvikoski, T., Waaler, E., Alfredsson, J., Pihlgren, C., Holmström, A., Johnson, A., . . . Nordström, A. L. (2011). Reduced ADHD symptoms in adults with ADHD after structured skills training group: Results from a randomized controlled trial. *Behaviour Research and Therapy*, *49*(3), 175–185.

Hirvikoski, T., Waaler, E., Lindström, T., Bölte, S., & Jokinen, J. (2015). Cognitive behavior therapy-based psychoeducational groups for adults with ADHD and their significant others (PEGASUS): an open clinical feasibility trial. *ADHD Attention Deficit and Hyperactivity Disorders*, *7*(1), 89–99.

Hodgson, K., Hutchinson, A. D., & Denson, L. (2012). Nonpharmacological treatments for ADHD: A meta-analytic review. *Journal of Attention Disorders*, *18*(4), 275–282.

Holland, K., & Higuera, V. (2015). The history of ADHD: A timeline. Retrieved from http://www.healthline.com/health/adhd/history#Overview1

Hölzel, B. K., Lazar, S. W., Gard, T., Schuman-Olivier, Z., Vago, D. R., & Ott, U. (2011). How does mindfulness meditation work? Proposing mechanisms of action from a conceptual and neural perspective. *Perspectives on Psychological Science*, *6*(6), 537–559.

Hong, L., & Page, S. E. (2004). Groups of diverse problem solvers can outperform groups of high-ability problem solvers. *Proceedings of the National Academy of Sciences of the United States of America, 101*(46), 16385–16389.

Hoza, B., Smith, A. L., Shoulberg, E. K., Linnea, K. S., Dorsch, T. E., Blazo, J. A., . . . McCabe, G. P. (2015). A randomized trial examining the effects of aerobic physical activity on attention-deficit/hyperactivity disorder symptoms in young children. *Journal of Abnormal Child Psychology, 43*(4), 655–667.

Huber, R. S., Kim, T. S., Kim, N., Kuykendall, M. D., Sherwood, S. N., Renshaw, P. F., & Kondo, D. G. (2015). Association between altitude and regional variation of ADHD in youth. *Journal of Attention Disorders*. Online advance publication.

ICD10Data.com. (2015). 2016 ICD-10-CM diagnosis code. Retrieved from http://www.icd10data.com/Search.aspx?search=F90

Jachimowicz, G., & Geiselman, R. E. (2004). Comparison of ease of falsification of attention deficit hyperactivity disorder diagnosis using standard behavioral rating scales. *Cognitive Science Online, 2*(1), 6–20.

Jarrett, M. A., Rapport, H. F., Rondon, A. T., & Becker, S. P. (2014). ADHD dimensions and sluggish cognitive tempo symptoms in relation to self-report and laboratory measures of neuropsychological functioning in college students. *Journal of Attention Disorders*. Advance online publication.

Jerome, L., Segal, A., & Habinski, L. (2006). What we know about ADHD and driving risk: A literature review, meta-analysis and critique. *Journal of the Canadian Academy of Child and Adolescent Psychiatry, 15*(3), 105–125.

Johnston, C., Mash, E. J., Miller, N., & Ninowski, J. E. (2012). Parenting in adults with attention-deficit/hyperactivity disorder (ADHD). *Clinical Psychology Review, 32*(4), 215–228.

Jurado, M. B., & Rosselli, M. (2007). The elusive nature of executive functions: A review of our current understanding. *Neuropsychology Review, 17*(3), 213–233.

Kemp, J. J., Lickel, J. J., & Deacon, B. J. (2014). Effects of a chemical imbalance causal explanation on individuals' perceptions of their depressive symptoms. *Behaviour Research and Therapy, 56*, 47–52.

Kent, K. M., Pelham, W. E.Jr., Molina, B. S., Sibley, M. H., Waschbusch, D. A., Yu, J., . . . Karch, K. M. (2011). The academic experience of male high school students with ADHD. *Journal of Abnormal Child Psychology, 39*(3), 451–462.

Kerson, C. (2013). A proposed multisite double-blind randomized clinical trial of neurofeedback for ADHD: Need, rationale, and strategy. *Journal of Attention Disorders, 17*(5), 420–436.

Kessler, R. C., Adler, L., Barkley, R., Biederman, J., Conners, C. K., Demler, O., . . . Zaslavsky, A. M. (2006). The prevalence and correlates of adult ADHD in the United States: Results from the National Comorbidity Survey Replication. *The American Journal of Psychiatry, 163*(4), 716–723.

Kessler, R. C., Adler, L. A., Barkley, R., Biederman, J., Conners, C. K., Faraone, S. V., . . . Üstün, T. B. (2005). Patterns and predictors of ADHD persistence into adulthood: Results from the National Comorbidity Survey Replication. *Biological Psychiatry, 57*(11), 1442–1451.

Kessler, R. C., Adler, L. A., Barkley, R., Biederman, J., Conners, C. K., Greenhill, L. L. & Spencer, T. (2011). The prevalence and correlates of adult ADHD. In J. Buitelaar, C. C. Kan, & P. J. Asherson (Eds.), *ADHD in adults: Characterization, diagnosis, and treatment* (pp. 9–17). Cambridge, UK: Cambridge University Press.

Kessler, R. C., Adler, L. A., Gruber, M. J., Sarawate, C. A., Spencer, T., & Van Brunt, D. L. (2007). Validity of the World Health Organization Adult ADHD Self-Report Scale (ASRS) screener in a representative sample of health plan members. *International Journal of Methods in Psychiatric Research, 16*(2), 52–65.

Kessler, R. C., Green, J. G., Adler, L. A., Barkley, R. A., Chatterji, S., Faraone, S. V., . . . Van Brunt, D. L. (2010). Structure and diagnosis of adult attention-deficit/hyperactivity disorder: Analysis of expanded symptom criteria from the Adult ADHD Clinical Diagnostic Scale. *Archives of General Psychiatry, 67*(11), 1168–1178.

Kessler, R. C., Lane, M., Stang, P. E., & Van Brunt, D. L. (2009). The prevalence and workplace costs of adult attention deficit hyperactivity disorder in a large manufacturing firm. *Psychological Medicine, 39*(1), 137–147.

Kirsch I., Deacon B. J., Huedo-Medina T. B., Scoboria A., Moore T. J., & Johnson B. T. (2008). Initial severity and antidepressant benefits: A meta-analysis of data submitted to the Food and Drug Administration. *PLoS Med, 5*(2), 260–268.

Knouse, L. E., Bagwell, C. L., Barkley, R. A., & Murphy, K. R. (2005). Accuracy of self-evaluation in adults with ADHD: Evidence from a driving study. *Journal of Attention Disorders, 8*(4), 221–234.

Knouse, L. E., Cooper-Vince, C., Sprich, S., & Safren, S. A. (2008). Recent developments in the psychosocial treatment of adult ADHD. *Expert Review of Neurotherapeutics, 8*(10), 1537–1548.

Knouse, L. E., & Mitchell, J. T. (2015). Incautiously optimistic: Positively valenced cognitive avoidance in adult ADHD. *Cognitive and Behavioral Practice, 22*(2), 192–202.

Knouse, L. E., & Safren, S. A. (2010). Current status of cognitive behavioral therapy for adult attention-deficit hyperactivity disorder. *Psychiatric Clinics of North America, 33*(3), 497–509.

Knouse, L. E., & Safren, S. A. (2011). Psychosocial treatment of adults with attention-deficit/hyperactivity disorder. In S. W. Evans & B. Hoza (Eds.), *Treating attention deficit hyperactivity disorder* (pp. 12-1–12-21). Kingston, NJ: Civic Research Institute.

Knouse, L. E., & Safren, S. A. (2013). Psychosocial treatment for adult ADHD. In C. B. H. Surman (Ed.), *ADHD in adults: A practical guide to evaluation and management* (pp. 119–136). New York: Humana Press.

Kolar, D., Keller, A., Golfinopoulos, M., Cumyn, L., Syer, C., & Hechtman, L. (2008). Treatment of adults with attention-deficit/hyperactivity disorder. *Neuropsychiatric Disease and Treatment, 4*(2), 389–403.

Kooij, S. J., Bejerot, S., Blackwell, A., Caci, H., Casas-Brugué, M., Carpentier, P. J., . . . Gaillac, V. (2010). European consensus statement on diagnosis and treatment of adult ADHD: The European network adult ADHD. *BMC Psychiatry, 10*(1), 67.

Kooij, J. S., Boonstra, A. M., Swinkels, S. H. N., Bekker, E. M., de Noord, I., & Buitelaar, J. K. (2008). Reliability, validity, and utility of instruments for self-report and informant report concerning symptoms of ADHD in adult patients. *Journal of Attention Disorders, 11*(4), 445–458.

Kubik, J. A. (2009). Efficacy of ADHD coaching for adults with ADHD. *Journal of Attention Disorders, 13*(5), 442–453.

Kuester, D. A., & Zentall, S. S. (2012). Social interaction rules in cooperative learning groups for students at risk for ADHD. *The Journal of Experimental Education, 80*(1), 69–95.

Kühn, S., Ritter, S. M., Müller, B. C., Baaren, R. B., Brass, M., & Dijksterhuis, A. (2014). The importance of the default mode network in creativity: A structural MRI study. *The Journal of Creative Behavior, 48*(2), 152–163.

Küpper, T., Haavik, J., Drexler, H., Ramos-Quiroga, J. A., Wermelskirchen, D., Prutz, C., & Schauble, B. (2012). The negative impact of attention-deficit/hyperactivity disorder on occupational health in adults and adolescents. *International Archives of Occupational and Environmental Health, 85*(8), 837–847.

Kuriyan, A. B., Pelham, W. E. Jr., Molina, B. S., Waschbusch, D. A., Gnagy, E. M., Sibley, M. H., . . . Kent, K. M. (2013). Young adult educational and vocational outcomes of children diagnosed with ADHD. *Journal of Abnormal Child Psychology, 41*(1), 27–41.

Kvaale, E. P., Haslam, N., & Gottdiener, W. H. (2013). The "side effects" of medicalization: A meta-analytic review of how biogenetic explanations affect stigma. *Clinical Psychology Review, 33*(6), 782–794.

Lackschewitz, H., Hüther, G., & Kröner-Herwig, B. (2008). Physiological and psychological stress responses in adults with attention-deficit/hyperactivity disorder (ADHD). *Psychoneuroendocrinology, 33*(5), 612–624.

Lahey, B. B., & Willcutt, E. G. (2010). Predictive validity of a continuous alternative to nominal subtypes of attention-deficit/hyperactivity disorder for DSM–V. *Journal of Clinical Child & Adolescent Psychology, 39*(6), 761–775.

Lakhan, S. E., & Kirchgessner, A. (2012). Prescription stimulants in individuals with and without attention deficit hyperactivity disorder: Misuse, cognitive impact, and adverse effects. *Brain and Behavior, 2*(5), 661–677.

Lally, P., Van Jaarsveld, C. H., Potts, H. W., & Wardle, J. (2010). How are habits formed: Modelling habit formation in the real world. *European Journal of Social Psychology, 40*(6), 998–1009.

Lally, P., Wardle, J., & Gardner, B. (2011). Experiences of habit formation: A qualitative study. *Psychology, Health & Medicine, 16*(4), 484–489.

Lis, S., Baer, N., Stein-en-Nosse, C., Gallhofer, B., Sammer, G., & Kirsch, P. (2010). Objective measurement of motor activity during cognitive performance in adults with attention-deficit/hyperactivity disorder. *Acta Psychiatrica Scandinavica, 122*(4), 285–294.

Ljung, T., Chen, Q., Lichtenstein, P., & Larsson, H. (2014). Common etiological factors of attention-deficit/hyperactivity disorder and suicidal behavior: A population-based study in Sweden. *JAMA Psychiatry, 71*(8), 958–964.

Loo, S. K., Hale, T. S., Macion, J., Hanada, G., McGough, J. J., McCracken, J. T., & Smalley, S. L. (2009). Cortical activity patterns in ADHD during arousal, activation and sustained attention. *Neuropsychologia, 47*(10), 2114–2119.

Lovett, B. J., & Leja, A. M. (2013). ADHD symptoms and benefit from extended time testing accommodations. *Journal of Attention Disorders, 19*(2), 167–172.

Machan, D. (2011, August 2). Why some entrepreneurs call ADHD a superpower. Market Watch. Retrieved from http://www.marketwatch.com/story/entrepreneurs-superpower-for-some-its-adhd-1310052627559

Mahone, M. (2016, January). Neuropsychological phenotype(s) of ADHD: Developmental models, sexual dimorphism, and comorbid conditions. Paper presented at the annual meeting of the American Professional Society of ADHD and Related Disorders, Washington, DC.

Malloy-Diniz, L., Fuentes, D., Leite, W. B., Correa, H., & Bechara, A. (2007). Impulsive behavior in adults with attention deficit/hyperactivity disorder: Characterization of attentional, motor and cognitive impulsiveness. *Journal of the International Neuropsychological Society, 13*(4), 693–698.

Mancini, C., Van Ameringen, M., Oakman, J. M., & Figueiredo, D. (1999). Childhood attention deficit/hyperactivity disorder in adults with anxiety disorders. *Psychological Medicine, 29*(03), 515–525.

Manor, I. (2016, January). Beyond the empirical data base: Assessment and treatment of ADHD in older adults. Symposium presented at the annual meeting of the American Professional Society of ADHD and Related Disorders, Washington, DC.

Manos, M. J. (2010). Nuances of assessment and treatment of ADHD in adults: A guide for psychologists. *Professional Psychology: Research and Practice, 41*(6), 511–517.

Mariani, J. J., & Levin, F. R. (2007). Treatment strategies for co-occurring ADHD and substance use disorders. *American Journal of Addictions, 16*(Suppl. 1), 45–56.

Matte, B., Rohde, L. A., Turner, J. B., Fisher, P. W., Shen, S., Bau, C. H., . . . Grevet, E. H. (2015). Reliability and validity of proposed DSM-5 ADHD symptoms in a clinical sample of adults. *The Journal of Neuropsychiatry and Clinical Neurosciences, 27*(3), 228–236.

Mattfeld, A. T., Gabrieli, J. D., Biederman, J., Spencer, T., Brown, A., Kotte, A., . . . Whitfield-Gabrieli, S. (2014). Brain differences between persistent and remitted attention deficit hyperactivity disorder. *Brain, 137*, 2423–2428.

Mayer, K., Wyckoff, S. N., & Strehl, U. (2013). One size fits all? Slow cortical potentials Neurofeedback: A review. *Journal of Attention Disorders, 17*(5), 393–409.

Mazza, M., Pomponi, M., Janiri, L., Bria, P., & Mazza, S. (2007). Omega-3 fatty acids and antioxidants in neurological and psychiatric diseases: An overview. *Progress in Neuro-Psychopharmacology and Biological Psychiatry, 31*(1), 12–26.

McBurnett, K. (2016, January). Sluggish cognitive tempo in 2016: What we've learned so far. Paper presented at the annual meeting of the American Professional Society of ADHD and Related Disorders, Washington, DC.

McCann, B. S., Scheele, L., Ward, N., & Roy-Byrne, P. (2000). Discriminant validity of the Wender Utah Rating Scale for attention-deficit/hyperactivity disorder in adults. *The Journal of Neuropsychiatry and Clinical Neurosciences, 12*(2), 240–245.

McCarthy, S., Asherson, P., Coghill, D., Hollis, C., Murray, M., Potts, L., . . . Wong, I. C. (2009). Attention-deficit hyperactivity disorder: Treatment discontinuation in adolescents and young adults. *The British Journal of Psychiatry, 194*(3), 273–277.

McClernon, F. J., & Kollins, S. H. (2008). ADHD and smoking. *Annals of the New York Academy of Sciences, 1141*(1), 131–147.

McGough, J. J. (2014). *ADHD: Oxford American psychiatry library*. New York: Oxford University Press.

McGough, J. J., & Barkley, R. A. (2004). Diagnostic controversies in adult attention deficit hyperactivity disorder. *The American Journal of Psychiatry, 161*(11), 1948–1956.

McGough, J. J., Smalley, S. L., McCracken, J. T., Yang, M., Del'Homme, M., Lynn, D. E., & Loo, S. (2005). Psychiatric comorbidity in adult attention deficit hyperactivity disorder: Findings from multiplex families. *The American Journal of Psychiatry, 162*(9), 1621–1627.

McLoughlin, G., Albrecht, B., Banaschewski, T., Rothenberger, A., Brandeis, D., Asherson, P., & Kuntsi, J. (2009). Performance monitoring is altered in adult ADHD: A familial event-related potential investigation. *Neuropsychologia, 47*(14), 3134–3142.

Melby-Lervóg, M., & Hulme, C. (2013). Is working memory training effective? A meta-analytic review. *Developmental Psychology, 49*(2), 270–291.

Merkel, R. L. (2010). Safety of stimulant treatment in attention deficit hyperactivity disorder: Part II. *Expert Opinion on Drug Safety, 8*(6), 917–935.

Merkel, R. L., & Kuchibhatla, A. (2009). Safety of stimulant treatment in attention deficit hyperactivity disorder: Part I. *Expert Opinion on Drug Safety, 8*(6), 655–668.

Meyer, H. (2010). Framing disability: Comparing individualist and collectivist societies. *Comparative Sociology, 9*, 1–17.

Michielsen, M., Semeijn, E., Comijs, H. C., van de Ven, P., Beekman, A. T., Deeg, D. J., & Kooij, J. S. (2012). Prevalence of attention-deficit hyperactivity disorder in older adults in the Netherlands. *The British Journal of Psychiatry, 201*(4), 298–305.

Miller, L. A., Lewandowski, L. J., & Antshel, K. M. (2015). Effects of extended time for college students with and without ADHD. *Journal of Attention Disorders, 19*(8), 678–686.

Minde, K., Eakin, L., Hechtman, L., Ochs, E., Bouffard, R., Greenfield, B., & Looper, K. (2003). The psychosocial functioning of children and spouses of adults with ADHD. *Journal of Child Psychology and Psychiatry, 44*(4), 637–646.

Mitchell, J. T., Benson, J. W., Knouse, L. E., Kimbrel, N. A., & Anastopoulos, A. D. (2013). Are negative automatic thoughts associated with ADHD in adulthood? *Cognitive Therapy and Research, 37*(4), 851–859.

Mitchell, J. T., McIntyre, E. M., English, J. S., Dennis, M. F., Beckham, J. C., & Kollins, S. H. (2013). A pilot trial of mindfulness meditation training for ADHD in adulthood: Impact on core symptoms, executive functioning, and emotion dysregulation. *Journal of Attention Disorders*. Advance online publication. doi:10.1177/1087054713513328

Mitchell, J. T., Pratt, R., Davis, N. O., Lunsford-Avery, J., Schechter, J., Sonuga-Barke, E. & Kollins, S. H. (2016, January). Psychometric properties of the Quick Delay Questionnaire (QDQ) in an adult outpatient sample seeking ADHD assessment. Poster presented at the annual meeting of the American Professional Society of ADHD and Related Disorders, Washington, DC.

Mitchell, J. T., Robertson, C. D., Kimbrel, N. A., & Nelson-Gray, R. O. (2011). An evaluation of behavioral approach in adults with ADHD. *Journal of Psychopathology and Behavioral Assessment, 33*(4), 430–437.

Mitchell, J. T., Zylowska, L., & Kollins, S. H. (2015). Mindfulness meditation training for attention-deficit/hyperactivity disorder in adulthood: Current empirical support, treatment overview, and future directions. *Cognitive and Behavioral Practice, 22*(2), 172–191.

Moffitt, T. E., Houts, R., Asherson, P., Belsky, D. W., Corcoran, D. L., Hammerle, M., . . . Poulton, R. (2015). Is adult ADHD a childhood-onset neurodevelopmental disorder? Evidence from a four-decade longitudinal cohort study. *The American Journal of Psychiatry, 172*(10), 967–977.

Mollayeva, T., Thurairajah, P., Burton, K., Mollayeva, S., Shapiro, C. M. & Colantonio, A. (2016). The Pittsburgh Sleep Quality Index as a screening tool for sleep dysfunction in clinical and non-clinical samples: A systematic review and meta-analysis. *Sleep Medicine Reviews, 25*, 52–73.

Morgan, P. L., Staff, J., Millemeier, M. M., Farkas, G. & Maczuga, S. (2013). Racial and ethnic disparities in ADHD diagnosis from kindergarten to eighth grade. *Pediatrics, 132*(1), 85–93.

Moriyama, T. S., Polanczyk, G. V., Terzi, F. S., Faria, K. V. M., & Rohde, L. A. P. (2013). Psychopharmacology and psychotherapy for the treatment of adults with ADHD: A systematic review of available meta-analyses. *CNS Spectrums, 18*(6), 296–306.

Mostofsky, S. (2016, January). Moving to improve behavioral control in ADHD. Paper presented at the annual meeting American Professional Society of ADHD and Related Disorders, Washington, DC.

Murphy, K. (2005). Psychosocial treatments for ADHD in teens and adults: A practice-friendly review. *Journal of Clinical Psychology, 61*(5), 607–619.

Murphy, K. R., Barkley, R. A., & Bush, T. (2002). Young adults with attention deficit hyperactivity disorder: Subtype differences in comorbidity, educational, and clinical history. *The Journal of Nervous and Mental Disease, 190*(3), 147–157.

Murphy, K. R., & Gordon, M. (2006). Assessment of adults with ADHD. In R. A. Barkley (Ed.), *Attention-deficit hyperactivity disorder: A handbook for diagnosis and treatment* (3rd ed., pp. 425–450). New York: Guilford Press.

Murphy, P., & Schachar, R. (2000). Use of self-ratings in the assessment of symptoms of attention deficit hyperactivity disorder in adults. *The American Journal of Psychiatry*, 157(7), 1156–1159.

Murray, C., & Johnston, C. (2006). Parenting in mothers with and without attention-deficit/hyperactivity disorder. *Journal of Abnormal Psychology, 115*(1), 52–61.

Musser, E. D., Hawkey, E., Kachan-Liu, S. S., Lees, P., Roullet, J. B., Goddard, K., . . . Nigg, J. T. (2014). Shared familial transmission of autism spectrum and attention-deficit/hyperactivity disorders. *Journal of Child Psychology and Psychiatry, 55*(7), 819–827.

Nadeau, K. G. (2005). Career choices and workplace challenges for individuals with ADHD. *Journal of Clinical Psychology, 61*(5), 549–563.

Naseem, S., Chaudhary, B., & Collop, N. (2001). Attention deficit hyperactivity disorder in adults and obstructive sleep apnea. *CHEST Journal, 119*(1), 294–296.

National Heart, Lung and Blood Institute Working Group on Restless Legs Syndrome. (2000). Restless legs syndrome: Detection and management in primary care. Retrieved from http://www.aafp.org/afp/2000/0701/p108.html

National Resource Center on AD/HD. (2003). Succeeding in the workplace. What we know. Retrieved from http://www.ldaofky.org/ADHD%20&%20Workplace%20Success.pdf

Naumann, A., Bellebaum, C., & Daum, I. (2006). Cognitive deficits in narcolepsy. *Journal of Sleep Research, 15*(3), 329–338.

Naumann, A., & Daum, I. (2003). Narcolepsy: Pathophysiology and neuropsychological changes. *Behavioural Neurology, 14*(3–4), 89–98.

Neale, B. M., Medland, S. E., Ripke, S., Asherson, P., Franke, B., Lesch, K. P., . . . Psychiatric GWAS Consortium: ADHD Subgroup. (2010). Meta-analysis of genome-wide association studies of attention deficit/hyperactivity disorder. *Journal of the American Academy of Child & Adolescent Psychiatry, 49*(9), 884–897.

Newark, P. E., & Stieglitz, R. D. (2010). Therapy-relevant factors in adult ADHD from a cognitive behavioural perspective. *ADHD Attention Deficit and Hyperactivity Disorders, 2*(2), 59–72.

Newcorn, J. H., Halperin, J. M., Jensen, P. S., Abikoff, H. B., Arnold, L. E., Cantwell, D. P., . . . Hechtman, L. (2001). Symptom profiles in children with ADHD: Effects of comorbidity and gender. *Journal of the American Academy of Child & Adolescent Psychiatry, 40*(2), 137–146.

Nigg, J. T. (2006). *What causes ADHD? Understanding what goes wrong and why.* New York: Guilford Press.

Nigg, J. T. (2010). Attention-deficit/hyperactivity disorder: Endophenotypes, structure and etiological pathways. *Current Directions in Psychological Science, 19*(1), 24–29.

Nigg, J. T. (2012). ADHD: Heterogeneity and etiology [Video]. Retrieved from https://www.youtube.com/watch?v=iqa9GL47Kv8

Nigg, J. T. (2013). Attention-deficit/hyperactivity disorder and adverse health outcomes. *Clinical Psychology Review, 33*(2), 215–228.

Nigg, J. T., Lewis, K., Edinger, T., & Falk, M. (2012). Meta-analysis of attention-deficit/hyperactivity disorder or attention-deficit/hyperactivity disorder symptoms, restriction diet, and synthetic food color additives. *Journal of the American Academy of Child & Adolescent Psychiatry, 51*(1), 86–97.

Nigg, J. T., Nikolas, M., Mark Knottnerus, G., Cavanagh, K., & Friderici, K. (2010). Confirmation and extension of association of blood lead with attention-deficit/hyperactivity disorder (ADHD) and ADHD symptom domains at population-typical exposure levels. *Journal of Child Psychology and Psychiatry, 51*(1), 58–65.

Nigg, J. T., Stavro, G., Ettenhofer, M., Hambrick, D. Z., Miller, T., & Henderson, J. M. (2005). Executive functions and ADHD in adults: Evidence for selective effects on ADHD symptom domains. *Journal of Abnormal Psychology, 114*(4), 706–717.

Ninowski, J. E., Mash, E. J., & Benzies, K. M. (2007). Symptoms of attention-deficit/hyperactivity disorder in first-time expectant women: Relations with parenting cognitions and behaviors. *Infant Mental Health Journal, 28*(1), 54–75.

Nolen-Hoeksema, S., Wisco, B. E., & Lyubomirsky, S. (2008). Rethinking rumination. *Perspectives on Psychological Science, 3*(5), 400–424.

Nonacs, R. (2014). Clinical update: Use of methylphenidate during pregnancy. Retrieved from https://womensmentalhealth.org/posts/clinical-update-use-methylphenidate-pregnancy/

Nutt, D. J., Fone, K., Asherson, P., Bramble, D., Hill, P., Matthews, K., . . . Weiss, M. (2007). Evidence-based guidelines for management of attention-deficit/hyperactivity disorder in adolescents in transition to adult services and in adults: Recommendations from the British Association for Psychopharmacology. *Journal of Psychopharmacology, 21*(1), 10–41.

Ohayon, M. M., & Roth, T. (2002). Prevalence of restless legs syndrome and periodic limb movement disorder in the general population. *Journal of Psychosomatic Research, 53*, 547–554.

Ohio Sleep Medicine Institute. (2015). Periodic limb movement disorder. Retrieved from http://sleepmedicine.com/disorders.cfm?disorder=6

Ohlmeier, M. D., Peters, K., Kordon, A., Seifert, J., Te Wildt, B., Wiese, B., . . . Schneider, U. (2007). Nicotine and alcohol dependence in patients with comorbid attention-deficit/hyperactivity disorder (ADHD). *Alcohol and Alcoholism, 42*(6), 539–543.

Ohlmeier, M. D., Peters, K., Te Wildt, B. T., Zedler, M., Ziegenbein, M., Wiese, B., . . . Schneider, U. (2008). Comorbidity of alcohol and substance dependence with attention-deficit/hyperactivity disorder (ADHD). *Alcohol and Alcoholism, 43*(3), 300–304.

Olfson, M., Blanco, C., Wang, S., & Greenhill, L. L. (2013). Trends in office-based treatment of adults with stimulants in the United States. *The Journal of Clinical Psychiatry, 74*(1), 43–50.

Oliver, M. L., Nigg, J. T., Cassavaugh, N. D., & Backs, R. W. (2012). Behavioral and cardiovascular responses to frustration during simulated driving tasks in young adults with and without attention disorder symptoms. *Journal of Attention Disorders, 16*(6), 478–490.

Page, S. E. (2007). Making the difference: Applying a logic of diversity. *The Academy of Management Perspectives, 21*(4), 6–20.

Pagoto, S., Curtin, C., Appelhans, B. M., & Alonso-Alonso, M. (2012). Attention deficit/hyperactivity disorder and the clinical management of obesity. *Current Obesity Reports, 1*(2), 80–86.

Pagoto, S. L., Curtin, C., Lemon, S. C., Bandini, L. G., Schneider, K. L., Bodenlos, J. S., & Ma, Y. (2009). Association between adult attention deficit/hyperactivity disorder and obesity in the US population. *Obesity, 17*(3), 539–544.

Park, S., Cho, M. J., Chang, S. M., Jeon, H. J., Cho, S. J., Kim, B. S., . . . Hong, J. P. (2011). Prevalence, correlates, and comorbidities of adult ADHD symptoms in Korea: Results of the Korean epidemiologic catchment area study. *Psychiatry Research, 186*(2), 378–383.

Parker, D. R., Hoffman, S. F., Sawilowsky, S., & Rolands, L. (2011). An examination of the effects of ADHD coaching on university students' executive functioning. *Journal of Postsecondary Education and Disability, 24*(2), 115–132.

Pennington, B. F., McGrath, L. M., Rosenberg, J., Barnard, H., Smith, S. D., Willcutt, E. G., . . . Olson, R. K. (2009). Gene × environment interactions in reading disability and attention-deficit/hyperactivity disorder. *Developmental Psychology, 45*(1), 77–89.

Pera, G. (2016). Sexual intimacy. In G. Pera & A. L. Robin (Eds.), *Adult ADHD-focused couple therapy*. New York: Routledge.

Philipsen, A. (2012). Psychotherapy in adult attention deficit hyperactivity disorder: Implications for treatment and research. *Expert Review of Neurotherapeutics, 12*(10), 1217–1225.

Philipsen, A., Feige, B., Hesslinger, B., Scheel, C., Ebert, D., Matthies, S., . . . Lieb, K. (2009). Borderline typical symptoms in adult patients with attention deficit/hyperactivity disorder. *ADHD Attention Deficit and Hyperactivity Disorders, 1*, 11–18.

Philipsen, A., Jans, T., Graf, E., Matthies, S., Borel, P., Colla, M., . . . Sobanski, E. (2015). Effects of group psychotherapy, individual counseling, methylphenidate, and placebo in the treatment of adult attention-deficit/hyperactivity disorder: A randomized clinical trial. *JAMA Psychiatry, 72*(12), 1199–1210.

Plichta, M. M., & Scheres, A. (2014). Ventral–striatal responsiveness during reward anticipation in ADHD and its relation to trait impulsivity in the healthy population: A meta-analytic review of the fMRI literature. *Neuroscience & Biobehavioral Reviews, 38*, 125–134.

Plichta, M. M., Vasic, N., Wolf, R. C., Lesch, K. P., Brummer, D., Jacob, C., . . . Grön, G. (2009). Neural hyporesponsiveness and hyper-responsiveness during immediate and delayed reward processing in adult attention-deficit/hyperactivity disorder. *Biological Psychiatry, 65*(1), 7–14.

Polanczyk, G., de Lima, M. S., Horta, B. L., Biederman, J., & Rohde, L. A. (2007). The worldwide prevalence of ADHD: A systematic review and meta-regression analysis. *The American Journal of Psychiatry, 164*(6), 942–948.

Prox, V., Dietrich, D. E., Zhang, Y., Emrich, H. M., & Ohlmeier, M. D. (2007). Attentional processing in adults with ADHD as reflected by event-related potentials. *Neuroscience Letters, 419*(3), 236–241.

Rabiner, D. L. (2013). Stimulant prescription cautions: Addressing misuse, diversion and malingering. *Current Psychiatry Report, 15*(7), 1–8.

Rabiner, D. L., Anastopoulos, A. D., Costello, J., Hoyle, R. H., & Swartzwelder, H. S. (2008). Adjustment to college in students with ADHD. *Journal of Attention Disorders, 11*(6), 689–699.

Raichle, M. E. (2010). The brain's dark energy. *Scientific American, 302*(3), 44–49.

Ramsay, J. R. (2007). Current status of cognitive-behavioral therapy as a psychosocial treatment for adult attention-deficit/hyperactivity disorder. *Current Psychiatry Reports, 9*(5), 427–433.

Ramsay, J. R. (2010a). CBT for adult ADHD: Adaptations and hypothesized mechanisms of change. *Journal of Cognitive Psychotherapy, 24*(1), 37–45.

Ramsay, J. R. (2010b). *Nonmedication treatments for adult ADHD: Evaluating impact on daily functioning and well-being.* Washington, DC: American Psychological Association.

Ramsay, J. R. (2012). "Without a net": CBT without medications for an adult with ADHD. *Clinical Case Studies, 11*(1), 48–65.

Ramsay, J. R., Giwerc, D., McGrath, R. E. & Niemiec, R. (2016, January). Are there character strengths associated with adult ADHD? Comparison of ADHD adults and controls on the VIA Inventory of Strengths. Poster presented at annual meeting of the American Professional Society of ADHD and Related Disorders, Washington, DC.

Ramsay, J. R., & Rostain, A. L. (2005). Adapting psychotherapy to meet the needs of adults with attention-deficit/hyperactivity disorder. *Psychotherapy: Theory, Research, Practice, Training, 42*(1), 72–84.

Ramsay, J. R., & Rostain, A. L. (2007). Psychosocial treatments for attention-deficit/hyperactivity disorder in adults: Current evidence and future directions. *Professional Psychology: Research and Practice, 38*(4), 338–346.

Ramsay, J. R., & Rostain, A. L. (2008a). Adult ADHD research: Current status and future directions. *Journal of Attention Disorders, 11*(6), 624–627.

Ramsay, J. R., & Rostain, A. L. (2008b). *Cognitive-behavioral therapy for adult ADHD: An integrative psychosocial and medical approach.* New York: Routledge.

Ramsay, J. R., & Rostain, A. L. (2011). CBT without medications for adult ADHD: An open pilot study of five patients. *Journal of Cognitive Psychotherapy, 25*(4), 277–286.

Ramsay, J. R., & Rostain, A. L. (2015). *Cognitive-behavioral therapy for adult ADHD.* New York: Routledge.

Ramsay, J. R., & Rostain, A. L. (2016). Adult attention-deficit/hyperactivity disorder as an implementation problem: Clinical significance, underlying mechanisms, and psychosocial treatment. *Practice Innovations, 1*(1), 36–52.

Rapport, M. D., Orban, S. A., Kofler, M. J., & Friedman, L. M. (2013). Do programs designed to train working memory, other executive functions, and attention benefit children with ADHD? A meta-analytic review of cognitive, academic, and behavioral outcomes. *Clinical Psychology Review, 33*(8), 1237–1252.

Ratey, J. J., Greenberg, M. S., Bemporad, J. R., & Lindem, K. J. (1992). Unrecognized attention-deficit hyperactivity disorder in adults presenting for outpatient psychotherapy. *Journal of Child and Adolescent Psychopharmacology, 2*(4), 267–275.

Reimherr, F. (2016, January). Update on emotional dysregulation in adult ADHD. Paper presented at annual meeting of the American Professional Society of ADHD and Related Disorders, Washington, DC.

Reimherr, F., Marchant, B. K., Strong, R. E., Hedges, D. W., Adler, L., Spencer, T. J., West, S. A., & Soni, P. (2005). Emotional regulation in adult ADHD and response to atomoxetine. *Biological Psychiatry, 58*, 125–131.

Reimherr, F. W., Williams, E. D., Strong, R. E., Mestas, R., Soni, P., & Marchant, B. K. (2007). A double-blind, placebo-controlled, crossover study of osmotic release oral system methylphenidate in adults with ADHD with assessment of oppositional and emotional dimensions of the disorder. *The Journal of Clinical Psychiatry*, *68*(1), 93–101.

Retz, W., & Rösler, M. (2009). The relation of ADHD and violent aggression: What can we learn from epidemiological and genetic studies? *International Journal of Law and Psychiatry*, *32*(4), 235–243.

Retz, W., Stieglitz, R. D., Corbisiero, S., Retz-Junginger, P., & Rösler, M. (2012). Emotional dysregulation in adult ADHD: What is the empirical evidence? *Expert Review of Neurotherapeutics*, *12*(10), 1241–1251.

Ricard, M., Lutz, A., & Davidson, R. J. (2014). Mind of the meditator. *Scientific American*, *311*(5), 38–45.

Riccardi, G. (2015, April). Sometimes it takes two. *Attention*, 28–29.

Riccio, C. A., Wolfe, M., Davis, B., Romine, C., George, C., & Lee, D. (2005). Attention deficit hyperactivity disorder: manifestation in adulthood. *Archives of Clinical Neuropsychology*, *20*(2), 249–269.

Richards, T. L., Deffenbacher, J. L., Rosén, L. A., Barkley, R. A., & Rodricks, T. (2006). Driving anger and driving behavior in adults with ADHD. *Journal of Attention Disorders*, *10*(1), 54–64.

Rieger, M., Mayer, G., & Gauggel, S. (2003). Attention deficits in patients with narcolepsy, *Sleep*, *26*(1), 36–43.

Roberts, K. (2016). Cyber addictions. In G. Pera & A. L. Robin (Eds.), *Adult ADHD-focused couple therapy* (pp. 197–205). New York: Routledge.

Robison, R. J., Reimherr, F. W., Marchant, B. K., Faraone, S. V., Adler, L. A., & West, S. A. (2008). Gender differences in 2 clinical trials of adults with attention-deficit/hyperactivity disorder: A retrospective data analysis. *The Journal of Clinical Psychiatry*, *69*(2), 213–221.

Rommelse, N. N., Franke, B., Geurts, H. M., Hartman, C. A., & Buitelaar, J. K. (2010). Shared heritability of attention-deficit/hyperactivity disorder and autism spectrum disorder. *European Child & Adolescent Psychiatry*, *19*(3), 281–295.

Rosenfield, B. M., Ramsay J. R. & Rostain, A. L. (2008). Extreme makeover: The case of a young adult man with severe ADHD. *Clinical Case Studies*, *7*(6), 471–490.

Rösler, M., Ginsberg, Y., Arngrim, T., Adamou, M., Niemelä, A., Dejonkheere, J., . . . Schäuble, B. (2013). Correlation of symptomatic improvements with functional improvements and patient-reported outcomes in adults with attention-deficit/hyperactivity disorder treated with OROS methylphenidate. *The World Journal of Biological Psychiatry*, *14*(4), 282–290.

Rostain, A. L., Ramsay, J. R., & Waite, R. (2015). Culturally competent strategies for assessing and treating ADHD in African American adults. *The Journal of Clinical Psychiatry*, *76*(5), 592–596.

Roth, R. M., Isquith, P. K., & Gioia, G. A. (2005). *BRIEF-A: Behavior Rating Inventory of Executive Function–Adult version*. Lutz, FL: Psychological Assessment Resources.

Roth, R. M., Lance, C. E., Isquith, P. K., Fischer, A. S., & Giancola, P. R. (2013). Confirmatory factor analysis of the Behavior Rating Inventory of Executive Function-Adult version in healthy adults and application to attention-deficit/hyperactivity disorder. *Archives of Clinical Neuropsychology*, *28*, 425–434.

Rothe, E. M. (2005). Considering cultural diversity in the management of ADHD in Hispanic patients. *Journal of the National Medical Association, 97*(10 Suppl.), 17S–23S.

Rubia, K., Halari, R., Cubillo, A., Mohammad, A. M., Brammer, M., & Taylor, E. (2009). Methylphenidate normalises activation and functional connectivity deficits in attention and motivation networks in medication-naive children with ADHD during a rewarded continuous performance task. *Neuropharmacology, 57*(7), 640–652.

Rucklidge, J. J., Frampton, C. M., Gorman, B., & Boggis, A. (2014). Vitamin-mineral treatment of attention-deficit hyperactivity disorder in adults: Double-blind randomised placebo-controlled trial. *The British Journal of Psychiatry, 204*(4), 306–315.

Rucklidge, J. J., & Kaplan, B. J. (1997). Psychological functioning of women identified in adulthood with attention-deficit/hyperactivity disorder. *Journal of Attention Disorders, 2*(3), 167–176.

Rybak, Y. E., McNeely, H. E., Mackenzie, B. E., Jain, U. R., & Levitan, R. D. (2006). An open trial of light therapy in adult attention-deficit/hyperactivity disorder. *The Journal of Clinical Psychiatry, 67*(10), 1527–1535.

Safren, S. A., Otto, M. W., Sprich, S., Winett, C. L., Wilens, T. E., & Biederman, J. (2005). Cognitive-behavioral therapy for ADHD in medication-treated adults with continued symptoms. *Behaviour Research and Therapy, 43*(7), 831–842.

Safren, S. A., Perlman, C. A., Sprich, S., & Otto, M. W. (2005). *Mastering your adult ADHD: A cognitive-behavioral treatment program client workbook.* New York: Oxford University Press.

Safren, S. A., Sprich, S., Mimiaga, M. J., Surman, C., Knouse, L., Groves, M., & Otto, M. W. (2010). Cognitive behavioral therapy vs relaxation with educational support for medication-treated adults with ADHD and persistent symptoms: A randomized controlled trial. *JAMA, 304*(8), 875–880.

Safren, S. A., Sprich, S., Perlman, C. A. & Otto, M. W. (2005). *Mastering your adult ADHD: A cognitive-behavioral treatment program therapist guide.* New York: Oxford University Press.

Salakari, A., Virta, M., Grönroos, N., Chydenius, E., Partinen, M., Vataja, R., . . . Iivanainen, M. (2010). Cognitive-behaviorally oriented group rehabilitation of adults with ADHD: Results of a 6-month follow-up. *Journal of Attention Disorders, 13*(5), 516–523.

Saxbe, C., & Barkley, R. A. (2014). The second attention disorder? Sluggish cognitive tempo vs. attention-deficit/hyperactivity disorder: Update for clinicians. *Journal of Psychiatric Practice, 20*(1), 38–49.

Schatz, D. B., & Rostain, A. L. (2006). ADHD with comorbid anxiety: A review of the current literature. *Journal of Attention Disorders, 10*(2), 141–149.

Schecklmann, M., Ehlis, A. C., Plichta, M. M., Romanos, J., Heine, M., Boreatti-Hümmer, A., . . . Fallgatter, A. J. (2009). Diminished prefrontal oxygenation with normal and above-average verbal fluency performance in adult ADHD. *Journal of Psychiatric Research, 43*(2), 98–106.

Schoenberg, P. L., Hepark, S., Kan, C. C., Barendregt, H. P., Buitelaar, J. K., & Speckens, A. E. (2014). Effects of mindfulness-based cognitive therapy on neurophysiological correlates of performance monitoring in adult attention-deficit/hyperactivity disorder. *Clinical Neurophysiology, 125*(7), 1407–1416.

Schwarz, A. (2014, April 19). Workers seeking productivity in a pill are abusing A.D.H.D. drugs. *The New York Times*. Retrieved from http://www.nytimes.com/2015/04/19/us/workers-seeking-productivity-in-a-pill-are-abusing-adhd-drugs.html

Schwartz, J. R., Nelson, M. T., Schwartz, E. R., & Hughes, R. J. (2004). Effects of modafinil on wakefulness and executive function in patients with narcolepsy experiencing late-day sleepiness. *Clinical Neuropharmacology*, *27*(2), 74–79.

Seidman, L. J. (2006). Neuropsychological functioning in people with ADHD across the lifespan. *Clinical Psychology Review*, *26*(4), 466–485.

Sexton, C. C., Gelhorn, H., Bell, J., & Classi, P. (2011). The co-occurrence of reading disorder and ADHD: Epidemiology, treatment, psychosocial impact, and economic burden. *Journal of Learning Disabilities*, *45*(6), 538–564.

Shaw, P., Eckstrand, K., Sharp, W., Blumenthal, J., Lerch, J. P., Greenstein, D. E. E. A., . . . Rapoport, J. L. (2007). Attention-deficit/hyperactivity disorder is characterized by a delay in cortical maturation. *Proceedings of the National Academy of Sciences of the United States of America*, *104*(49), 19649–19654.

Shaw, P., Stringaris, A., Nigg, J., & Leibenluft, E. (2014). Emotion dysregulation in attention deficit hyperactivity disorder. *The American Journal of Psychiatry*, *171*(3), 276–293.

Shaw-Zirt, B., Popali-Lehane, L., Chaplin, W., & Bergman, A. (2005). Adjustment, social skills, and self-esteem in college students with symptoms of ADHD. *Journal of Attention Disorders*, *8*(3), 109–120.

Sheline, Y. I., Barch, D. M., Price, J. L., Rundle, M. M., Vaishnavi, S. N., Snyder, A. Z., . . . Raichle, M. E. (2009). The default mode network and self-referential processes in depression. *Proceedings of the National Academy of Sciences of the United States of America*, *106*(6), 1942–1947.

Shiels, K., & Hawk, L. W. (2010). Self-regulation in ADHD: The role of error processing. *Clinical Psychology Review*, *30*(8), 951–961.

Sibley, M. H., Pelham, W. E.Jr., Molina, B. S., Gnagy, E. M., Waschbusch, D. A., Garefino, A. C., . . . Karch, K. M. (2012a). Diagnosing ADHD in adolescence. *Journal of Consulting and Clinical Psychology*, *80*(1), 139–150.

Sibley, M. H., Pelham, W. E.Jr., Molina, B. S., Gnagy, E. M., Waxmonsky, J. G., Waschbusch, D. A., . . . Kuriyan, A. B. (2012b). When diagnosing ADHD in young adults emphasize informant reports, DSM items, and impairment. *Journal of Consulting and Clinical Psychology*, *80*(6), 1052–1061.

Simon, V., Czobor, P., Bálint, S., Mészáros, Á., & Bitter, I. (2009). Prevalence and correlates of adult attention-deficit hyperactivity disorder: Meta-analysis. *The British Journal of Psychiatry*, *194*(3), 204–211.

Skirrow, C., & Asherson, P. (2013). Emotional lability, comorbidity and impairment in adults with attention-deficit hyperactivity disorder. *Journal of Affective Disorders*, *147*(1), 80–86.

Skirrow, C., McLoughlin, G., Kuntsi, J., & Asherson, P. (2009). Behavioral, neurocognitive and treatment overlap between attention-deficit/hyperactivity disorder and mood instability. *Expert Review of Neurotherapeutics*, *9*(4), 489–503.

Sklar, R. H. (2013). *Hyperfocus in adult ADHD: An EEG study of the differences in cortical activity in resting and arousal states* (Unpublished doctoral dissertation). University of Johannesburg, Johannesburg, South Africa.

Smalley, S. (2008). Reframing ADHD in the genomic era: The emerging view of ADHD in the 21st century: More complex than previously believed. *Psychiatric Times*, *25*(7), 74–74.

Smith, A. L., Hoza, B., Linnea, K., McQuade, J. D., Tomb, M., Vaughn, A. J., . . . Hook, H. (2013). Pilot physical activity intervention reduces severity of ADHD symptoms in young children. *Journal of Attention Disorders, 17*(1), 70–82.

Smith, J. M., & Alloy, L. B. (2009). A roadmap to rumination: A review of the definition, assessment and conceptualization of this multifaceted construct. *Clinical Psychology Review, 29*(2), 116–128.

Sobanski, E., Paslakis, G., Schredl, M., Daffner, S. & Alm, B. (2013). Managing ADHD in adults with common comorbidities. In C. B. H. Surman (Ed.), *ADHD in adults: A practical guide to evaluation and management* (pp. 137–154). New York: Humana Press.

Sobanski, E., Schredl, M., Kettler, N., & Alm, B. (2008). Sleep in adults with attention deficit hyperactivity disorder (ADHD) before and during treatment with methylphenidate: A controlled polysomnographic study. *Sleep, 31*(3), 375–381.

Söderlund, G., Sikström, S., & Smart, A. (2007). Listen to the noise: Noise is beneficial for cognitive performance in ADHD. *Journal of Child Psychology and Psychiatry, 48*(8), 840–847.

Solanto, M. V. (2002). Dopamine dysfunction in AD/HD: Integrating clinical and basic neuroscience research. *Behavioural Brain Research, 130*(1–2), 65–71.

Solanto, M. V. (2011). *Cognitive-behavioral therapy for adult ADHD: Targeting executive dysfunction*. New York: Guilford Press.

Solanto, M. V., Marks, D. J., Mitchell, K. J., Wasserstein, J., & Kofman, M. D. (2008). Development of a new psychosocial treatment for adult ADHD. *Journal of Attention Disorders*, 11(6), 728–736.

Solanto, M. V., Marks, D. J., & Wasserstein, J. (2011). Development of a cognitive-behavioral treatment for adult ADHD. *The ADHD Report, 19*(1), 7–13.

Solanto, M. V., Wasserstein, J., Marks, D. J., & Mitchell, K. J. (2012). Diagnosis of ADHD in adults: What is the appropriate DSM-5 symptom threshold for hyperactivity-impulsivity? *Journal of Attention Disorders, 16*(8), 631–634.

Solanto, M. V., Marks, D. J., Wasserstein, J., Mitchell, K., Abikoff, H., Alvir, J. M. J., & Kofman, M. D. (2010). Efficacy of meta-cognitive therapy for adult ADHD. *The American Journal of Psychiatry, 167*(8), 958–968.

Sollman, M. J., Ranseen, J. D., & Berry, D. T. (2010). Detection of feigned ADHD in college students. *Psychological Assessment, 22*(2), 325–335.

Sonuga-Barke, E. J. (2015). Editorial: Diet and children's behaviour problems–Disentangling urban myth from clinical reality. *Journal of Child Psychology and Psychiatry, 56*(5), 497–499.

Sonuga-Barke, E. J., Brandeis, D., Cortese, S., Daley, D., Ferrin, M., Holtmann, M., . . . Dittmann, R. W. (2013). Nonpharmacological interventions for ADHD: Systematic review and meta-analyses of randomized controlled trials of dietary and psychological treatments. *The American Journal of Psychiatry, 170*, 275–289.

Sonuga-Barke, E., Brandeis, D., Holtmann, M., & Cortese, S. (2014). Computer-based cognitive training for ADHD: A review of current evidence. *Child and Adolescent Psychiatric Clinics of North America, 23*(4), 807–824.

Sonuga-Barke, E. J., Sergeant, J. A., Nigg, J., & Willcutt, E. (2008). Executive dysfunction and delay aversion in attention deficit hyperactivity disorder: Nosologic and diagnostic implications. *Child and Adolescent Psychiatric Clinics of North America, 17*(2), 367–384.

Spencer, T. (2016, January). Evidence of a pharmacological dissociation between the robust effects of methylphenidate on ADHD symptoms and weaker effects on working memory. Paper presented at the annual meeting of the American Professional Society of ADHD and Related Disorders, Washington, DC.

Spencer, T. J., Biederman, J., & Mick, E. (2007). Attention-deficit/hyperactivity disorder: Diagnosis, lifespan, comorbidities, and neurobiology. *Journal of Pediatric Psychology, 32*(6), 631–642.

Spencer, T. J., Brown, A., Seidman, L. J., Valera, E. M., Makris, N., Lomedico, A., . . . Biederman, J. (2013). Effect of psychostimulants on brain structure and function in ADHD: A qualitative literature review of magnetic resonance imaging-based neuroimaging studies. *The Journal of Clinical Psychiatry, 74*(9), 902–917.

Spencer, T. J., Mick, E., Surman, C. B., Hammerness, P., Doyle, R., Aleardi, M., . . . Biederman, J. (2011). A randomized, single-blind, substitution study of OROS methylphenidate (Concerta) in ADHD adults receiving immediate release methylphenidate. *Journal of Attention Disorders, 15*(4), 286–294.

Sprich, S. E., Knouse, L. E., Cooper-Vince, C., Burbridge, J., & Safren, S. A. (2012). Description and demonstration of CBT for ADHD in adults. *Cognitive and Behavioral Practice, 17*(1), 9–15.

Stevens, J., Harman, J. S., & Kelleher, K. J. (2005). Race/ethnicity and insurance status as factors associated with ADHD treatment patterns. *Journal of Child & Adolescent Psychopharmacology, 15*(1), 88–96.

Stevens, L. J., Kuczek, T., Burgess, J. R., Hurt, E., & Arnold, L. E. (2010). Dietary sensitivities and ADHD symptoms: Thirty-five years of research. *Clinical Pediatrics, 50*(4), 279–293.

Stevens, S. E., Sonuga-Barke, E. J., Kreppner, J. M., Beckett, C., Castle, J., Colvert, E., . . . Rutter, M. (2008). Inattention/overactivity following early severe institutional deprivation: Presentation and associations in early adolescence. *Journal of Abnormal Child Psychology, 36*(3), 385–398.

Stevenson, J., Buitelaar, J., Cortese, S., Ferrin, M., Konofal, E., Lecendreux, M., . . . Sonuga-Barke, E. (2014). Research review: The role of diet in the treatment of attention-deficit/hyperactivity disorder—An appraisal of the evidence on efficacy and recommendations on the design of future studies. *Journal of Child Psychology and Psychiatry, 55*(5), 416–427.

Stevenson, C. S., Whitmont, S., Bornholt, L., Livesey, D., & Stevenson, R. J. (2002). A cognitive remediation programme for adults with attention deficit hyperactivity disorder. *Australian & New Zealand Journal of Psychiatry, 36*(5), 610–616.

Stray, L. L., Kristensen, Ø., Lomeland, M., Skorstad, M., Stray, T., & Tonnessen, F. E. (2013). Motor regulation problems and pain in adults diagnosed with ADHD. *Behavioral and Brain Functions, 9*(1), 18.

Ströhle, A., Stoy, M., Wrase, J., Schwarzer, S., Schlagenhauf, F., Huss, M., . . . Juckel, G. (2008). Reward anticipation and outcomes in adult males with attention-deficit/hyperactivity disorder. *NeuroImage, 39*(3), 966–972.

Strohmeier, C. W., Rosenfield, B., DiTomasso, R. A., & Ramsay, J. R. (2016). Assessment of the relationship between self-reported cognitive distortions and adult ADHD, anxiety, depression and hopelessness. *Psychiatry Research, 238*, 153–158.

Surman, C. B. H. (2013a). Clinical assessment of ADHD in adults. In C. B. H. Surman (Ed.), *ADHD in adults: A practical guide to evaluation and management* (pp. 19–44). New York: Humana Press.

Surman, C. B. H. (2013b). Treatment planning for adults with ADHD. In C. B. H. Surman (Ed.), *ADHD in adults: A practical guide to evaluation and management* (pp. 45–58). New York: Humana Press.

Surman, C. B., Adamson, J. J., Petty, C., Biederman, J., Kenealy, D. C., Levine, M., . . . Faraone, S. V. (2009). Association between attention-deficit/hyperactivity disorder and sleep impairment in adulthood: Evidence from a large controlled study. *The Journal of Clinical Psychiatry, 70*(11), 1523–1529.

Surman, C. B., Biederman, J., Spencer, T., Miller, C. A., McDermott, K. M., & Faraone, S. V. (2013). Understanding deficient emotional self-regulation in adults with attention deficit hyperactivity disorder: A controlled study. *ADHD Attention Deficit and Hyperactivity Disorders, 5*(3), 273–281.

Surman, C. B., Biederman, J., Spencer, T., Yorks, D., Miller, C. A., Petty, C. R., & Faraone, S. V. (2011). Deficient emotional self-regulation and adult attention deficit hyperactivity disorder: A family risk analysis. *The American Journal of Psychiatry, 168*(6), 617–623.

Surman, C., Hammerness, P., Petty, C., Doyle, R., Chu, N., Gebhard, N., . . . Biederman, J. (2010). Atomoxetine in the treatment of adults with subthreshold and/or late onset attention-deficit hyperactivity disorder–not otherwise specified (ADHD-NOS): A prospective open-label 6-week study. *CNS Neuroscience & Therapeutics, 16*(1), 6–12.

Surman, C. B., Hammerness, P. G., Pion, K., & Faraone, S. V. (2013). Do stimulants improve functioning in adults with ADHD? A review of the literature. *European Neuropsychopharmacology, 23*(6), 528–533.

Swanson, J. M., Kinsbourne, M., Nigg, J., Lanphear, B., Stefanatos, G. A., Volkow, N., . . . Wadhwa, P. D. (2007). Etiologic subtypes of attention-deficit/hyperactivity disorder: Brain imaging, molecular genetic and environmental factors and the dopamine hypothesis. *Neuropsychology Review, 17*(1), 39–59.

Taylor, A., Deb, S., & Unwin, G. (2011). Scales for the identification of adults with attention deficit hyperactivity disorder (ADHD): A systematic review. *Research in Developmental Disabilities, 32*(3), 924–938.

Thapar, A., Cooper, M., Eyre, O., & Langley, K. (2013). Practitioner review: What have we learnt about the causes of ADHD? *Journal of Child Psychology and Psychiatry, 54*(1), 3–16.

Thapar, A., Langley, K., O'Donovan, M., & Owen, M. (2006). Refining the attention deficit hyperactivity disorder phenotype for molecular genetic studies. *Molecular Psychiatry, 11*, 714–720.

Theiling, J., & Petermann, F. (2014). Neuropsychological profiles on the WAIS-IV of ADHD adults. *Journal of Attention Disorders*. Advance online publication.

Thompson, J. M. D., Waldie, K. E., Wall C. R., Murphy, R., Mitchell, E. A., & ABC Study Group. (2014). Associations between acetaminophen use during pregnancy and ADHD symptoms measured at ages 7 and 11 years. *PLoS One, 9*(9), e108210. Retrieved from http://journals.plos.org/plosone/article?id=10.1371/journal.pone.0108210

Tierney, J. (2012, February 13). What's new? Exuberance for novelty has benefits. *The New York Times*. Retrieved from http://www.nytimes.com/2012/02/14/science/novelty-seeking-neophilia-can-be-a-predictor-of-well-being.html

Toone, B. (2004). Attention deficit hyperactivity disorder in adulthood. *Journal of Neurology, Neurosurgery & Psychiatry, 75*(4), 523–525.

Turgay, A., Goodman, D. W., Asherson, P., Lasser, R. D., Babcock, T. F., Pucci, M. L., & Barkley, R. (2012). Lifespan persistence of ADHD: The life transition model and its application. *The Journal of Clinical Psychiatry, 73*(2), 192–201.

Tsai, C. S., Huang, Y. S., Wu, C. L., Hwang, F. M., Young, K. B., Tsai, M. H., & Chu, S. M. (2013). Long-term effects of stimulants on neurocognitive performance of Taiwanese children with attention-deficit/hyperactivity disorder. *BMC Psychiatry, 13*(1), 1–10.

Tuckman, A. (2007). *Integrative treatment for adult ADHD: A practical, easy-to-use guide for clinicians*. Oakland, CA: New Harbinger.

Tuttle, L. J., Ahmann, E., & Wright, S. D. (2016, January). Emerging evidence for the efficacy of ADHD coaching. Poster presented at the annual meeting of the American Professional Society of ADHD and Related Disorders, Washington, DC.

Tymms, P., & Merrell, C. (2011). ADHD and academic attainment: Is there an advantage in impulsivity? *Learning and Individual Differences, 21*(6), 753–758.

Upadhyaya, H. P. (2007). Managing attention-deficit/hyperactivity disorder in the presence of substance use disorder. *The Journal of Clinical Psychiatry, 68*, 23–30.

Van Ameringen, M., Mancini, C., Simpson, W., & Patterson, B. (2011). Adult attention deficit hyperactivity disorder in an anxiety disorders population. *CNS Neuroscience & Therapeutics, 17*(4), 221–226.

van de Glind, G., Konstenius, M., Koeter, M. W., van Emmerik-van Oortmerssen, K., Carpentier, P. J., Kaye, S., . . . Moggi, F. (2014). Variability in the prevalence of adult ADHD in treatment seeking substance use disorder patients: Results from an international multi-center study exploring DSM-IV and DSM-5 criteria. *Drug and Alcohol Dependence, 134*, 158–166.

Van Voorhees, E. E., Hardy, K. K., & Kollins, S. H. (2011). Reliability and validity of self- and other ratings of symptoms of ADHD in adults. *Journal of Attention Disorders, 15*(3), 224–234.

Verheul, I., Block, J., Burmeister-Lamp, K., Thurik, R., Tiemeier, H., & Turturea, R. (2015). ADHD-like behavior and entrepreneurial intentions. *Small Business Economics, 45*(1), 85–101.

Verret, C., Guay, M. C., Berthiaume, C., Gardiner, P., & Béliveau, L. (2012). A physical activity program improves behaviour and cognitive functions in children with ADHD: An exploratory study. *Journal of Attention Disorders*, 16(1), 71–80.

Vidal, R., Bosch, R., Nogueira, M., Gómez-Barros, N., Valero, S., Palomar, G., . . . Ramos-Quiroga, J. A. (2013). Psychoeducation for adults with attention deficit hyperactivity disorder vs. cognitive behavioral group therapy: A randomized controlled pilot study. *The Journal of Nervous and Mental Disease, 201*(10), 894–900.

Vidal-Estrada, R., Bosch-Munso, R., Nogueira-Morais, M., Casas-Brugue, M., & Ramos-Quiroga, J. A. (2012). Psychological treatment of attention deficit hyperactivity disorder in adults: A systematic review. *Actas Españolas de Psiquiatría, 40*, 147–154.

Voinescu, B. I., Szentagotai, A., & David, D. (2012). Sleep disturbance, circadian preference and symptoms of adult attention deficit hyperactivity disorder (ADHD). *Journal of Neural Transmission, 119*(10), 1195–1204.

Volkow, N. D., & Swanson, J. M. (2013). Adult attention deficit–hyperactivity disorder. *The New England Journal of Medicine, 369*(20), 1935–1944.

Volkow, N. D., Wang, G. J., Newcorn, J. H., Kollins, S. H., Wigal, T. L., Telang, F., . . . Swanson, J. M. (2011). Motivation deficit in ADHD is associated with dysfunction of the dopamine reward pathway. *Molecular Psychiatry, 16*(11), 1147–1154.

Waite, R., & Ramsay, J. R. (2010a). Adults with ADHD: Who are we missing? *Issues in Mental Health Nursing, 31*(10), 670–678.

Waite, R., & Ramsay, J. R. (2010b). Cultural proficiency: A Hispanic woman with ADHD—A case example. *Journal of Attention Disorders, 13*(4), 424–432.

Wallis, D., Russell, H. F., & Muenke, M. (2008). Review: Genetics of attention deficit/hyperactivity disorder. *Journal of Pediatric Psychology, 33*(10), 1085–1099.

Walters, A. S., Silvestri, R., Zucconi, M., Chandrashekariah, R., & Konofal, E. (2008). Review of the possible relationship and hypothetical links between attention deficit hyperactivity disorder (ADHD) and the simple sleep related movement disorders, parasomnias, hypersomnias, and circadian rhythm disorders. *Journal of Clinical Sleep Medicine, 4*(6), 591–600.

Wasserstein, J. (2005). Diagnostic issues for adolescents and adults with ADHD. *Journal of Clinical Psychology, 61*(5), 535–547.

Weiss, M., Gibbins, C. & Hunter, J. D. (2011). Attention-deficit hyperactivity disorder and anxiety disorders in adults. In J. K. Buitelaar, C. C. Kan, & P. J. Asherson (Eds.), *ADHD in adults: Characterization, diagnosis and treatment* (pp. 130–137). New York: Cambridge University Press.

Weiss, M., & Murray, C. (2003). Assessment and management of attention-deficit hyperactivity disorder in adults. *Canadian Medical Association Journal, 168*(6), 715–722.

Weiss, M., Murray, C., Wasdell, M., Greenfield, B., Giles, L., & Hechtman, L. (2012). A randomized controlled trial of CBT therapy for adults with ADHD with and without medication. *BMC Psychiatry, 12*(1), 30.

Weiss, M., Safren, S. A., Solanto, M. V., Hechtman, L., Rostain, A. L., Ramsay, J. R., & Murray, C. (2008). Research forum on psychological treatment of adults with ADHD. *Journal of Attention Disorders, 11*(6), 642–651.

Weisz, J. R., Ng, M. Y., & Bearman, S. K. (2014). Odd couple? Reenvisioning the relation between science and practice in the dissemination-implementation era. *Clinical Psychological Science, 2*(1), 58–74.

Wender, P. H. (1995). *Attention-deficit hyperactivity disorder in adults.* New York: Oxford University Press.

Wender, P. H., Wolf, L. E., & Wasserstein, J. (2001). Adults with ADHD. *Annals of the New York Academy of Sciences, 931*(1), 1–16.

Westmoreland, P., Gunter, T., Loveless, P., Allen, J., Sieleni, B., & Black, D. W. (2010). Attention deficit hyperactivity disorder in men and women newly committed to prison clinical characteristics, psychiatric comorbidity, and quality of life. *International Journal of Offender Therapy and Comparative Criminology, 54*(3), 361–377.

Weyandt, L. L., & DuPaul, G. J. (2008). ADHD in college students: Developmental findings. *Developmental Disabilities Research Reviews, 14*(4), 311–319.

White, H. A., & Shah, P. (2006). Uninhibited imaginations: Creativity in adults with attention-deficit/hyperactivity disorder. *Personality and Individual Differences, 40*(6), 1121–1131.

White, H. A., & Shah, P. (2011). Creative style and achievement in adults with attention-deficit/hyperactivity disorder. *Personality and Individual Differences, 50*(5), 673–677.

White, J. W., & Buehler, C. (2012). Adolescent sexual victimization, ADHD symptoms, and risky sexual behavior. *Journal of Family Violence, 27*(2), 123–132.

Wierzbicki, M. (2005). Reliability and validity of the Wender Utah Rating Scale for college students. *Psychological Reports, 96*(3), 833–839.

Wietecha, L., Williams, D., Shaywitz, S., Shaywitz, B., Hooper, S. R., Wigal, S.B., . . . McBurnett, K. (2013). Atomoxetine improved attention in children and adolescents with attention-deficit/hyperactivity disorder and dyslexia in a 16 week, acute, randomized, double-blind trial. *Journal of Child and Adolescent Psychopharmacology, 23*(9), 605–613.

Wiklund, J., Patzelt, H., & Dimov, D. (2016). Entrepreneurship and psychological disorders: How ADHD can be productively harnessed. *Journal of Business Venturing Insights, 6*, 14–20.

Wilens, T. E. (2004). ADHD and the substance use disorders: The nature of the relationship, who is at risk, and treatment issues. *Primary Psychiatry, 11*, 63–70.

Wilens, T. E. (2006). Attention deficit hyperactivity disorder and substance use disorders. *The American Journal of Psychiatry, 163*(12), 2059–2063.

Wilens, T. E. (2011). Attention-deficit hyperactivity disorder and the substance use disorders. In J. K. Buitelaar, C. C. Kan, & P. J. Asherson (Eds.), *ADHD in adults: Characterization, diagnosis and treatment* (pp. 138–150). New York: Cambridge University Press.

Wilens, T. E., Biederman, J., Faraone, S. V., Martelon, M., Westerburg, D., & Spencer, T. J. (2009). Presenting ADHD symptoms, subtypes, and comorbid disorders in clinically referred adults with ADHD. *The Journal of Clinical Psychiatry, 70*(11), 1557–1562.

Wilens, T. E., Faraone, S. V., & Biederman, J. (2004). Attention-deficit/hyperactivity disorder in adults. *JAMA, 292*(5), 619–623.

Wilens, T. E., Faraone, S. V., Biederman, J., & Gunawardene, S. (2003). Does stimulant therapy of attention-deficit/hyperactivity disorder beget later substance abuse? A meta-analytic review of the literature. *Pediatrics, 111*(1), 179–185.

Wilens, T. E., Martelon, M., Joshi, G., Bateman, C., Fried, R., Petty, C., & Biederman, J. (2011). Does ADHD predict substance-use disorders? A 10-year follow-up study of young adults with ADHD. *Journal of the American Academy of Child & Adolescent Psychiatry, 50*(6), 543–553.

Willcutt, E. G., Chhabildas, N., Kinnear, M., DeFries, J. C., Olson, R. K., Leopold, D. R., . . . Pennington, B. F. (2014). The internal and external validity of sluggish cognitive tempo and its relation with DSM–IV ADHD. *Journal of Abnormal Child Psychology, 42*(1), 21–35.

Willcutt, E. G., Doyle, A. E., Nigg, J. T., Faraone, S. V., & Pennington, B. F. (2005). Validity of the executive function theory of attention-deficit/hyperactivity disorder: A meta-analytic review. *Biological Psychiatry, 57*(11), 1336–1346.

Willcutt, E. G., Nigg, J. T., Pennington, B. F., Solanto, M. V., Rohde, L. A., Tannock, R., . . . Lahey, B. B. (2012). Validity of DSM-IV attention deficit/hyperactivity disorder symptom dimensions and subtypes. *Journal of Abnormal Psychology, 121*(4), 991–1010.

Willer, J. (2014). *The beginning psychotherapist's companion* (2nd ed.). New York: Oxford University Press.

Wilmshurst, L., Peele, M., & Wilmshurst, L. (2011). Resilience and well-being in college students with and without a diagnosis of ADHD. *Journal of Attention Disorders,* 15(11), 11–17.

Wood, W., & Neal, D. T. (2007). A new look at habits and the habit–goal interface. *Psychological Review, 114*(4), 843–863.

World Health Organization. (1993). *The ICD-10 classification of mental and behavioural disorders: Diagnostic criteria for research.* Geneva: Author. Retrieved from http://www.who.int/classifications/icd/en/GRNBOOK.pdf

World Health Organization. (2003). *Adult ADHD Self-Report Scale-V1.1 (ASRS-V1.1): Symptoms checklist.* Geneva: Author. Retrieved from http://www.hcp.med.harvard.edu/ncs/ftpdir/adhd/18Q_ASRS_English.pdf

World Health Organization. (2015). *International statistical classification of diseases and related health problems, 10th revision. Chapter V: Mental and behavioural disorders (F00-F99).* Geneva: Author. Retrieved from http://apps.who.int/classifications/icd10/browse/2015/en#/F90-F98

Wymbs, B. T., & Molina, B. S. (2015). Integrative couples group treatment for emerging adults with ADHD symptoms. *Cognitive and Behavioral Practice, 22*(2), 161–171.

Wymbs, B. T., Molina, B., Pelham, W., Cheong, J., Gnagy, E., Belendiuk, K., . . . Waschbusch, D. (2012). Risk of intimate partner violence among young adult males with childhood ADHD. *Journal of Attention Disorders, 16*(5), 373–383.

Yoon, S. Y. R., Jain, U., & Shapiro, C. (2012). Sleep in attention-deficit/hyperactivity disorder in children and adults: Past, present, and future. *Sleep Medicine Reviews, 16*(4), 371–388.

Young, S., Bramham, J., Gray, K., & Rose, E. (2007). The experience of receiving a diagnosis and treatment of ADHD in adulthood: A qualitative study of clinically referred patients using interpretative phenomenological analysis. *Journal of Attention Disorders, 11*(4), 493–503.

Young, S., Morris, R., Toone, B., & Tyson, C. (2007). Planning ability in adults with attention-deficit/hyperactivity disorder. *Neuropsychology, 21*(5), 581–589.

Young, T., Peppard, P. E., & Gottlieb, D. J. (2002). Epidemiology of obstructive sleep apnea: A population health perspective. *American Journal of Respiratory and Critical Care Medicine, 165*, 1217–1239.

Zhang, L., Jin, X., & Zhang, Y. (2011). Effect of methylphenidate on intelligence quotient scores in Chinese children with attention-deficit/hyperactivity disorder. *Journal of Clinical Psychopharmacology, 31*(1), 51–55.

Zentall, S. S., Kuester, D. A., & Craig, B. A. (2011). Social behavior in cooperative groups: Students at risk for ADHD and their peers. *The Journal of Educational Research, 104*(1), 28–41.

Zhu, X., Wang, X., Xiao, J., Liao, J., Zhong, M., Wang, W., & Yao, S. (2012). Evidence of a dissociation pattern in resting-state default mode network connectivity in first-episode, treatment-naive major depression patients. *Biological Psychiatry, 71*(7), 611–617.

Zylowska, L., Ackerman, D. L., Yang, M. H., Futrell, J. L., Horton, N. L., Hale, T. S., . . . Smalley, S. L. (2008). Mindfulness meditation training in adults and adolescents with ADHD: A feasibility study. *Journal of Attention Disorders, 11*(6), 737–746.

Zylowska, L., Smalley, S. L., & Schwartz, J. M. (2009). Mindful awareness and ADHD. In Fabrizio Didonna (Ed.), *Clinical handbook of mindfulness* (pp. 319–338). New York: Springer.

ABOUT THE AUTHOR

Jan Willer, Ph.D., is a licensed clinical psychologist in independent practice in Chicago, Illinois. *Could it Be Adult ADHD? Recognition, Assessment, and Treatment* is her second book, following *The Beginning Psychotherapist's Companion*. She enjoys teaching, lecturing, writing, and working with psychotherapy clients. She has five Chicago theater subscriptions, three volunteer positions, two rescue cats, and one beloved husband.

INDEX

www.ingramcontent.com/pod-product-compliance
Lightning Source LLC
Chambersburg PA
CBHW061608180926
51615CB00006B/19
9780190256319